SEMEIA 53

THE FOURTH GOSPEL FROM A LITERARY PERSPECTIVE

Guest Editors:

R. Alan Culpepper
Fernando F. Segovia

©1991
by the Society of Biblical Literature

Published by
SCHOLARS PRESS
P.O. BOX 15399
Atlanta, GA 30333-0399

Correction:

The essay by Bernard Brandon Scott, "The Birth of the Reader," *Semeia* 52 (1990): 83-102, should have included the following note: This essay is reprinted with the permission of the publisher from *Faith and History: Essays in Honor of Paul W. Meyer*, edited by John T. Caroll, Charles H. Cosgrove, and E. Elizabeth Johnson (Atlanta: Scholars Press, 1990) 35-54.

ISBN 978-1-58983-491-0 (paper : alk. paper)

Printed in the United States of America
on acid-free paper

CONTENTS

Contributors to this Issue v

Introduction 1
    Fernando F. Segovia

Main Papers:

I.   The Journey(s) of the Word of God:
    A Reading of the Plot of the Fourth Gospel 23
    Fernando F. Segovia

II. Stumbling in the Dark, Reaching for the Light:
    Reading Character in John 5 and 9 55
    Jeffrey L. Staley

III. Johannine Metaphor—Meaning and Function:
    A Literary Case Study of John 10:1–18 81
    Robert Kysar

IV. Putting Life Back into the Lazarus Story and Its Reading:
    The Narrative Rhetoric of John 11 as the Narration of Faith 113
    Wilhelm Wuellner

V.   The Johannine *Hypodeigma*: A Reading of John 13:1–38 133
    R. Alan Culpepper

VI. "I Have Overcome the World" (John 16:33):
    Narrative Time in John 13—17 153
    Gail R. O'Day

VII. The Final Farewell of Jesus:
    A Reading of John 20:30–21:25 167
    Fernando F. Segovia

Response Papers:

"Response from a European Perspective" 191
    Johannes Beutler

"A Response from a Literary Perspective" 203
    Mary Ann Tolbert

CONTRIBUTORS TO THIS ISSUE

Johannes Beutler
  Philosophisch-Theologische Hochschule Sankt Georgen
  Offenbacher Landstrasse 224
  D 6000 Frankfurt 70
  Germany

R. Alan Culpepper
  Baylor University
  Waco, Texas 76798

Robert Kysar
  Lutheran Theological Seminary
  7301 Germantown Avenue
  Philadelphia, Pennsylvania 19119

Gail R. O'Day
  Candler School of Theology
  Emory University
  Atlanta, Georgia 30322

Fernando F. Segovia
  The Divinity School
  Vanderbilt University
  Nashville, Tennessee 37240

Jeffrey L. Staley
  Department of Theology
  The University of Portland
  5000 N. Willamette Boulevard
  Portland, Oregon 97203

Mary Ann Tolbert
 The Divinity School
 Vanderbilt University
 Nashville, Tennesee 37240

Wilhelm Wuellner
 Pacific School of Religion
 1798 Scenic Avenue
 Berkeley, California 94709

TOWARDS A NEW DIRECTION IN JOHANNINE SCHOLARSHIP: THE FOURTH GOSPEL FROM A LITERARY PERSPECTIVE

Fernando F. Segovia
Vanderbilt Divinity School

The broad title adopted for the present volume of *Semeia*, *The Fourth Gospel from a Literary Perspective*, represents by no means a simply fortuitous or accidental choice. As a matter of fact, its rather vague and open-ended formulation has been explicitly and deliberately chosen for a variety of different reasons, all of which have to do with a distinct and pressing need for a new direction, a new thrust, in contemporary Johannine scholarship and research, in keeping with the recent course of gospel studies in general.

First of all, the title specifically recalls the momentous shift in New Testament studies that began to take place towards the end of the 1970s and the beginning of the 1980s. In effect, the long-reigning and widely accepted paradigm represented by the historical critical method in all of its many guises and variations—by that time well into its final stage of composition criticism to which redaction criticism had been gradually yielding in the 1970s—began to show rather ominous cracks at its very foundations and eventually gave way, within a remarkably brief period of time, to two very different directions of scholarly research, which may be generally characterized as literary criticism and social world criticism. Both of these directions have dominated the field through the 1980s and at this point, at the beginning of the final decade of the century, continue to show only increasing strength and sophistication, though still rather limited mutual engagement. The title does point, therefore, to the present volume as a direct and specific contribution to one of these two dominant directions in the field today, namely, that of literary criticism.

Secondly, with this fundamental shift in orientation, the traditional paradigm of historical critical studies not only came to a rather abrupt and decisive halt—at least in the North American scene—but also failed to be replaced by any new and all-encompassing paradigm as such. In fact, what the two new directions in research have brought have been a multiplicity of paradigms, introducing thereby an incredible and heretofore unknown measure of richness and diversity in the field as a whole. Thus, with the turn to literary criticism came a full reliance upon and employment of literary theory, involving the wide range of the theoretical spectrum (e.g., narratology; feminist theory; rhetorical criticism; communications theory; reader-response criticism) as well as the full range of each individual area within such a spectrum; similarly, with the turn to social world criticism came a full use of and dependence upon sociological and anthropological theory, again comprehending not only the wide range of the theoretical spectrum (e.g., sectarianism; millenarian studies; social dynamics and roles; sociology of knowledge; mediterranean studies) but also the entire range of each area within the spectrum. The title also points, therefore, to the deliberate and explicit openness of this volume with regard to theoretical orientation and methodological procedure, whereby complete freedom was allowed each contributor from the very beginning in the selection of topic to be addressed, text to be considered, and mode of development to be followed.

Finally, though this fundamental shift in orientation has now been in place for more than ten years, its effects on Johannine research and scholarship have been and continue to be, on the whole, rather limited and occasional in character, both from the literary and the social world perspective, lagging well behind such efforts in the broader field of gospel studies. In fact, a number of the participants in this volume have been directly responsible for what little effort there has been in the appropriation and application of literary criticism with regard to the Fourth Gospel. In many ways, therefore, the traditional paradigm has continued to exercise a predominant role in Johannine studies, far beyond its rate of survival and acceptability in the discipline as a whole; as a result, one still finds very much of a continued search for literary strata, for sources and redactions, and a persistent reading of the Gospel from a compositional, diachronic perspective. As such, the title further points to the volume as a very concrete way of giving added emphasis and momentum to the literary turn in general, both in the interest of wider research and methodological sophistication, regardless of the particular area to be pursued or the specific theoretical orientation to be followed.

The overall result of this combined effort has proved to be, as the present collection of essays will readily testify, quite varied and quite rich indeed, pointing to the many benefits and insights to be reaped in Johannine studies from the adoption of a such a fresh interpretive approach. These essays not only touch upon a wide variety of texts from every major section of the Gospel (the Gospel as a whole; John 5 and 9; John 10; John 11; John 13; John 13—17; and John 21) but also address a wide variety of different areas or topics (plot; characterization; metaphorical usage; narrative rhetoric; narrative strategy; narrative time; and narrative structure) from a similarly wide variety of theoretical perspectives (literary conventions of ancient narrative; mode of characterization in ancient narrative; parable research and study of figurative language; contemporary rhetorical theory; literary functions of time; and reader response criticism). In the end, these very suggestive and insightful essays raise far more questions, open up far more possibilities, and point in far more directions than those addressed or pursued, thus leaving the door wide open for further, sustained, and open-ended analysis of the Gospel from a literary perspective which is broadly conceived and broadly applied.

In what follows I provide a detailed presentation of the collection in two major sections, in keeping with the generic distinction employed between major or interpretive papers and response or critical papers. In the first section, therefore, I summarize the main thrust and orientation of each major paper. In so doing I follow the order of the essays in the volume, which order follows in turn the sequence of the Gospel narrative itself; in other words, the various essays have been arranged, for lack of a more appropriate design, according to the location of the texts addressed in the Gospel narrative, since all but one—duly placed at the beginning of the volume—focus on specific narrative units or scenes of the Gospel. A general overview of these major papers follows in terms of significant trends or developments to be discerned within them, so that the full contribution and impact of the collection as a whole may be more readily perceived and appreciated. In the second section, then, I summarize the gist of the response papers, again both individually and collectively, as a very specific way of gauging the very first critical reaction to and reception of the collection.

A. MAJOR PAPERS

1. In my essay on the plot of the Gospel, I propose a literary-rhetorical reading of the plot which is directly informed by both generic conventions of ancient biographies and literary conventions of ancient narrative. First of all, I believe the Gospel to be an example of ancient biography of the holy man as son of god type: a biography of Jesus as the Word of God made flesh. As such, I argue for a plot which follows the overall threefold structural division of such biographies: a beginning narrative of origins (1:1–18); a long central narrative of the public life or career of the hero (1:19–17:26); and a concluding narrative of death and lasting significance (18:1–21:25). Secondly, I further believe that the Gospel reveals a very important and interrelated use of two common literary conventions of ancient narrative: the motif of the travel account or journey and the use of patterns of repetition and recurrence. Such conventions I see as a further key to the plot of the Gospel.

On the one hand, I argue for a mythological, cosmic journey as providing a further overall framework for the plot: the Word of God as undertaking a journey from the world of God to the world of human beings, becoming flesh as Jesus of Nazareth and carrying out the mission of the Father in and to the world (1:1–18); upon completion of this mission, the Word of God returns to the world of God (18:1–21:25). On the other hand, I also argue for a series of geographical journeys as governing the central narrative of the public life (1:19–17:26): as the Word of God made flesh, Jesus of Nazareth undertakes a series of four journeys to the city of Jerusalem in the course of his mission, journeys which are accompanied by a constellation of other and varying patterns of repetition. The result is a reading which relies on the dominant motif of the repeated journeys of Jesus, both into the world and in the world itself, within the larger framework of his biographical narrative as the Word of God made flesh.

Such a reading is ultimately informed as well by reader-response criticism and placed within the broader theoretical discussion concerning the very meaning of the concept of plot. Thus, the proposed reading is advanced not as the sole, definitive, and objective reading of the Gospel's plot but rather as one possible reading thereof, directly shaped and influenced by my own social location as the reader of this text. At the same time, the proposed reading is specifically situated within the three-dimensional matrix advanced by K. Egan for a proper understanding of the notion of plot in critical theory: at the center of the particular-to-abstract axis, with an emphasis on the geometry or pattern of the narrative; at the diachronic end of the synchronic-diachronic axis, with an emphasis on the sequential or dynamic element of the narrative; and at the center of the content-emotion axis, with an emphasis on the close correspondence between the patterns of the narrative and the patterns of emotional reaction. The result is a reading that is comprehensive and coherent; that reflects a very definite sense of movement and development; and that argues for a close connection between narrative organization and emotional effect.

2. The essay by J. Staley focuses on two very similar miracle stories of the Fourth Gospel, the Sabbath healings of John 5:1–18 and 9:1–41, from the point of view of characterization in the Gospel. Staley is directly informed by two different though very much interrelated theoretical orientations. First of all, he argues that the two characters in question—the lame man and the blind man, respectively—represent examples of a mode of characterization in the Gospel which has not received proper scholarly attention, namely, a Hebrew model of character with personal development rather than ethical type as the main focus of interest. In his analysis

of these two characters from the Gospel, therefore, Staley turns to recent studies of characterization in ancient Hebrew narrative by R. Alter, A. Berlin, and M. Sternberg. Given the general position of these studies to the effect that such characterization strategically withholds crucial pieces of narrative exposition from the reader, Staley follows their lead in paying particular attention to certain rhetorical features of such characterization: the role of repetition and variation; the role of direct discourse; and the subtle use of narration. Secondly, Staley further argues that such analysis is particularly open to the concerns of reader response criticism, with its sensitivity to the successive unfolding judgments that take place during the reading experience. What follows, therefore, is a close reading of the two central characters of these stories with a special emphasis on the dynamics of the reading process in the formation of character.

Such a reading produces much more complex and nuanced interpretations of these two characters. In the case of the lame man, Staley in effect goes against established opinion to the effect that this man represents not at all an ingrate or a betrayer, as generally argued, but rather a faithful witness to the sign performed: a man who acts twice, positively and unquestioningly, upon Jesus' commands, even to the point of proclaiming Jesus as the charismatic healer in question to the authorities. In the case of the blind man, Staley does follow established opinion but provides a further refinement thereof by focusing on the man's behavior vis-à-vis the authorities: the man not only acts as a faithful witness to the sign performed but also attempts, repeatedly and from the very beginning, to protect Jesus from attack by the authorities on the possible charge of a Sabbath violation. Both characters emerge, therefore, as examples of what Staley calls the double-edged joy of Christian living, an experience that is ultimately summarized as stumbling in the dark while reaching for the light.

3. In his essay on John 10:1–18, R. Kysar turns his attention to the use of metaphors in the Fourth Gospel. Three specific theoretical concerns are at work in this paper. First of all, pointing to the persistent lack of interest in the metaphors of Jesus in the Fourth Gospel, in direct contrast to the great deal of attention bestowed on the parables of Jesus in the Synoptic Gospels, Kysar specifically argues for a renewed and vigorous study of the use and function of Johannine metaphors, a discussion which he himself initiates by focusing on the problematic example of John 10:1–18. Secondly, Kysar further points out that the literary unity of this passage has quite often been called into question on account of its seemingly confused use of metaphors, leading to a general view of the passage as a literary composite involving different literary strata, with considerable disagreement regarding their number and scope, and different kinds of

metaphorical language, with considerable disagreement once again regarding their proper designation or genre. As such, Kysar argues for a reading of the passage and its entire metaphorical development as meaningful and coherent as it presently stands in the Gospel narrative. Finally, given the very sharp disagreements in the traditional historical critical approach to the passage, Kysar argues as well for a reading of John 10:1–18 in terms of reader response criticism, with a view of meaning as residing in the imaginative interaction between reader and text and a corresponding focus on the response of the reader to the strategies and rhetoric of the text. Consequently, Kysar undertakes an analysis of Johannine metaphors with specific reference to John 10:1–18 as a meaningful and coherent unit of the Gospel and from the standpoint of reader response criticism.

The proposed reading follows a threefold development centered on the experience of the reader with regard to the structure, the integrity, and the genre of the passage.

With regard to structure, first of all, Kysar sees John 10:1–18 as consisting of five interrelated images: four interlocking "human" images (dealing with the relationship between Jesus and human beings), with an expansion of the last image, and a concluding "theological" image (dealing with the relationship between Jesus and God), each of which is developed by way of contrast; this contrast involves in each case the use of at least one positive image and one negative image, though the arrangement of such contrasts is quite varied from image to image. Other characteristics are noted as well: (a) clear patterns in the varying use of contrasts: not only does each image conclude with a positive image, but the entire series begins with a negative image and concludes with a positive image; (b) rapid transitions among the images; and (c) the use of various aids to reading, such as the narrator's comment of 10:6–7a. The effects of this structure upon the reader are described as follows: while the variations in the use of contrasts keeps the reader off guard and surprised, the overall patterns continuously emphasize the positive in the reader's mind; the swift transition from image to image provides a further challenge as well, constantly drawing the reader onwards from picture world to picture world; and the various aids to reading serve as effective guides for the reader through the seeming confusion of imagery of the passage. For the reader, therefore, the structure is said to provide both abruptness and consistency, surprise and regularity.

Secondly, with regard to integrity, Kysar sees John 10:1–18 as highly unified throughout, both with regard to the passage as a whole and its component parts: (a) each image constitutes a self-contained whole; (b) each pair of human images also constitutes a self-contained whole, revealing a wide number of close interconnections; (c) following upon the narrator's comment of 10:6-7a, the second pair of images introduces a strong tone of personal immediacy, with an explicit shift from implicit to explicit metaphors, as well as a strong sense of motion in time and space; (d) the expansion within the fourth image brings to a close the human imagery of the first four images; and (e) the final, theological image breaks open the human realm to reveal the divine presence in the human. Such unity is said to have very definite effects upon the reader as well, whereby the reader is progressively caught up in a world of movement and drawn closer into intimacy with Jesus, led in tantalizing fashion in and through the human realm to the divine realm, and finally asked to reflect on the identity of Jesus from the point of view of the human experience of relationship (father/son).

Finally, with regard to genre, Kysar sees John 10:1-18 as functioning very much like the synoptic parables, drawing the reader further into the bosom of the implied author by means of tension: on the one hand, through its abrupt series of images, the passage causes amazement, confusion, lack of understanding on the part of the reader, leading to a certain sense of distance from Jesus and a certain identification with the outsiders, with those who fail to understand, in the text; on the other hand, through its portrayal of such outsiders and its own aids to reading, the passage also creates a certain sense of pleasure and hope on the part of the reader, leading to a continued search for further clarification and resolution. As with the Synoptic parables, therefore, Kysar characterizes these metaphors as diaphors or poetic metaphors: metaphors with the power to initiate a new kind of reality in the reader, given their participatory, shocking, paradoxical, contrastive, and decisional qualities. For Kysar, in the end, the usual distinctions drawn between the Synoptic parables and the Johannine metaphors, responsible in turn for the exhaustive analysis of the former and the almost complete disregard for the latter, prove to be quite ironic, given their great functional similarity with regard to the reader.

4. W. Wuellner's essay on John 11 deals with the narrative rhetoric of John 11, with the raising of Lazarus not as a narration of one of Jesus' many signs but rather as a narration of faith, that is to say, as a narration for the purpose of enhancing and confirming the belief of the readers in Jesus as the Christ and the Son of God and thereby confirming and enhancing their possession of life in his name. As such, a rhetorical reading of the text, grounded in modern rhetorical criticism, is proposed, whereby both the narration of faith and the response of the reader to the reading of the narration of faith may be better appreciated. Such a rhetorical reading involves three different though very much interrelated

dimensions: (a) the rhetoric in John—a focus on the argumentative or persuasive function of the textual constraints, the literary and linguistic devices internal to the text, produced by the author and the narrator in order to facilitate the production of meaning by the reader; (b) the rhetoric of John—a focus on the experience of the reader in the reading of the text, on the evaluative responses of the reader to the argumentative or persuasive force of the text both during and after reading; and (c) the rhetoric of rhetorical criticism—a focus on the argumentative or persuasive nature of what the scholarly critical readers themselves share in the process of their critical deliberations about their findings. With regard to John 11 itself, Wuellner focuses above all on the first and second dimensions of such a reading.

To begin with, Wuellner approaches the rhetoric in the Lazarus story in terms of a fivefold process involving an analysis of the rhetorical unit or argument, its rhetorical situation or intentionality, its rhetorical structure or disposition, its rhetorical techniques or style, and its rhetorical or argumentative coherence.

As a rhetorical unit, first of all, the Lazarus story is defined as beginning and ending with two conflict settings: 10:39–42, in itself the closure of the previous unit, and 11:54–57, the overture to the next unit as well; as argument, this unit is further described in terms of a threefold conflict of value positions, involving not only the call for help and the later reproofs of the sisters of Lazarus but also the opposition by the Jewish religious authorities and the protestations of Jesus' own disciples. Secondly, Wuellner identifies the rhetorical situation of the unit in terms of an oxymoron, namely, glorification through death—the juxtaposition of the reality of God's glory and the appearance of sickness and death for believers; as such, its plausibility is described as contrary to all common sense, regardless of how the norms and values of common sense be defined in any given culture. Thirdly, the unit's rhetorical structure is described as consisting of seven narrative scenes whose purpose it is to argue for this oxymoron of glorification through death as well as for Jesus' identity as the agent of God, given the conflict setting of 10:40–42, and thereby move the reader to believe by accepting another criterion of reality. In fact, Wuellner argues that the structure of the unit ultimately reveals three stories all together embedded in the surface plot, thus paralleling in effect the three conflicts of value positions identified within the unit: not only the glorification through death of Lazarus, but also the glorification through death of both Jesus and his disciples. As such, the story of Lazarus' raising also represents a narration of faith regarding values tested and contested concerning the presence of God in Jesus as God's agent and in the disciples as Jesus' agents. Fourthly, Wuellner shows how various rhetorical techniques of the story are used to achieve plausibility for the oxymoron of glorification through death with regard to all three stories present within John 11. Finally, the rhetorical coherence of the story is seen in terms of God's continuing action in and disruption of history and the habitual ambiguous reaction of the people of God to God's agent as conveyed both by means of its internal consistency and its many textual gaps, surplus features, and inconsistencies.

At the end, Wuellner turns to the rhetoric of the Lazarus story and the evaluative responses of the reader to the reading of such a narration of faith, which responses are regarded as commitments or performance rather than appraisals or analysis (i.e., acceptance or rejection, full or partial) and further characterized as corporate and cultural, ongoing and ever-changing, as well as specific to the cultural context and the media-choice. Thus, for example, the reader may experience this narration of faith as the narrating of the living God who manifests life in the midst of every generation and be moved thereby to evoke life, hope, and wholeness where others only see death, despair, and fragmentation. Similarly, the reader may also experience the unbelief among God's own people to be found within this narration of faith as the narrating of a latent unbelief present in all persons, conventions, and institutions and be moved as a result to see faith as a process involving constant renewal and deepening. Finally, the reader may further experience the disciples' experience of having God revealed to them in this narration of faith as the narrating of a faith which will be tested and contested by prevailing cultural identities and institutional power structures and be moved thereby to adopt a stance which is in conflict with the old and in harmony with the new. Given the possibility of such transformations, for Wuellner in the end the proposed rhetorical reading of John 11 represents a way of putting life back into the story of Lazarus and its reading.

5. The essay by R. A. Culpepper on John 13 reveals a twofold theoretical thrust. On the one hand, Culpepper pursues a reading of this chapter as a cohesive segment of the Gospel. Thus, in the light of the many attempts in the scholarly literature to make sense of this text by dividing it into different literary strata and reading it only in terms of its compositional history, Culpepper specifically argues for a reading of John 13 as coherent and meaningful in its present state. On the other hand, Culpepper also pursues a reading of the chapter from the perspective of reader response criticism, with an explicit focus on the process of reading and interpreting the text, that is to say, on how the text guides the reader in the construction of meaning and on the responses elicited by the text from the reader. Such a reading is further placed within a much wider reading of the plot of the Gospel in terms of an ongoing conflict between

belief and unbelief with regard to Jesus, the revealer. This conflict is said to be developed by means of a series of repetitive episodes which set forth a variety of responses to Jesus; as such, the Gospel is seen as exposing throughout the errors of unbelief while constantly guiding the reader to faith in Jesus. For Culpepper, therefore, John 13 represents, as it presently stands, one of these many episodes of the Gospel that seek to elicit such responses from the reader and should be read accordingly.

The proposed reading bears a structural, a literary, as well as an affective dimension. From a structural point of view, first of all, Culpepper argues for the whole of John 13:1–38 as a self-contained narrative unit of the Gospel, consisting of six subunits which function as a guide to the reader in the process of reading. Secondly, from a literary point of view, Culpepper sees John 13 as developing a contrast between the knowledge of Jesus and the ignorance of the disciples: while reporting what Jesus knew and the actions that followed from such knowledge, the chapter also reports what the disciples did not know and the results of such ignorance; given their failure to understand, therefore, the disciples are said to function in the chapter as a foil for Jesus. On the one hand, the knowledge of Jesus has to do with the arrival of his "hour" and leads to love for his own, the footwashing, and death; on the other hand, given their failure to understand the arrival of "the hour," the ignorance of the disciples leads to denial and betrayal, the very opposite of the ethic laid out by Jesus. Finally, from an affective point of view, the disciples are said to function as a foil for the readers as well, whereby the readers are called to be more perceptive and responsive to Jesus than the disciples were, to avoid thereby the disastrous consequences of the latter's behavior, and to follow instead the ethic of Jesus as conveyed by the footwashing.

Within such a reading, then, the footwashing itself emerges as both an interpretation of Jesus' death on the cross and a model for the Johannine community to follow. On the one hand, therefore, the footwashing becomes a proleptic and metaphorical interpretation of Jesus' death: a symbolic act of love for his own whereby the social norms of the world are entirely displaced and reordered. Similarly, on the other hand, the footwashing also becomes a *hypodeigma* or example for the disciples to follow: to do for one another as Jesus has done for them, to love one another as Jesus has loved them, again putting aside the social norms of this world and serving one another to the point of death if need be. Through the footwashing, therefore, the death of Jesus is interpreted as the norm of life and conduct for the believing community, as the very grounds for a new and radical ethic indeed. It is this ethic, therefore, that the readers of the Gospel are specifically called upon to accept and follow by witnessing the failure of the disciples to understand and the ultimate consequences of such ignorance.

6. In her essay on the farewell discourse of John 13–17, G. O'Day turns to a study of narrative time in the Gospel. Given the constant shifting in temporal focus within the farewell discourse—most clearly exemplified by the changing temporal standpoint of Jesus as speaker: from a Jesus who speaks as if his crucifixion-resurrection-ascension were a past event, to a Jesus who speaks as if his departure were imminent, to a Jesus who speaks as if he were in the very process of departing—O'Day points to narrative time and, more specifically, temporal sequence or order as pivotal concerns for the discourse as a whole. At the same time, however, O'Day argues that the temporal complexity of these chapters is such that even sophisticated critical categories used to analyze temporal order in narrative, such as those devised by G. Genette (analepsis or prolepsis, internal or external), fail to do justice to the temporal idiosyncracy of the farewell discourse. Consequently, she argues for a study of temporal sequence in John 13–17 that moves beyond any and all such critical taxonomies to consider the literary and theological functions of time in the discourse.

From a literary point of view, first of all, the discourse as a whole is seen as proleptic and thus out of place in the temporal sequence of the narrative, insofar as it brings the future and the present in one narrative moment in ways that challenge conventional notions of time. In effect, the Jesus that speaks in these chapters is described as a Jesus whose "hour" of glorification has come, that is to say, not a Jesus who is about to undergo the process of crucifixion-to-resurrection but rather a Jesus who is already risen, a Jesus who by his words brings the future into the present, anticipating thereby not only the future of the gospel narrative but also the future lying outside the end of the narrative. Secondly, from a theological point of view, given the arrival of "the hour," the Jesus who speaks is also described as a Jesus who speaks with full confidence and certainty about the future, a Jesus who knows no temporal bounds or categories, a Jesus who has already overcome the world (16:33). As such, not only the disciples as characters in the story but also all subsequent readers of the Gospel are given access to the voice of the risen Jesus and assured thereby of an unwavering future, of his own abiding presence among them, and of his victory over the world. For O'Day, therefore, the farewell discourse represents a perfect melding of narrative form and theological claim: the arrival of "the hour" constitutes both the governing narrative reality and the governing theological reality of the discourse.

7. In my essay on John 21, I propose once again a literary-rhetorical reading of this narrative scene which is directly informed by a number of

literary conventions of ancient narrative. In so doing, I bypass entirely the traditional scholarly discussion concerning the specific provenance of this scene in the Gospel, a discussion characterized by a wide consensus regarding its very late addition to an already fairly complete narrative in the compositional history of the Gospel as well as by a search for literary layers within the scene itself. I approach it instead as the very final scene of the Gospel as it stands, namely, as the final resurrection appearance of Jesus within the narrative of death and lasting significance (18:1–21:25)—as identified in the essay on plot—and, more specifically, within the very final section of this concluding narrative, which focuses on the promised aftermath of the death itself and thus further reveals the lasting significance of the figure of Jesus (20:1–21:25). As such, I pursue a reading of this scene as quite meaningful and coherent in the Gospel narrative as it presently stands. Two common literary conventions of ancient narrative particularly serve to guide such a reading: the use of patterns of repetition and recurrence and the use of the farewell type-scene.

On the one hand, I argue for a highly unified and carefully developed scene based on a number of highly interrelated patterns of repetition, a narrative scene composed of John 20:30–21:25 and consisting of three narrative units arranged in an overall pattern of inclusion—while the outer units contain explicit comments by the narrator regarding the nature, purpose, and origins of Jesus' biography (20:30–31; 21:24–25), the central unit portrays the fourth and final resurrection appearance of Jesus (21:1–23). On the other hand, I also argue for the central unit itself as an example of a farewell type-scene, quite common to both Graeco-Roman and Hebrew narrative: the last farewell of the risen Jesus to his disciples prior to his full glorification or apotheosis with the Father, following upon a long farewell before death, farewell words at the scene of death, and three resurrection appearances in the farewell after death itself. In the end, I see this final farewell of the risen Jesus as focusing specifically on the proper and correct role of the disciples in the world after his return to the Father and thus bringing the entire narrative of death and lasting significance—and the Gospel itself—to a close by showing in a very concrete way the lasting significance of Jesus' mission, ministry, and death as lying in the very praxis of the disciples themselves, in their own mission to the world as well as in their own love for one another as Jesus had loved them. In so doing, furthermore, I see a number of highly interrelated and interdependent strategic aims at work within this final farewell, of which the didactic and the exhortative emerge as primary.

In the end, therefore, I propose a reading of this scene as not only quite meaningful and coherent but also quite appropriate and pointed in the Gospel narrative as it presently stands. As with the reading of the plot, this proposed reading of John 20:30–21:25 is ultimately informed as well by reader response criticism. Once again, therefore, the reading advanced is by no means presented as the sole, definitive, and objective reading of this narrative scene, but as only one possible reading of it, directly influenced and shaped by my own social location as the reader of this scene. However, in this particular reading I do begin to approach, albeit in very limited fashion, the very nature of this complex relationship between social location and biblical interpretation.

Concluding Comments. The preceding summary of the interpretive or major papers immediately points to a number of rather distinctive and recurrent trends or developments in this collection; I confine myself to the three I consider to be the most important for Johannine studies in general: (1) a unified and comprehensive reading of narrative units or scenes of the Gospel traditionally regarded as quite problematic from a literary point of view, given their many perceived aporias or literary difficulties, as quite meaningful and coherent as they presently stand in the Gospel narrative; (2) a turn to literary theory characterized by a view of theory itself not as a strict and unyielding grid to which the text in question must be submitted but rather as a point of departure for an informed analysis of the text as unique in itself; (3) a decided preference for some form of reader response criticism, involving an explicit move away from the text as the sole locus of meaning and hence as an object to be analyzed to a view of the text as a guide to the reader in the construction of meaning, both semantic and practical, and of meaning itself as residing in the interaction between text and reader.

1. To begin with, all of the essays in this volume deal with texts of varying length from the Gospel which have been traditionally and quite often regarded as either the product of various literary strata involving sources and redactions or as late additions, in whole or in part, to an already existent and rather complete Gospel narrative, or both. In all such cases a very similar line of argumentation can be readily discerned: (a) the text in question reveals any number of literary difficulties or aporias of an insurmountable sort; (b) the presence of such difficulties points to the text not as a literary unity but rather as a literary composite, consisting of any number of sources and redactions, more often than not in conflicting relationship to one another; (c) a meaningful and coherent reading of the text is possible only in the light of its redactional or compositional history, properly reconstructed and sequentially followed.

Such has certainly been the case with regard to the miracle stories of John 5:1–18 and 9:1–41, the metaphorical discourse of John 10:1–18, the raising story of John 11, and the meal scene of John 13, all of which have been quite frequently divided into various literary layers of different provenance. Such has been the case as well with regard to the long farewell discourse of John 13–17 and the final farewell scene of John 21, both of which have been very frequently considered, either in part (John 15–17) or as a whole (John 21), as coming from the very last stage or stages in the compositional history of the Gospel narrative, along with further subdivision to be sure into constitutive literary layers. In fact, what applies to individual units or scenes ultimately applies as well to the narrative as a whole, and the very same judgment has been consistently rendered with regard to the entire Gospel narrative: a narrative so full of difficulties of all sorts that only a proper division into its various literary strata and a proper reading of such strata in diachronic fashion could lead to a meaningful and coherent reading of the whole.

All of the essays in this text call into question at a very fundamental level indeed this traditional line of argumentation by arguing that in every case a meaningful and coherent reading of the text as it presently stands is quite possible, whether that text be a brief narrative unit, an extended narrative scene, or the Gospel as a whole. A comprehensive and thorough reading is shown to be possible without any need for a diachronic inquiry, whether with regard to the textual prehistory of any one unit or scene or the compositional history of the narrative as a whole. At the same time, however, a number of these essays also proceed to point out that they are by no means ruling out in principle the search for the prehistory of the text in question and indeed go out of their way to acknowledge the theoretical validity and usefulness of the historical critical method and its characteristic excavative concerns. Thus, while making allowances for source-redaction inquiries throughout, these essays completely bypass all such excavative concerns, implicitly call into question the very grounds for the existence of such concerns, and come very close at times to an explicit rejection of the need for such concerns with regard to the particular text under analysis.

Despite such common and repeated allowances, however, there can be little doubt that the gulf between the more traditional approach and the newer approaches becomes increasingly wide and extremely difficult to negotiate: the more any text is shown to be meaningful and coherent as it stands, the more difficult it becomes to accept the presence of aporias as traditionally conceived and defined, to argue for substantial reconstructions of underlying sources and subsequent redactions, and to begin with the prehistory of the text in the search for meaning. As much as one might want to allow in theory for the mutual validity and usefulness of such different approaches to the text, it will become increasingly hard to do so in the future, except perhaps in the case of a few salient examples, and even then excavative approaches will be forced to become much more sophisticated and critical from a theoretical point of view if they are to remain at all viable and persuasive in the discipline.

2. All of the essays in this volume further demonstrate a thorough acquaintance with the wider realm of literary theory as well as an informed use of the insights and principles of such theory in the analysis of the different texts in question. As a result, a wide recourse to theory can be readily observed in a number of different areas: the critical understanding of plot; the conception of characterization in ancient narrative; the meaning and function of figurative language; the tools of modern rhetorical criticism; the analysis of narrative time and temporal order; the relationship between narrative strategy and reader response; and the use of literary conventions of ancient narrative. From a theoretical point of view, therefore, it is clear that biblical interpretation, in turning outwards for support and guidance, becomes much more self-conscious and sophisticated and hence much more rigorous and exacting.

It is also clear from these essays that such a turning outwards, such a recourse to theory, is not of the purely slavish or imitative sort, with theory functioning as a convenient grid through which to examine the text and obtain the desired results. Rather, what these essays reveal is a critical approach to theory itself whether in terms of a critical awareness of the history of and ongoing discussion within theory itself or a critical use of theory as a necessary and informed point of departure for the analysis of a text which in itself calls for a creative and imaginative use of such theory. The turn to theory shows, therefore, two very important and interrelated dimensions: on the one hand, a view of theory as not at all static and uniform, but rather as quite varied and ongoing; on the other hand, a view of theory as subservient to rather than domineering over the text. Consequently, in the turn to theory, biblical interpretation not only becomes much more sophisticated and rigorous, but also much more self-confident and self-critical.

3. Finally, most of the essays in this volume explicitly call for and follow an interpretation of the given text from the perspective of reader response criticism. One of the major developments within the turn to literary criticism in biblical studies has been, in effect, the emergence of reader response criticism, a theoretical orientation which has gained increasing momentum and importance through the 1980s. Its impact and importance for the discipline as a whole may be more readily described and appreciated by way of contrast with the traditional paradigm.

In the traditional paradigm of the historical critical method, the meaning of the text was invariably located either in the world represented by the text or in the intention of the author of the text, giving rise thereby to a search for the sole, definitive, and objective meaning of the text, a search marked nonetheless by wide and profound disagreement regarding the meaning of any text and a corresponding attack on all other meanings but that of the interpreter as in some way defective or incorrect. With the rise of reader response criticism, however, such claims to universality and objectivity are effectively called into question. To begin with, the meaning of the text is now located within a much wider spectrum ranging from the reader as member of an interpretive community to the interaction between reader and text, with a decided preference for the latter position within biblical interpretation. As such, the focus of attention shifts to the reader and to the process of negotiation between text and reader in the construction of meaning, in other words, to the response of the reader to the textual constraints and strategies of the text. Consequently, the former search for a sole and objective meaning yields to an acceptance of a plurality of meanings, while the former mode of discussion by means of attack and dismissal gives way to an emphasis on the social location of the various readers of the text.

Such claims come readily to the fore in many of these papers, though the identity and temporal location of the "reader" in question does vary widely from paper to paper, with the following spectrum in evidence: a seemingly universal reader, reading the text for the first time and responding to it primarily during the process of reading; a seemingly universal reader, though with occasional references to particular insights of first-century readers, reading the text for the first time and responding to it primarily during the process of reading; a seemingly universal reader, reading the text for the first time and responding to it mostly after the reading itself; a seemingly universal though socially conditioned reader, reading the text at some point and responding to it mostly after the reading itself; and a contemporary and socially conditioned reader, though with a reconstruction of the implied readers of the text, reading the text at some point and responding to it after the reading itself.

It is interesting to note in this regard that, aside for a brief discussion in one essay, the social location of the contemporary reader, of each and every one of these authors, is not pursued in and of itself, either in the case of those who posit the construct of a seemingly universal reader, of whatever stripe, or in the case of those who argue for a socially conditioned reader, again of whatever stripe. Though subscribing to reader response criticism and accepting, to one extent or another, the locus of meaning as lying in the process of negotiation between reader and text in the construction of meaning, these essays still preserve for the most part the reluctance of the traditional paradigm to let any aspect of the individual interpreter come into full view with regard to sociocultural context (e.g., class, gender, racial or ethnic origins, religious affiliation, ideological stance, etc.) and continue to adopt a certain stance of objectivity with regard to the text. While the plurality of meanings is granted, the plurality of readers continues to be largely disguised. Nevertheless, the tremendous richness and diversity that reader response criticism brings to the interpretive task, especially given its enormous variety of standpoints, remains quite clear.

In many and significant ways, therefore, the collection does represent, as intended, a major contribution to Johannine studies. Given its consistently unified and coherent readings of the Gospel as it presently stands, it calls for much greater care and caution regarding the presence and acknowledgment of aporias or literary difficulties in the text, for a much greater sense of theoretical sophistication and self-criticism in the search for and reconstruction of the prehistory of the text, as well as for a preeminent emphasis on a synchronic reading of the text. Given its critical turn to and use of theory, it calls for ever increasing sophistication, rigorousness, and self-criticism with regard to theory itself, and for a view of theory as indispensable but also as a way or tool rather than a grid. Given its explicit focus on the reader and the process of reading, it calls for a different mode of scholarly discourse centered on a plurality of meanings, a greater emphasis on the social location of all readers, and a concern for the influence of such a social location upon the interpretation of the text. Finally, given its richness and diversity, both with regard to theoretical orientation and interpretive results, the collection also calls for an ongoing and sustained analysis of the Fourth Gospel from a literary perspective, broadly conceived and broadly applied.

B. RESPONSE PAPERS

1. In his analysis of the volume from the perspective of contemporary European scholarship, J. Beutler approaches the collection from four different theoretical perspectives: (a) methodological focus; (b) underlying hermeneutical stance; (c) relationship between literature and history; and (d) theological implications. On the one hand, Beutler compares throughout the overall orientation and concerns of these essays with recent currents in European scholarship. On the other hand, Beutler provides in each of these areas a critical reading of the collection leading to a number of insightful and cautionary observations.

a. From the point of view of method, Beutler focuses on three distinctive characteristics of the collection: the emphasis on the present text of the Gospel as meaningful and coherent—the preference for a synchronic approach to the text; the adoption of reader response criticism as its main theoretical stance; and the use of rhetorical criticism.

First, Beutler observes that the synchronic emphasis of the collection is accompanied by a recurring element of comparative research, namely, a focus on the generic features of the text in question and hence a type of form criticism. Given such a continued use of form criticism, he wonders whether source and tradition criticism can be altogether bypassed or excluded in the interpretation of biblical texts, whether such formal elements of the text do not also include material elements which are realized outside and inside the Gospels. On both sides of the Atlantic, he concludes, the methodological place of form criticism continues to be problematic. Second, Beutler points out that the type of reader response criticism practiced in this volume is not unlike the quest for the pragmatics of a text in European schools—a third step in synchronic exegesis, following upon syntactical analysis and semantics. However, he finds the corresponding emphasis on the relationship of the reader to the text as constitutive not only for the purpose but also the meaning of the text to serve as an appropriate reminder of the fundamental connection between the semantics and the pragmatics of a text. On both sides of the Atlantic, he concludes, it is the step from the implied readers of the text to contemporary readers that remains the most difficult one. Third, for Beutler the use of classical rhetorical theory in Gospel interpretation is problematic, insofar as such laws were developed with speeches in mind, not narrative; consequently, such laws, he concludes, can only be properly applied to the Gospel with reference to the discourses of Jesus.

b. From the point of view of hermeneutics, Beutler singles out three specific consequences of the volume's emphasis on the literary dimensions of the text. First, such emphasis leads to a neglect of the social conditions of author and readers and hence to a neglect of a hermeneutical approach that attempts to see such conditions as a paradigm for an understanding of the text. Second, though the volume is sensitive to previous interpretations of the texts in question, there is a much greater need to take into account the history and impact of the interpretation of any given text in its interpretation for today. Third, while arguing for meaning as the result of a negotiation between text and reader, the authors fail, for the most part, to reflect on themselves as subjects of interpretation. For Beutler, such preoccupation with formal questions is quite characteristic of the First World on both sides of the Atlantic and quite different from the emphasis of the Third World on social location.

c. With regard to the problematic relationship between literature and history, Beutler offers a twofold word of caution concerning the present approach to the Fourth Gospel as a literary document. On the one hand, he points out that such an approach abstracts from the historical reality of the persons, facts, and speeches mentioned or reported in the text; such a reading, however, is said to be in direct contrast to the intention of the author as expressed in the Gospel itself—the Gospel as a witness to facts. On the other hand, he observes that such an approach should not deny all historical value to the text; historical criticism, despite its many shortcomings, has proved to be of immense value in many ways. Consequently, the literary approach, Beutler concludes, should never be seen as the one and sole method of Johannine research; a historical approach remains indispensable.

d. With regard to the theological implications of such a literary approach, Beutler again offers a threefold word of caution. First, given the abstract reader at work in this collection and the corresponding neglect for the social roots of such a reader in history, Beutler sees the emergence of a theological anthropology without a proper concern for ecclesiology. Second, with the adoption of reader response, he sees the focus of concern as shifting from christology to discipleship; though such a shift has yielded many positive results, Beutler also argues for a continuing interest in christology. Third, given its emphasis on the response of the reader, Beutler points out that reader response could lead to a view of human activity rather than divine activity as the main purpose of the Gospel; consequently, he argues for a view of such a response as a response of faith equal to the acceptance of God's love and saving word.

Beutler has provided an excellent reading of the collection. It is a sympathetic and appreciative reading, a reading which acknowledges the need for such a line of inquiry in the light of Johannine scholarship. It is also a broad and informative reading, a reading which situates such a line of inquiry within recent and prevailing exegetical practices on the European continent. Finally, it is a critical and challenging reading as well, a reading which is not afraid to point out important shortcomings and omissions in such a line of inquiry.

2. M. A. Tolbert approaches the volume from the point of view of its overall location, as a self-described exercise in biblical literary criticism, within the broader discipline of contemporary literary theory. The analysis focuses on two specific issues: (a) the question of text and meaning; and (b) the emergence of theoretical coalitions and ideological analysis. In each case the theoretical orientation of the collection as a whole is outlined and a fundamental critique offered.

a. Tolbert approaches the first issue of text and meaning in terms of the development of literary studies of the New Testament in the last thirty years, a development which has followed since its inception the broader course of literary theory and criticism. Three stages are distinguished in all. (1) The first stage was dominated by New Criticism (1930s to early 1960s), with its focus on the text as an autonomous literary object, to be investigated on its own terms and without reference to author, audience, or sociocultural context. Such early works, appearing in the 1960s, were characterized by a formalist analysis of the literary dynamics of biblical texts. (2) The second stage was directly influenced by the displacement of New Criticism in favor of a variety of literary theories (e.g., myth criticism; Marxism; psychoanalysis; structuralism) with a continuing focus on the text itself but now going outside the aesthetic realm of the text for their theoretical grounding (early 1960s to late 1970s). Such works, published in the 1970s, pursued their analysis of the biblical texts from such different perspectives as psychology or linguistics. (3) The third stage is marked by the increasing prominence of reader or audience response criticism, with its focus on the interaction between text and reader (end of 1970s through the present). Within this broad theoretical position, some emphasize the relative power of the text and preserve many of the formalist features of New Criticism, while others stress the relative power of the reader and have recourse to the insights of psychology, sociology, and ideology.

It is within this third stage of biblical literary criticism that Tolbert places the present volume and, more particularly, toward its text-oriented pole: the strong formalist tendencies of the collection reveal a very definite connection with the text-dominant positions within reader response criticism and thus ultimately with New Criticism as well. Two criticisms are offered as a result. First, given its emphasis on the text, the volume avoids, for the most part, the ongoing critical discussion concerning differences among readers and the legitimacy of multiple readings; thus, its authors continue to hide behind the masks of analytical constructs such as the ideal reader, failing to own up thereby to such critical readings as their own. Second, given its focus on isolated sections of a longer story, the volume also goes against, for the most part, the reading strategy and rules of reader response criticism, with its clear emphasis on the final form of the whole text; consequently, its authors should, at the very least, locate their studies of such brief units within the context of the overall development of the story.

b. The second issue of theoretical coalitions and ideological analysis is approached from the point of view of a further development in literary theory in the 1980s, a development with a broad cross-disciplinary background and scope. First, under the direct influence of French deconstructionism, the decade witnessed the formation of a number of theoretical coalitions giving rise to a body of theory shared by a wide number of fields of study; in effect, such disciplines began to see their subject matter as "texts"—human constructions supporting certain viewpoints while bypassing or negating others. Second, reader-dominant positions within reader response criticism readily joined such coalitions and further contributed to this emerging body of theory; in effect, such "texts" require "readers" for interpretation and such "readings" reflect discourses of power. With this incorporation of ideological analysis into literary theory in the mid to late 1980s, such factors as gender, race, and sociocultural contexts began to be seen as human constructions and their influence on the production and reading of texts examined.

With regard to the present volume, Tolbert points out that, for the most part, the collection fails to reflect such theoretical developments not only in contemporary literary theory but also within reader response criticism itself. As a result, its authors not only hide their own selves behind their analytical masks but also fail to engage in a critical analysis of their own social location as readers; in so doing, they fail to integrate one of the most important theoretical developments of the last decade—the many critiques of the ideal, universal reader.

Tolbert's reading of the collection is equally excellent. It is clearly sympathetic and appreciative: the insights of text-dominant reader response criticism, evident in the volume, are readily acknowledged and praised. It is also broad and informative: the volume is well situated within the wider context of biblical literary criticism and contemporary literary theory. Finally, it is properly critical and challenging: fundamental shortcomings and omissions—in themselves reflective of contemporary biblical literary criticism in general—are openly pointed out and explained.

Concluding Comments. These two critical readings represent a major and invaluable contribution to the volume, especially given their very different theoretical perspectives and sociocultural contexts. As a first indication of its reception, they sharply but graciously analyze both its strengths and its weaknesses. A common and very important observation does come to the fore: despite its overall subscription to reader response criticism, the authors as readers remain largely in hiding. Such a critical comment is not only true but also calls for immediate attention: readers of biblical texts must read themselves as well as their texts, since no reading of the latter can be said to be complete, appropriate, or even healthy without a reading of the former. In these times of heightened awareness of global diversity, it is indeed imperative for readers to own up to their readings and their social locations as readers. As the new chair of the Johannine Literature Section of the Society of Biblical Literature, I hope to take up this serious challenge to literary studies of the Fourth Gospel by means of an ongoing, multiyear series on "Readers and Readings of the

Fourth Gospel." The time is certainly ripe for readers of the Fourth Gospel—and indeed of any biblical texts—to begin reading themselves as well.

THE JOURNEY(S) OF THE WORD OF GOD:
A READING OF THE PLOT OF THE FOURTH GOSPEL

Fernando F. Segovia
The Divinity School, Vanderbilt University

ABSTRACT

This study advances a literary-rhetorical reading of the plot of the Fourth Gospel based on the following methodological criteria: the Gospel as an example of ancient biographical literature; the Gospel's use of the common motif of the journey in ancient narrative; and the Gospel's use of the common literary technique of patterns of repetition and recurrence in ancient narrative. Following generic conventions, the study argues for an overall threefold division of the plot in terms of the Gospel as a biography of Jesus, the Word of God: a narrative of origins (1:1–18), a narrative of the public life or career of Jesus (1:19–17:26), and a narrative of death and lasting significance (18:1–21:25). Following narrative conventions, the study also argues for the dominant role of the journey motif in the plot of the Gospel: on the one hand, a mythological, cosmic journey of the Word of God from the world of God to the world of human beings, becoming flesh in Jesus of Nazareth, which provides a further overall framework for the plot; on the other hand, a series of repeated geographical journeys in the course of the public life or career of Jesus as the Word of God, with an accompanying constellation of other repeated motifs. The study further provides a critical analysis of the broader theoretical discussion regarding the very concept of plot itself; a critical examination of previous approaches to the plot of the Gospel in Johannine scholarship; and an account of the various interrelated and interdependent strategic functions of the proposed plot.

1. INTRODUCTION

There is simply no fast and easy way to arrive at any type of consensus definition with regard to the meaning and use of the term "plot" in poetics and critical literature, let alone identify and describe the plot of any one work of narrative, whether ancient or modern. As recent literary criticism of the canonical gospels has already pointed out, the wider critical discussion concerning how "plot" is to be understood and how it is to be analyzed in any particular narrative work is not only quite extensive but also very diverse (Rhoads and Michie:73; Culpepper:79–80; Matera:235–36); indeed, such an assessment of the wider critical discussion is often encountered within that very same literature (Egan:455–57; Chatman:84–95; Brooks:5–7; Caserio:3–4; Martin:81–129).

At the same time and in direct reaction to a certain traditional and rather widespread disregard, even disdain at times, for the study of plot in general (Caserio:3-4), one also finds within this literature a growing emphasis on the importance of this particular element of narrative. Thus, for example, while Egan speaks of plot as "a crucial term in criticism and poetics" (456), Brooks argues that "plot is somehow prior to those elements most discussed by most critics, since it is the very organizing line, the thread of design, that makes narrative possible because finite and comprehensible" (4).

I believe that the critical analysis and interpretation of the canonical gospels can only stand to benefit from a proper consideration of the plot of each gospel in the light of an informed theoretical framework regarding the very concept of "plot" itself, a theoretical framework which goes beyond either an uncomplicated adoption of one particular use of the term or an essentially synthetic appropriation of various such usages. In the present study, therefore, I have three specific goals in mind. I should like to offer, first of all, an initial reading of the plot of the Fourth Gospel as it presently stands, that is to say, from the point of view of the present Gospel as a unified and coherent work, thus bypassing altogether any discussion of literary strata underlying the present Gospel, no matter how complete or extensive such strata may be (see Fortna), or of the process of redaction and accretion resulting in the present text of the Gospel. While such excavative concerns are certainly justified and worth pursuing, they are not at all relevant to the main thrust of this study. Secondly, I should like to stress as well the preceding description of this proposal as "initial," not only because it represents a first attempt on my part to come to terms with a very complex issue, but also because I hope to develop such a reading in much greater detail in a future work on the Gospel.[1] Thirdly, I should also like to preface this reading by addressing the fundamental question of an informed theoretical framework so that I can ultimately locate my own approach within such a framework.

A final comment is further in order by way of introduction. As the subtitle of this study clearly indicates, the present reading of the plot of the Fourth Gospel is by no means offered as the sole, definitive, and objective reading of this narrative feature of the Gospel but only as one possible reading thereof. With pragmatic or reader-response criticism (Abrams, 1953:3-29; Freund:1-20), I believe the reader to be a very important pole of the reading task. In effect, I believe all readings to be perspectival, a negotiation between text and reader in the construction of meaning. In such a negotiation the reader becomes as important as the text: while features of the text (e.g., plot, characters, point of view, narrator, literary conventions, sociocultural context) guide the reader, the very identification and emphasis of the features in question by the reader is influenced by a number of highly complex and interrelated factors (e.g., gender, race or ethnic origins, class, ideology, sociocultural context). No reading is final and scientific: methodological questions are as important as hermeneutical questions. In the present study, however, I shall confine myself to the former rather than to the latter questions, to my reading of the text as such without any explicit consideration of my own social location or ideological stance in the reading of this text.[2]

2. Critical Approaches to the Notion of a Plot

Despite the extensive and diverse character of the existing critical literature on "plot," I believe that the work of K. Egan provides a very satisfactory point of entry in this regard. In effect, Egan approaches the various understandings and uses of the term "plot" in the critical literature in terms of three intersecting axes, of which one is regarded as primary, as the basic continuum for most uses of "plot," while the other two are said to weave around it, intersecting the first axis here and there (455–57). Though Egan himself ultimately abandons this three-dimensional matrix as too extended and irregular in favor of what he claims to be a much more rigorous model based on linguistics, such a matrix does provide in my opinion a very clear and effective way of drawing together and contrasting the major thrusts of a great variety of different critical approaches to an understanding of plot.

a. The primary axis or basic continuum within this three-dimensional matrix is identified as the particular-to-abstract axis. Towards one end of this axis, plot is used to mean an outline or skeleton of the main events or incidents of the narrative, that is to say, a relatively detailed description which remains very close to the narrative itself (Scholes and Kellogg:12, 207–8; Perrine:42–43). Then, as one moves away from this particular end of the axis, a greater degree of abstraction is to be found, leading to a more or less pronounced content/form distinction. Such a distinction is less pronounced at an intermediate stage of abstraction, where plot is seen in terms of the overall arrangement of the incidents or as the relationship among incidents or between each incident and the whole and thus in terms of the pattern or geometry of the narrative (Chatman:43–56). The distinction becomes much more pronounced towards the abstract end of the axis, where plot is understood not so much in terms of the incidents it organizes but rather in terms of the mind that does the organizing and, consequently, as a primary property of minds rather than narratives, ultimately yielding a limited classification or typology of plots (Crane:238–40; Friedman:154–66; Frye:33–67, 158–239; cf. Brooks:35–36).

b. A second axis is then described as the synchronic-diachronic axis. At the synchronic end of this axis, plot is seen as a synthetic or structural whole, a *mythos*, open to a kind of static analysis; within such a whole causal completion determines the overall sense of unity and all parts serve the final end, which thus emerges as the very soul of the work itself (Crane:241–42; Friedman:148–50, 165–66). At the diachronic end of the axis, plot is seen as the process of causal completion, and the dynamic or sequential element of the narrative becomes the main focus of attention. As a result, plot is seen as the source of movement from beginnings, where anything can happen, to middles, where things become probable, to ends, where everything is necessary (Scholes and Kellogg:207–8). As one moves from the synchronic to the diachronic end of the axis, the content/form distinction becomes, once again, increasingly pronounced: narrative is seen more and more as a mass of subject matter that cannot move until the end or destination is known.

c. The third and final axis is characterized as the content-emotion axis. At the content end of this axis, plot is seen in terms of patterns of narrative, while at the emotion end it is seen in terms of patterns of emotions. This axis is further described in terms of the common distinction drawn in the literature between "plot" and "story": at the former end of the axis, plot becomes the arrangement and connection of the events according to the orderly sequence of presentation in the narrative—in other words, how the reader learns of the story (Perrine:48–50); at the latter end of the axis, plot is seen as the organization of these events for maximum emotional effect and thematic interest—in other words, how the reader is affected by the story (Crane:239–40; Friedman:149–51). The content/form distinction becomes increasingly pronounced, once again, from one end of the axis to the other: the sequence of events is seen more and more in terms of its emotional effects.

3. THE PLOT OF THE FOURTH GOSPEL: PREVIOUS APPROACHES
AND METHODOLOGY

a. *Traditional Approaches.* Though not pursued in such terms until the advent of literary criticism and its explicit incorporation of literary theory in New Testament studies in the 1980s, it would be quite incorrect to suppose that the analysis of the plot of the canonical gospels was completely unknown and unpracticed until quite recently. In fact, all through the period of redaction and composition criticism in gospel studies, from the 1950s to the 1970s, one can detect in the scholarly literature—and above all in the commentary tradition—an ever sharper concern for plot under the guise of "structure," with more and more attention devoted to the given arrangement and sequence of events in the gospel in question. The scholarly literature on the Fourth Gospel is no exception in this regard.

Indeed, a look at a few of the major commentaries that appeared in these decades shows an increasing concern for the organization and development of the work as a whole.

1. Thus, for example, in his two-volume commentary on John of the mid to late 1960s, R. Brown offers an overall fourfold division for the Gospel, "suggested by the Gospel itself," consisting of a Prologue (1:1–18), a Book of Signs (1:19–12:50), a Book of Glory (13:1–20:31), and an Epilogue (21) (1:xi–xii, cxxxviii–cxxxix; 2:xiii–xiv). This overall division is explained as follows: (a) the first large division largely concerns Jesus' miracles or "signs" and discourses explaining the signs; (b) the second large division develops the theme of Jesus' return to the Father or glorification, with the risen Jesus as Lord and God; (c) while the signs of the former anticipate the glory of Jesus in a figurative way for those who believe, the action of the latter, directed to those who believed in the signs, accomplishes in reality what was anticipated in signs. Each of these large divisions is then subdivided into smaller sections (five in 1:19–12:50; four in 13:1–20:31), and these are in turn further subdivided into smaller units of varying lengths. The various divisions in question, from the major to the minor, are posited on the basis of a combination of temporal, spatial, artistic, generic, and thematic-theological criteria, with a decided emphasis on the latter.

2. From the mid-1960s to the mid-1970s, R. Schnackenburg's three-volume commentary on the Fourth Gospel gradually appeared. A very similar outline for the structure of the Gospel is provided, though now in terms of an overall threefold division, with the given incorporation of "the prologue" into the first division itself: "Jesus Reveals Himself before the World" (1:1–12:50); "Jesus in the Circle of His Own" (13:1–20:31); and an Editorial Conclusion (21) (1:vii, 2:1, 3:vii). As the titles themselves indicate, however, a slight shift of focus may also be detected in the explanation behind such a division: the emphasis is now placed more on the audience or recipients than on the mode or means of Jesus' revelation— not so much signs-figurative/ glorification-in reality, as in Brown, but rather world/disciples. The large divisions are again subdivided into several and much smaller sections of differing lengths (fifteen in the former; seven in the latter), with a further subdivision of the longer sections within 13:1–20:31 into smaller units. The very same type of criteria may be observed at work once again: temporal, spatial, artistic, generic, and thematic-theological, with a clear emphasis on the latter as well.

3. In the early 1970s, after the full publication of Brown's work but prior to the completion of Schnackenburg's, B. Lindars advanced a very different overall division of the Gospel into fifteen sections of varying lengths, comprising anywhere from one to three chapters, with further

subdivision throughout into smaller units (70–73). While the prologue is again incorporated within the first such division, John 21 is also set apart, once again, as the final division, now characterized as "The Appendix" (21). This proposed structure is thematic-theological through and through, with a fundamental christological orientation throughout, as the very central and active mention of Jesus in all the titles for the main sections readily indicates.[3]

The approach to plot in all three works reveals certain fundamental similarities: on the whole, a rather limited explanation or discussion of the proposed plot or structure; the use of strictly internal criteria throughout; an overwhelming emphasis on criteria of a thematic-theological character; no theoretical orientation of any sort with regard to the concept of structure or plot; and the presence of redactional or diachronic concerns, especially with respect to John 21. From the point of view of the three-dimensional matrix outlined above, these works can be classified as follows: towards the center of the particular-to-abstract axis—with an emphasis on the geometry of the Gospel; towards the synchronic end of the second axis—with an emphasis on the Gospel as a synthetic whole; and towards the content end of the third axis—with an emphasis on patterns of narrative in the Gospel.

b. *Recent Approaches.* A much more explicit and self-conscious discussion of plot in the canonical gospels comes about as a result of the full turn to literary criticism in gospel studies in the 1980s. Within Johannine studies, two works have been especially important in this regard, both of whose authors are contributors to the present issue of *Semeia*: R. A. Culpepper and J. Staley.

1. In an early study of the general literary dimensions of the Gospel, published in 1983, Culpepper devoted a full chapter to the element of plot (79–98). The line of argumentation presents a clear fourfold development. First of all, a twofold summary of the wider discussion concerning plot itself is offered: a summary of the central features of plot, taken from M. H. Abrams' glossary of literary terms (sequence; causality; unity; and affective power) (1971:127), with a brief explanation of some of these terms; and a summary of different classifications of plots (Crane; Chatman; Friedman; Frye), with some brief comparisons made here and there between these various classifications and the plot of John. In the end, a decision is made to approach the plot of John away from all such classifications and in terms of a close study of the Gospel itself— "the careful crafting of a unified sequence and a logic of causality which is developed through the repetition of scenes and dialogues in the Gospel" (87).

Secondly, Culpepper then proceeds to identify both the central focus of the plot (Jesus' fulfillment of his mission to reveal the Father and authorize the children of God) and its specific mode of development (the repeated recognition or lack of recognition of Jesus' identity and mission, so that each episode not only further reveals Jesus' identity but also recapitulates the plot of the Gospel as a whole). Thirdly, in a chapter by chapter approach, Culpepper then goes on to describe the development of this plot in much greater detail. Finally, Culpepper returns to Abrams' four central features of plot and ranks them in order of importance with regard to the plot of the Fourth Gospel: sequence; causality; and affective power, which is characterized as by far its most important feature and described in terms of enclosing the reader in the company of faith.

A comparison with the earlier commentary tradition shows a full and extended discussion of the proposed plot of the Gospel; a consideration of external criteria, with a deliberate decision to rely on criteria of a strictly internal sort; a continued emphasis on criteria of a thematic-theological sort, as the identification of the plot's focus and mode of development readily shows; a full use of a theoretical orientation drawn from the wider literary discussion; and a lingering presence, again with regard to John 21, which is called a later epilogue, of redactional-diachronic concerns. In terms of the three-dimensional matrix, Culpepper's approach can be characterized as follows: within the first axis—towards the particular end, with an emphasis on the repeated episodes that recapitulate the plot as a whole; within the second axis—towards the diachronic end, with an emphasis on the process of causal completion; within the third axis—towards the emotion end, with a very strong emphasis on the affective power of the work.

2. Five years later, in 1988, Staley's dissertation on the rhetorical strategies of the Fourth Gospel appeared; a full chapter is again devoted to the question of the overall rhetorical structure or plot—defined as the "literary design" or "order in which words, phrases, and motifs appear in the text regardless of narrative level" (50, n. 4)—of the Gospel, beginning with the prologue (1:1–18) and then proceeding to the remainder of the narrative as a whole (1:19–21:25) (50–73). In all Staley proposes a fivefold overall division of the Gospel, with four major divisions outlined within 1:19–21:25: (a) the prologue (1:1–18); (b) the first ministry tour (1:19–3:36); (c) the second ministry tour (4:1–6:71); (d) the third ministry tour (7:1–10:42); and (e) the fourth ministry tour (11:1–21:25).

All of these divisions, including the prologue, reveal a very similar symmetrical, concentric structure; in fact, it is the first such division, the prologue, that provides the fundamental structural pattern for the four other major divisions of the narrative, thus accounting in effect for the twofold line of development pointed out above—namely, an analysis of the prologue followed by an analysis of the remainder of the narrative (72–73). To begin with, the prologue presents a sevenfold concentric structure: its outermost components (A) deal with the relationship of the Word of God to God, creation, and humankind; the intermediate components (B) present the witness of John; the innermost components (C) depict the journey of the Word of God into the world; while the central component (D) describes the gift of empowerment to those who believe. In the subsequent divisions of the narrative, then, this structure is reproduced in various degrees: in the first such division, one finds a fivefold development, beginning with the witness of John as its outer components (A), continuing with journeys of Jesus as its innermost component (B), and concluding with a central component describing the actions of Jesus (C); in the three final divisions, one finds a threefold development instead, whose outer components consist of further journeys of Jesus (A) and whose central component again focuses on the actions of Jesus (B). In addition, this symmetrical, concentric structure reveals two other distinctive characteristics as well: not only is each division within it larger than the one before it, but also each division introduces a minor discordant story problem at the very beginning which it then proceeds to resolve climactically at the end.

This proposed delineation of the overall rhetorical structure of the Gospel is ultimately based on four basic criteria. As the very titles ("ministry tours") given to these divisions indicate, the first of these criteria, the motif of the journey, is by far the most important one. Thus, following the initial pattern of the prologue, all four ministry tours of 1:19–21:25 mention a journey of Jesus—the innermost components of the prologue—at the beginning and at the end; in the case of the first such tour, this concentric pattern is expanded, again following the pattern of the prologue, through the further incorporation of the latter's intermediate components, the witness of John, immediately before and after such journeys. All of these ministry tours further reveal various other signs of symmetry that confirm this basic concentric pattern, such as the geographical location of the various components in question, the kinds of episodes contained within them, and thematic content and development.

The other three basic criteria serve as further confirmation for such a tightly-knit structure in all four ministry tours: the given interplay between narration and direct speech, whereby the spatial notations of the narrator regarding the geographical locations of the major characters in the opening scenes are resumed in the final scenes and used metaphorically in direct speech by the major characters; other specific aspects of plot development, such as the relationship of the various characters in question to one another; and the use of distinctive *Leitwörter* or keywords.

Finally, Staley addresses the question of the overall function of this proposed rhetorical structure. On the one hand, he does agree with Culpepper to the effect that through the use of such a plot the implied reader is pulled into an intimate relationship with the implied author whereby the former is brought to share in the latter's convictional system (the enclosing of the reader in the company of faith). On the other hand, he also goes beyond Culpepper in arguing that the symmetrical, concentric structures of this plot play a major role in this regard: (a) such structures help to produce an implied reader who is brought to a sense of closure insofar as he or she is repeatedly brought to the original starting place; (b) however, such a sense of closure is never final, insofar as the implied reader is constantly forced to reevaluate the opening scene in the light of the closing scene and thus to delve below surface appearances; (c) consequently, through such "a second look" the implied reader is always brought to a new level of understanding and faith.

A comparison with Culpepper's approach shows, once again, a full and extended explanation of the proposed plot or structure of the Gospel; a continued reliance on criteria of a strictly internal sort; a clear move away from an emphasis on thematic-theological criteria to a corresponding emphasis on criteria of an artistic nature; a full use of a theoretical orientation derived from the wider literary discussion, though not so much with regard to the very concept of plot itself; and a complete move away from all concerns of a redactional-diachronic sort, even with regard to John 21. From the point of view of the three-dimensional matrix proposed by Egan, Staley's approach can be characterized as follows: in terms of the first axis, towards the center—with an emphasis on the structure or geometry of the narrative; in terms of the second axis, towards the synchronic end—with an emphasis on the Gospel as a synthetic whole; and in terms of the third axis, towards the center—with a more or less equal emphasis on both patterns of narrative and patterns of reaction.

3. *Present Proposal*. In the light of the preceding scholarly discussion, I should like to set forth at this point, prior to the outline of the plot itself, the three basic methodological criteria to be used in my own approach to the plot of the Gospel: (a) the Fourth Gospel as an example of ancient biographies; (b) the Fourth Gospel's adoption of the common motif of the journey or travel account in ancient narrative; and (c) the Fourth Gospel's use of the common technique of patterns of repetition or recurrence in ancient narrative. It is an approach that I would characterize as literary-rhetorical in character.

a. The first methodological criterion has to do with issues of genre and generic conventions. To begin with, then, I believe that the Fourth Gospel does represent an example of ancient biography and, as such, follows the basic conventions of ancient biographical writing (Scholes and Kellogg:210–18; Fairweather:266–75; Cox:45–65; Aune:46–63); I further believe that a proper attention to and consideration of such biographical conventions can be very fruitful indeed in coming to terms with the plot of the Gospel. I limit myself at this point to three very important conventions in this regard.

First of all, ancient biographies usually present a threefold structural framework: a beginning narrative of origins and youth, a central and extended narrative of the public life or career of the hero, and a concluding narrative of death and lasting significance. The narrative of origins and the narrative of death function, therefore, as a frame for the central division depicting the public life or career of the hero; this frame, however, is ultimately optional, so that either one or both of these outer divisions can be omitted from any one work (Cox:54–55; Aune:27, 47–49). Secondly, ancient biographies generally present two different types of development: the chronological, which follows a historical or temporal approach to the public life of the hero, portraying the individual events of his career in order of occurrence; or the topical, which follows a systematic approach instead, arranging such events in terms of the various different aspects of the hero's character (Cox:55–56; Aune:31–32). Thus, while the chronological type depicts the public life of the hero in terms of a succession of events that gradually lead to his *akme*—his most productive and creative period, usually said to begin at age forty—the topical type portrays the public life of the hero as if it were one continuous *akme* (Polman:171–72). Finally, in keeping with ancient conceptions of the individual as dyadic or group-oriented and of personality as static or unchanging (Malina:51–70), ancient biographies also present a stylized view of the hero's character and career—the hero not as a unique individual but rather as an example of a type, which type exhibits certain very characteristic traits or topoi and differs according to the individual in question, e.g., kings, generals, poets, orators, philosopher (Aune:28, 32–34).

In the case of the philosopher type, increasingly regarded as a divine sage or holy man by the first century A.D., these constitutive traits or topoi can be identified as follows (Cox:17–30): wisdom, insight into human nature, concern for the welfare of his fellow human beings, desire to communicate wisdom, and an ascetic lifestyle. In addition, the philosopher type admits of two subtypes in terms of the degree of divinity attributed to the hero: the holy man as either a son of god or godlike;

again, very specific traits or topoi distinguish the former from the latter: divine parentage, miracle-working, and misunderstanding by followers and enemies alike (Cox:30–44). On the whole, biographies of holy men were topical in nature, thus depicting their entire life as one continuous *akme*.

In the light of these biographical conventions, the portrayal of Jesus in the Fourth Gospel can be readily summarized as follows: (1) all three divisions of the overall structural framework—a narrative of origins and youth, of the public life or career, and of death and lasting significance—are present, though their precise demarcation is very much open to discussion and interpretation; (b) the chronological type of development is followed, though in fact no distinction is made between the public life and *akme* of Jesus (cf. 8:57); and (c) the type of the holy man is adopted and, more specifically, the subtype of the holy man as a son of god—in addition to the five essential traits enumerated above, Jesus' life also includes divine parentage, miracle-working, as well as a thorough misunderstanding by all, including his own circle of disciples.

b. The second methodological criterion has to do with matters of literary form. The Fourth Gospel has recourse to a very common literary motif of ancient narrative, namely, the journey or travel account (Scholes and Kellogg:73–79; Aune:122–24).[4] Beginning with the Homeric epic itself and the biblical writings, the journey or travel motif becomes a very important means of arranging the material in question at a macrostructural level, ultimately functioning as a host form and thus encompassing a wide variety of different literary forms; this journey or travel motif is used in a wide number of narrative forms (e.g., history, biography, and romance) and is ultimately developed by the Romans into first-person narrative (e.g., picaresque, the mock journey, and autobiography). Again, I believe that a close analysis of the presence and use of this motif in the Fourth Gospel can be of direct help in coming to terms with its plot.[5]

In the Gospel this journey or travel motif is developed in two rather different though highly interrelated directions. On the one hand, the Word of God is portrayed from the very beginning of the Gospel as undertaking—at the bequest of God the Father himself—a mythological, cosmic journey from the world of God to the world of human beings, ultimately becoming flesh as Jesus of Nazareth and thus carrying out the mission of the Father in and to the world; upon the completion of this mission, the Word of God returns from the world of human beings to the world of God. As such, this cosmic journey provides an overall framework for the plot of the Gospel: the biography of Jesus of Nazareth, messiah and son of God, is the biography of the Word of God made flesh in the world. On the other hand, as the Word of God made flesh, Jesus of

Nazareth is further portrayed throughout the Gospel as undertaking a series of geographical journeys in the course of his public life or ministry, thus continuing to carry out the mission of the Father in and to the world; with the completion of the last such journey, the mission itself comes to an end and the return to the world of God takes place. Within the overall framework of the mythological, cosmic journey, therefore, these geographical journeys provide a further and much more concrete framework for the plot of the Gospel: the biography of Jesus of Nazareth, the Word of God made flesh in the world, entails a number of journeys in the world of human beings as well.

c. The third methodological criterion has to do with matters of literary style and technique. The Fourth Gospel has recourse as well to a very common literary technique of ancient narrative, namely, the use of patterns of recurrence or repetition. Again beginning with the Homeric epic itself and the biblical writings, patterns of recurrence become very important indeed in arranging the material in question, both at a macrostructural and microstructrural level (Kawin:34–59; Miller:1–21; Alter:88–113). Accordingly, such repetitive patterns range from the very small to the very large, encompassing such different features as: words and other verbal elements (words in unbroken sequence; key-words or *Leitwörter*; figures of speech); motifs (concrete images, sensory qualities, actions, or objects; often in association with key-words); themes (ideas which form part of the value system of the work, again often in association with key-words or motifs); events or scenes within the same text, involving the same cluster of motifs; motifs from one plot or character in another plot or character within the same work (double plots; reenactments); motifs, themes, characters, events, or scenes from one work in another. In addition, such patterns of recurrence quite often involve an important element of variation as well, thus providing a very significant measure of richness and diversity in the very midst of repetition (Alter:88–91). Once again, I believe that a proper attention to and analysis of such patterns in the Fourth Gospel can be of immediate advantage in coming to terms with its plot.

In the Fourth Gospel such repetitive patterns are quite numerous indeed and encompass the full range of the spectrum. Given the goals and limitations of the present study, however, I shall focus for the most part on the motif of the journey or travel account already described in the preceding exposition of the second methodological criterion: not only does one encounter a very frequent recurrence of this motif in the Gospel, insofar as Jesus undertakes a wide number of geographical journeys throughout the course of his public life or ministry, but also a very frequent recurrence of a similar series of events surrounding such journeys, insofar as a cluster of subordinate motifs are also used repeatedly in the development of these journeys.

4 THE PLOT OF THE FOURTH GOSPEL: THE JOURNEY(S) OF THE WORD OF GOD

A. *The Narrative of Jesus' Origins (1:1–18)*

As indicated in the exposition of the first methodological criterion, the Fourth Gospel follows the standard threefold division of ancient biographies, with a narrative of origins and youth preceding and leading to a central and extended narrative of Jesus' public life or career. I believe that this first major division of the Gospel consists of John 1:1–18, that is to say, what has traditionally been referred to as "the prologue" of the Gospel (Brown:1.xi; Schnackenburg:1.197; Lindars:70).

This proposed demarcation is not entirely free of difficulties; indeed, a number of other options can be reasonably advanced as well. To begin with, one could extend this first division all the way through 2:12 (1:1–2:12), thus including the episode at Cana (2:1–11) and the subsequent visit to Capernaum (2:12), by arguing that Jesus' full public life begins only with 2:13, with his first visit to Jerusalem; that prior to 2:13, the Gospel is concerned with either the gathering of the first disciples, with little impact on anyone else, or with the witness of John to Jesus; and that the latter witness serves as a further introduction to Jesus' origins. Secondly, one could extend it as well through 1:51 (1:1–51), including thereby the calling of Jesus' first disciples (1:35–51), on the following grounds: the episode at Cana forms part of Jesus' public life, insofar as some do know what Jesus has done at the marriage feast; prior to Cana, the story is concerned only with individual disciples and the witness of John; and, again, the latter does function as an additional introduction to Jesus' origins. Thirdly, one could also extend it through 1:34 (1:1–34), through the very end of John's witness to Jesus (1:19–34), by arguing that there is no public activity of Jesus prior to this point, only the encounter with John and the witness of the latter, and that the public life begins with the gathering of the first disciples themselves.

In the end, however, I would argue for 1:18 as the most satisfactory option for the following reasons: such a delineation provides in and of itself a full account of Jesus' true origins, not in the world of human beings but rather in the world of God; the witness of John (1:19–1:34) begins the public life or career proper by alerting both the authorities of Jerusalem with regard to the figure of the one to come after him and his own disciples with regard to the identity of this figure; such witness is properly anticipated and summarized within the proposed narrative of origins itself (1:6–8, 15); and such witness also forms part of a repetitive pattern of narrative sections—thus paralleling the repeated references within 1:1–18 itself—dealing with the figure and witness of John to be found, with direct structural implications, throughout the public ministry of Jesus. Let the traditional "prologue" of John 1:1–18 serve therefore as the narrative of origins and youth of the Gospel.

Though providing the customary first and reliable glimpse into the character of the individual in question, such a narrative of origins proves to be quite unusual as well. On the one hand, it contains no standard account of Jesus' ancestors, birth, or youth; in fact, no information whatsoever of this kind is given at this point (cf. 1:45; 2:1, 13; 4:43–44; 6:42; 7:1–9, 40–41, 52; 19:25b–27). On the other hand, it goes well beyond the usual attribution of divine parentage granted to a son of god as such and bestows on Jesus a very high degree of divinity indeed: he is introduced thereby as the very Word of God itself.

This first major division of the Gospel reveals a threefold structure, with an overall pattern of repetition in the form of an inclusion (A B A): while its framing components address Jesus' origins with and relationship to God in the world above (1:1–2; 1:18)—his status and role as the Word of God, its central component describes his relationship as Word of God to the world below in terms of a progressive pattern of concretization (1:3–16)—from an initial focus on the creation of the world (1:3); to an intermediate focus on his cosmic journey into the world and his twofold reception by the world, rejection/unbelief and acceptance/belief (1:4–13); to a concluding focus on this second reception, on those who accepted him and believed in him, the children of God (1:14–17). In each of the last two sections of this central component, furthermore, one finds a further repetitive pattern consisting of references to the figure and witness of John (1:6–8, 15), summarizing thereby his proper relationship to the Word of God from the very beginning of the Gospel.

Through the outer components of such a structure, first of all, the narrative of origins reveals in full Jesus' status and role, his identity and mission, as the Word of God: he who was in the beginning with God and was God, the only-begotten God of the Father and the only one who has seen the Father, reveals the Father and makes him known. Through the central component of the structure, furthermore, the narrative of origins introduces as well—as already indicated in the exposition of the second methodological criterion—an overall framework of a mythological, cosmic journey to the story of Jesus that follows: as the Word of God made flesh, he came from the world of God into the world of human beings, which he himself had created, in order to carry out his mission of revealing the Father. Finally, through the unfolding process of concretization, the narrative of origins also introduces both a fundamental dimension of conflict and a fundamental assurance of victory and vindication into the story of Jesus about to be told: in revealing the Father in and to the world, the world, quite ironically, did not accept or believe in him, but rather opposed him and attempted to overcome him; however, the world did not succeed and, as a result, only those who did accept or believe in him were given the power to become the children of God, with the multitude of benefits such a status implies and entails.

B *The Narrative of Jesus' Public Life or Career (1:19–17:26)*

In keeping with the common biographical convention of a threefold structural division, the rather brief narrative of Jesus' origins of 1:1–18 is followed by an extended narrative of his public life or career. I believe that this central major division of the Gospel encompasses the whole of John 1:19–17:26, that is to say, from the very beginnings of John's witness concerning the one to come after him (1:19–34) through the prayer of Jesus to the Father at the conclusion of the farewell scene (17:1–26).

Once again, such a demarcation is not without difficulties, especially given the very important theme of "the hour" that is used to characterize the final stage of the Word of God's journey into the world, a period of time which comprises a rather wide number of constitutive events or components. Thus, several other options can be reasonably advanced as well, offering a very wide range of possibilities indeed. First of all, one could end this central division with 12:11 (1:19–12:11), after the Lazarus cycle of events (11:1–12:11) and prior to the final journey of Jesus to Jerusalem, at the very beginning of which the arrival of "the hour" is explicitly announced (12:23). Secondly, one could extend it through 12:19 (1:19–12:19), after the episode of the final entrance into the city (12:12–19) and immediately before the episode containing the explicit identification of the arrival of "the hour" upon the coming of some Greeks to see Jesus (12:20–36a). Thirdly, one could extend it even further through 12:50 (1:19–12:50), after all of the events concerning the final entry into Jerusalem are over, culminating with the narrator's summary of 12:36b–50 and Jesus' soliloquy of 12:44–50, and immediately prior to the farewell scene of 13:1–17:26. This is by far the most common division encountered in the scholarly literature (Brown:1.xi–xii; Schnackenburg:3.1–5; cf. Staley:66–68). Finally, one could take it all the way through 19:16 (1:19–19:16), after the appearance of Jesus before the Roman authorities (18:28–19:16) and immediately prior to the death scene proper (19:17–42).

In the end, however, I would argue for 17:26 as the most satisfactory option. First of all, such a delineation brings this central narrative of the public life or career of Jesus to a very proper and effective close with a depiction of the various public events surrounding the final entrance of Jesus into Jerusalem (12:12–50), an explicit identification of the arrival of "the hour" (12:20–23), and the portrayal of a long farewell scene with his disciples, where the fundamental meaning and consequences of this "hour" are disclosed and explained to the disciples prior to the occurrence of its impending climactic events (13:1–17:26). Secondly, such a central narrative would be followed immediately by the scene of Jesus' arrest in 18:1–12, a scene that sets into rapid motion the chain of events ultimately leading to his crucifixion and death. Finally, with this scene of the arrest at the beginning of chap. 18, Jesus is also formally separated from his disciples, thus bringing to an end a relationship that marks the whole of the public ministry, and brought into the custody and control of the ruling authorities, thus allowing for the climactic events of "the hour" to take their full and swift course. Let John 1:19–17:26 serve therefore as the central narrative of Jesus' public life or career in the Gospel.

As in the case of the narrative of origins, however, this narrative of the public life or career of Jesus proves to be quite unusual as well. On the one hand, as already pointed out above, while biographies of holy men generally follow a topical rather than chronological development, the Fourth Gospel portrays Jesus as the Word of God in terms of a chronological type of presentation, though again with an exclusive focus on his *akme*. To be sure, such a focus is readily understandable: as the Word of God made flesh in the world, the whole of Jesus' public ministry becomes his *akme*. On the other hand, when a chronological type of development is followed in biographical writing, the many events used to depict the course of the hero's public life—events which comprise a wide variety of different literary forms, such as anecdotes, maxims, discourses, catalogs, and miracles—are usually connected to one another by means of vague transitional notices of a chronological character, thus revealing the unchanging character of the hero in pastiche form, with a very simple concept of plot at work (Cox:55–58). In the Fourth Gospel, however, the portrayal of Jesus' public life or career goes well beyond such an uncomplicated connection of largely unrelated events and reveals instead a much more complex and artistic use of such events, a much more sophisticated use of plot.

It is precisely at this point, therefore, that the second and third methodological criteria outlined above—the extensive use of the journey or travel motif and the similarly extensive use of patterns of repetition—can play a major role in coming to terms with this much more artistic arrangement of Jesus' public life or career in the Fourth Gospel. In what follows, then, I shall rely expressly on both of these criteria as I proceed to outline, step by step, my own reading of the plot of the Gospel within this long central narrative of the public ministry. I shall argue, in effect, for the pivotal role of four different journeys to the city of Jerusalem: 1:19–3:36; 4:1–5:47; 6:1–10:42; and 11:1–17:26(21:25), the last part of which (18:1–21:25) constitutes the narrative of death and lasting significance; such a central pattern of repetition involves, furthermore, a number of other repetitive patterns as well, though with a great deal of variation throughout.

1. I have already made reference, in the preceding delineation of the narrative of origins, to an important pattern of repetition consisting of narrative sections dealing with the figure and witness of John, a pattern of repetition that ultimately parallels the repeated references to John within the narrative of origins itself; I would argue, in effect, that a first structural pattern of this central division of the Gospel can be discerned in the following sections dealing with the relationship between Jesus and John: 1:19–34; 3:22–36; and 10:40–42. Thus, while the first two sections surround the first journey to Jerusalem, the last two provide a frame for the second and third journeys; as such, the first three journeys of Jesus to Jerusalem are properly enclosed by the repeated witness of John.

The importance of these sections as literary markers is clearly enhanced by the use of explicit cross-references within them: both 3:22–36 (3:25–28, by way of both John himself and his disciples) and 10:40–42 (10:40–41, by way of the narrator and the people who had heard John) point back to the first section of 1:19–34. These three sections should be read, therefore, with direct reference to one another. Their importance as literary markers is further enhanced by their decreasing length, with each section smaller than the one preceding it, reflecting thereby not only the expanding public life of Jesus but also the declining public life of John, so well conveyed by both the narrator's disclosure of 3:24 (the eventual imprisonment of John) and John's own declaration of 3:30 (he must increase/I must decrease). In other words, by their very length these three narrative sections show how, as the ministry of Jesus begins to unfold, the ministry of John comes to an end.

The content of these sections further reflects such a change; indeed, a very clear progression with regard to the witness of John can be readily discerned. First of all, in 1:19–34—located in Bethany beyond the Jordan, prior to the beginning of Jesus' public ministry—John describes his own identity and mission, points forward to the figure of the one who is to come after him and who is greater than he, and identifies Jesus as such a one. Then, in 3:22–36—situated in the countryside of Judea, after the first major thrust of Jesus' public life and indeed occasioned by Jesus' own journey to and ministry in that area—John proceeds to describe his own identity and mission once again, points to the appointed end of his mission in the light of Jesus' own expanding mission, and gives further witness concerning Jesus. Finally, in 10:40–42—again in Bethany beyond the Jordan, after a significant part of Jesus' public life has already transpired—many who had heard John in that area (1:19–34) are now portrayed as accepting his witness regarding Jesus as true and hence as believing in Jesus. Through the sequence provided by these three sections, therefore, the appointed expansion of Jesus' ministry in and to the world is directly or indirectly contrasted with the appointed end of John's own ministry.

2. A second pattern of repetition within this central division, again with structural implications, consists of several journeys of Jesus to Galilee; three such journeys are undertaken in all: 1:35(43)–2:12; 4:1–54 (4:1–3, 43–52, with an intervening stop in Samaria); and 6:1–7:9. In direct contrast to the narrative sections dealing with John, each journey is developed in greater detail than the preceding one, thus reflecting the expanding mission of Jesus. Once again, the repeated witness of John provides a proper frame for all of these journeys of Jesus to Galilee: while the first two sections surround the first such journey, the last two sections enclose the second and third journeys.

The first journey (1:35[43]–2:12) takes place almost immediately after the first narrative section of John in Bethany beyond the Jordan (1:19–34) and forms an integral part of the initial gathering of the disciples, introduced by the transitional verses of 1:35–42; this first journey to Galilee is seemingly motivated, therefore, by Jesus' desire to expand the circle of disciples (1:43). Given the transitional character of 1:35–42, which record the movement from the disciples of John in Bethany beyond the Jordan to further disciples in Galilee, I see 1:35 as the beginning of this overall scene, with the journey proper encompassing 1:43–2:13. The second journey (4:1–54) follows immediately upon the second narrative section dealing with John, in the countryside of Judea (3:22–36), and is directly occasioned by Jesus' desire to avoid any type of encounter or confrontation with the Jewish authorities at this point (4:1–3). The third journey (6:1–7:9) is directly motivated by a similar desire on Jesus' part to avoid open persecution at the hands of the Jews in Judea (7:1). After 7:9 Jesus visits Galilee no more.

A very definite progression with regard to the expansion of Jesus' public ministry in Galilee can be immediately observed in the given sequence of these journeys: (a) The first journey proves to be quite successful, with a further gathering of disciples and a confirmation of the entire group's belief in Jesus after his first miraculous sign (2:11–12). (b) The second appears to be at first sight—quite aside from the results of the intervening Samaritan sojourn (4:4–42)—very successful as well, with a very positive reception by the Galileans (4:45) and the belief of an entire household in him as a result of a second miraculous sign (4:53–54); however, a prophetic note of rejection is attributed to Jesus by the narrator—Jesus will find no honor in his own country (4:43–44). (c) With the third journey, this prophecy of rejection in his own country comes true: despite a third miraculous sign and a further reaction of belief in him (6:1–15), the many who had followed him in Galilee eventually reject and abandon him, with the sole exception of a group of disciples now called "the twelve" (6:66–71); in fact, even his own brethren reject him as well (7:1–9; cf. 2:12). In sum, these repeated journeys of Jesus to Galilee lead from (a) rather limited though proper belief; to (b) massive though misguided belief as well as limited though proper belief; to (c) even more massive belief at first though followed by massive rejection, limited though proper belief, and further rejection by his own family.

3. Such journeys to Galilee are paralleled by a third pattern of repetition involving four journeys to the city of Jerusalem: 2:13–3:21; 5:1–47; 7:14–10:39; and 11:1–17:26(21:25). As in the case of the Galilean journeys and in contrast to the narrative sections that focus on John, each journey to Jerusalem is described in greater detail than the preceding one, thus reflecting once again the ever expanding mission of Jesus. As already indicated above, these journeys also constitute the pivotal repetitive pattern of the public ministry. Again, while the first three are properly enclosed by the narrative sections dealing with John, with one taking place between the first two sections and the other two between the last two sections, the fourth begins immediately after the last such section (10:40–42) and takes up the remainder of the Gospel.

a. The First Three Journeys of Jesus to Jerusalem

1. Two additional repetitive patterns may be observed with regard to the first three journeys: each one is directly associated with the celebration of a Jewish feast in Jerusalem; each one also follows immediately upon a corresponding journey to Galilee, thus accounting for three Galilee/Jerusalem cycles in a row: 1:35–3:21; 4:1–5:47; and 6:1–10:39.

Thus, the first journey of 2:13–3:21, which takes place during the Passover feast, follows the first Galilean journey that concludes with the brief stay of Jesus and his disciples in Capernaum (1:35–2:12). Similarly, the second journey of 5:1–47, which takes place on the occasion of an unidentified feast, follows immediately upon the second Galilean journey that concludes with the belief of an entire household in him (4:1–54). Finally, the third journey of 7:10–10:39, which begins during the feast of Tabernacles and extends through the feast of the Dedication, follows the third and final Galilean journey that ends with the massive rejection of

Jesus (6:1-7:9). After 7:10, therefore, Galilee disappears altogether from the narrative—except for the return of the disciples and the final appearance of Jesus in chap. 21—and Jerusalem becomes the most important focus of attention.

It should be further observed at this point that the narrative sections focusing on the figure and witness of John provide in fact a proper frame for these three Galilee/Jerusalem cycles: while the first cycle is enclosed by the first two sections, the second and third are surrounded by the last two sections.

2. A third repetitive pattern can be further observed at work with regard to these first three journeys to Jerusalem. Each journey leads to a negative reception of some sort in the city; in fact, as in the case of the Galilean journeys, a very definite progression with regard to the expansion of Jesus' ministry can be observed as well in the given sequence of these journeys to Jerusalem: the negative reception in question increases dramatically with each new journey.

In the first journey of 2:13-3:21, one finds a sharp questioning of Jesus on the part of the Jewish authorities (2:13-22); initial belief by many because of his many (unnarrated) miraculous signs in the city, though with a prophetic note of rejection, quite similar to the one found in the course of the subsequent second journey to Galilee, attached by the narrator (2:23-25); and a complete failure to understand on the part of one of the rulers of the Jews (3:1-21). In the second journey of 5:1-47, the prophetic note of rejection again begins to come true: Jesus' miraculous signs and declarations lead to open rejection and active hostility, with the intent to kill him on the part of the Jewish authorities (5:16-18). In the third journey of 7:10-10:42, Jesus' ongoing declarations and miraculous signs lead to even greater rejection and hostility, marked by a number of attempts to arrest him (7:30; 7:32, 44-52; 8:20; 10:39) as well as two attempts to kill him by stoning (8:59; 10:31), which in fact divide this third journey into two different cycles of events with the same climax (7:10-8:59; 9:1-10:42). With each journey to Jerusalem, therefore, one does indeed find—with some very limited exceptions of proper belief in him (9:1-41)—increasing rejection and open hostility, roughly paralleling the eventual course of the repeated journeys to Galilee, though in the latter case proper belief is somewhat more frequent and open hostility is altogether absent.

3. This last comment points to a fourth repetitive pattern within these first three journeys. Such a negative reception in the city of Jerusalem leads Jesus throughout to avoid further trouble and confrontation with the authorities by leaving the city and undertaking a journey to safer territory. For example, after the first journey of 2:13-3:21, Jesus first leaves

for the countryside of Judea (3:22-24), thus introducing the second narrative section dealing with John (3:22-36); eventually, he leaves this area as well in order to avoid further questioning by the Jewish authorities (4:1-3), thus giving rise to the second journey to Galilee and the second Galilee/Jerusalem cycle. Similarly, after the second journey of 5:1-47, Jesus leaves Jerusalem once again in order to avoid the first occasion of open hostility (5:16-18), giving rise thereby to the third journey to Jerusalem and the third Galilee/ Jerusalem cycle. Finally, after the third journey of 7:10-10:42, Jesus leaves Jerusalem yet again in order to avoid the second occasion of open hostility, with its twofold cycle and double attempt on his life; it should be noted that Jesus does not leave the city after the first attempt to kill him but only after the second, thus increasing tremendously the dramatic tension occasioned by this third journey. This time, however, instead of Galilee, where he goes no more until chap. 21, he proceeds to Bethany beyond the Jordan, thus giving rise to the third and final narrative section focusing on John (10:40-42).

To summarize, in 1:19-10:42, one finds the following sequence of events in the public ministry: (1) the first (direct) witness of John to Jesus in Bethany beyond the Jordan (1:19-34), pointing forward to the public life of Jesus; (2) the first Galilee/Jerusalem cycle (1:35-2:12/2:13-3:21), with a positive though limited reception in Galilee and a rather negative reception in Jerusalem, including questioning on the part of the authorities, surface acceptance by many with an accompanying prophecy of rejection to come, and a failure to understand on the part of one of the authorities—but with no open hostility; (3) the second (direct) witness of John in the countryside of Judea (3:22-36), occasioned by Jesus' first withdrawal from Jerusalem and pointing to the end of the public ministry of John in the light of the unfolding public ministry of Jesus; (4) the second Galilee/Jerusalem cycle (4:1-53/5:1-47), occasioned by a desire to avoid further questioning by the Jewish authorities, with surface acceptance by many and an accompanying prophecy of rejection to come in Galilee as well as outright rejection and open hostility in Jerusalem; (5) the third Galilee/Jerusalem cycle (6:1-7:9/7:10-10:39), occasioned by a desire to avoid persecution in Jerusalem, with massive rejection and very limited belief in Galilee and even sharper rejection and hostility in Jerusalem; and (6) the third (indirect) witness of John (10:40-42), occasioned by a desire to avoid persecution in Jerusalem and validating the witness of John concerning Jesus in the light of the latter's ever expanding public ministry.

b. The Fourth and Final Journey of Jesus to Jerusalem

Three of these repetitive patterns can be observed at work once again in the portrayal of the fourth and final journey of Jesus to the city of Jerusalem of 11:1–17:26(21:25), a visit which contains within itself the concluding narrative of death and lasting significance (18:1–21:25). This final journey is introduced by the Lazarus cycle of events (11:1–12:10), involving a further pattern of repetition: two different journeys to Bethany, a town quite close to Jerusalem itself and thus quite close to the very source of open hostility (11:1–53; 11:54–12:10); the final journey as such extends, therefore, from 12:11 through 17:26(21:25).

1. The first journey to Bethany (11:1–54) leads once again to rejection and hostility, now in terms of a decision on the part of the Jerusalem authorities to put Jesus to death on account of Jesus' raising of Lazarus (11:45–53), as well as another withdrawal of Jesus to safer territory, now Ephraim (11:54). The tension created by the preceding journeys to Jerusalem is directly continued and indeed increased by this journey to Bethany, not far from Jerusalem.

2. The second journey to Bethany (11:55–12:10) is again directly motivated by the celebration of a Jewish feast, the feast of Passover. The journey leads yet again to rejection and hostility (12:9–11); however, no withdrawal to safer territory takes place at this point. Instead, Jesus proceeds to Jerusalem for his final visit, a visit that will lead directly to his imprisonment and death and thus to his "hour."

3. This final journey to Jerusalem begins with a portrayal of the public events surrounding his very entrance into the city (12:12–50), in the course of which the arrival of "the hour" is explicitly identified, and continues with a long farewell scene (13:1–17:26), in the course of which the climactic events of "the hour" are anticipated (the farewell context: 13:1–30) and the fundamental meaning and consequences of such events disclosed and explained (the farewell discourse: 13:31–17:26) prior to their very occurrence. As already indicated above, its final components consist of the narrative proper of death and lasting significance.

To summarize, with the use of the same repetitive patterns employed in the development of the first three journeys, the final journey to Jerusalem continues to develop the ever-building rejection and hostility of the city towards Jesus in the course of his expanding mission: while the Lazarus cycle of events, with its repeated visits to the immediate area of Jerusalem and its further withdrawal of Jesus for safety, prepares the stage for the final journey itself through a dramatic increase in tension, the initial events of the journey proper clearly show that this final visit is undertaken with the appointed end of the mission in full view—the capture and death of Jesus at the hands of the ruling authorities of the world and their own ruler, specifically identified as the devil in the course of the farewell scene (13:1-3, 27, 30-31).

C. *The Narrative of Jesus' Death and Lasting Significance (18:1-21:25)*

Once again, following the standard biographical convention of a threefold structural framework, the central and extended narrative of the public life or career of Jesus gives way to a concluding narrative of death and lasting significance. Again, given the preceding argumentation for a delineation of the narrative of the public life as consisting of John 1:19-17:26, I believe that the narrative of Jesus' death and final significance extends from the scene of the arrest at the hands of the ruling authorities (18:1-12) to the final resurrection appearance to the disciples (21:1-25), thus encompassing all of John 18:1-21:25. As such, this final major division of the Gospel focuses directly on the last events of Jesus' final journey to the city of Jerusalem and thus on the climactic events of his "hour," whose arrival was explicitly announced at the very beginning of this final visit and whose meaning and consequences were subsequently disclosed and explained to the disciples in the course of the long farewell scene that follows immediately upon this final entry. Though the death of Jesus is certainly anticipated in the narrative before 18:1-12, it is only with this scene of the arrest that the portrayal of these climactic events begins in earnest. Let John 18:1-21:25 serve therefore as Jesus' narrative of death and lasting significance in the Gospel.

Five narrative sections—with all but the first involving several narrative units—may be readily identified within this final division of the Gospel. While the first three sections depict the preparatory events, the last two focus, respectively, on the death itself and its promised aftermath. The last section also makes for a quite unusual narrative of death and lasting significance: though an apotheosis of the hero and even appearances after death for a final farewell are by no means unknown (Fairweather:274-75), resurrection appearances certainly are. Through such appearances the fundamental assurance of victory and vindication introduced in the narrative of origins comes true: Jesus has survived death at the hands of his enemies and can now return to the world of God, thus bringing the cosmic journey to a proper closure.

The first section (18:1-12) provides an introduction: the arrest of Jesus in the garden beyond the Kidron valley by the ruling authorities of the world, a party composed of both Jewish and Gentile authorities and led by the ruler of the world, the evil one; his formal separation from the group of disciples; and a sign of his true status vis-à-vis the world and its rulers (18:4-8). The second and third sections then proceed to describe the appearance of Jesus before the ruling authorities in Jerusalem: the second before the Jewish authorities (18:13–27) and the third before the Roman authorities (18:28–19:16). The fourth section (19:17–42), the narrative of death proper, focuses on Jesus' death at the hands of the ruling authorities outside the city, from the very act of crucifixion itself to the removal of the body from the cross and burial in a nearby garden. The fifth and final narrative section (20:1–21:25) provides the proper and expected aftermath to the death itself: four resurrection appearances of Jesus to his disciples, both in Jerusalem and Galilee. This section reveals in a very unusual way, once again, the lasting significance of Jesus: in rising from the dead, his mission of revealing the Father is fully and triumphantly accomplished, his status and authority vis-à-vis the world and its rulers are vindicated, and a successor is bestowed upon the disciples so that they can proceed to undertake their own mission in and to the world.

Given the nature of the narrative of origins, however, one does fail to find a direct description or portrayal of the return of the Word of God from the world of human beings to the world of God, that is to say, a formal closure to the mythological, cosmic journey of the Word introduced in 1:1–18. To be sure, one does find explicit references to such a return by Jesus both prior to his death (e.g., 14:1–3; 13:31–32) and after his death (20:17). Consequently, there is indeed a conclusion to the mythological, cosmic journey introduced in 1:1–18, but only by way of future reference on the part of either the narrator or Jesus himself—upon the completion of his assigned mission, the Word of God returns to God from the world of human beings.

In the light of the preceding narrative of the public life or career, the present narrative of death brings the plot of the Gospel to a very proper and effective end. First of all, the fundamental conflict between the Word of God and the world introduced in 1:1–18 comes to a climax: the growing rejection and hostility of Jesus during the course of his public ministry, above all in the city of Jerusalem, leads to his arrest, condemnation, and execution by the Jerusalem authorities, both Gentile and Jewish. Secondly, the fundamental assurance of victory and vindication also comes to a climax: the end of the conflict—despite all appearances to the contrary, given Jesus' arrest, condemnation, and execution—is not at all a demise for Jesus. On the one hand, such an end forms part—indeed the central part—of the mission of revelation entrusted to him by the Father and is followed by his resurrection and resurrection appearances, demonstrating that the apparent demise is actually a triumph on his part. On the other hand, such an end also shows that the authority of the world and its rulers has been invalidated and subverted at a most fundamental level indeed.

5. THE STRATEGIC CONCERNS AND AIMS OF THE PLOT OF THE GOSPEL

I see this proposed plot for the Gospel as having a number of interrelated and interdependent strategic concerns and aims, yielding a rather complex variety of strategic functions for the Gospel as a whole:

a. I would argue for a very strong didactic function at work. The dominant motif of journeying allows Jesus, the Word of God, to engage in widespread and sustained teaching regarding the ways and values of God, his own status or identity as Word of God, and his role or mission in the world as entrusted to him by God. While the mythological, cosmic journey from the world of God firmly establishes the origins and provenance of Jesus and his message, the repeated geographical journeys in the world of human beings assure a widespread hearing and dissemination of such teaching and hence a repeated exposition and continuous development of such a revelation. As a result, as both Culpepper and Staley point out, the implied readers of the Gospel are indeed drawn thereby into the community of believers—initiated, confirmed, or reinforced as children of God, not only way of repetition and recapitulation (Culpepper) but also by way of expansion and intensification (Staley): the children of God are those who believe in Jesus and carry out his commands.

b. I would also argue for a very strong polemical function. Again, the dominant motif of journeying allows Jesus as the Word of God to undertake a broad and sustained attack on the ways and values of the world at large, a world whose own ruler is ultimately and explicitly identified as Satan himself. Through his mythological, cosmic journey from the world of God, Jesus introduces the ways and values of God into an unfriendly and hostile world ruled by the demonic powers; through his repeated geographical journeys in the world itself, Jesus also proceeds to call into question and attack the fundamental ways and values of the world; through his repeated visits to Jerusalem and his recurrent teaching in the Temple, Jesus further proceeds to do so at the very seat of power itself and in the very presence of the world's immediate rulers. As such, the implied readers of the Gospel are also systematically differentiated and separated thereby from the world at large, its own immediate rulers, as well as its ultimate ruler, the devil himself: the community of believers, the children of God, should see itself as deeply estranged from and at odds with the world, the children of the devil—in fact, they have been "taken out of" the world and are no longer "of the world."

c. I would argue for a very prominent admonitory function as well, closely tied to this polemical function. The broad and sustained attack on the world introduced by the journeys of Jesus provokes a very definite and sustained counterattack on the part of the world and its ruler(s).

Jesus' repeated geographical journeys lead to mounting questioning and massive rejection on the part of the world; his repeated journeys to the city of Jerusalem involve not only questioning and rejection but also outright hostility and persecution, culminating in his betrayal, arrest, condemnation, and execution at the hands of the world; and his mythological, cosmic journey into the world comes to an end with a forced and cruel departure from the world by way of crucifixion. Consequently, the implied readers of the Gospel are specifically warned thereby that an acceptance of the ways and values of God in the world implies and entails severe opposition from the world—pointed questioning, widespread rejection, active hostility, and perhaps even loss of life itself: the community of believers, the children of God, should expect nothing but hatred and oppression in and from the world.

d. Alongside this admonitory function I would further argue for a clear consolatory function. Despite such an inevitable and inescapable reaction on the part of the world, the dominant motif of journeying also allows for a great deal of comforting and consolation. The repeated geographical journeys of Jesus do meet with some success in the world—there are those who do believe in him, who accept his claims and his teaching; in addition, such a response is accompanied throughout by a host of promises and rewards, culminating not only with the designation of such believers as the new abiding place of God in the world but also with the solemn assurance of their own abiding places in the house of God. Similarly, the mythological, cosmic journey of Jesus does not come to an end with death at the hands of the world and its ruler(s) but rather gives way to resurrection and a glorious return to the world of God—in other words, to victory over the world and its ruler(s). As such, the implied readers of the Gospel are further assured that an acceptance of the ways and values of God in the world implies and entails a very privileged position indeed while in the world, ultimate victory over the world, and an abiding union with God in the world above: the community of believers, the children of God, shall receive glory not only in the world of human beings but also in the world of God.

e. Finally, I would argue for a very important exhortatory function as well. In the light of such warnings and promises, the dominant motif of journeying allows for sustained exhortation and encouragement as well. Thus, the repeated geographical journeys of Jesus show that the mission of the Father in and to the world must be undertaken as appointed regardless of the consequences involved—despite sharp questioning, overwhelming rejection, and severe hostility; similarly, the mythological, cosmic journey shows that the mission must be carried out regardless of its appointed end—arrest, condemnation, and execution. Only through trials and defeat in the world, therefore, can the teaching of God be properly disseminated and the mission properly accomplished. As a result, the implied readers of the Gospel are also urged thereby to carry on with their own mission in the world, regardless of dangers or consequences, in obedience to the plan of God and following the example of Jesus: the community of believers, the children of God, must bear much and constant fruit if they wish to abide in the vine of Jesus.

6. Conclusions

To begin with, a comparison of the proposed plot with those advanced by Culpepper and Staley reveals the following characteristics: (a) a similarly full and extended discussion of the proposed plot; (b) a much greater reliance on external criteria (generic and literary conventions), though with full attention to internal criteria as well—closer to Staley in this regard, but with a much more explicit discussion of such criteria from the point of view of ancient narrative; (c) with Staley, a clear move away from an emphasis on thematic-theological criteria in favor of artistic criteria; (d) a similarly full use of a theoretical orientation derived from the wider literary discussion; and (e) with Staley, a complete abandonment of all redactional-diachronic concerns. The result is a reading of the plot that relies on the dominant motif of the repeated journeys of Jesus, both into the world and in the world itself, within the larger framework of his biographical narrative as the Word of God made flesh.

In addition, given the three-dimensional matrix advanced by Egan, I would characterize my reading as follows: (a) with regard to the first axis, towards the center of the particular-abstract spectrum—with an emphasis on the pattern or geometry of the narrative, though with no claims to a final and definitive reading in this regard; (b) with regard to the second axis, towards the diachronic end—with an emphasis on the dynamic or sequential element of the narrative; (c) with regard to the third axis, towards the center—with an emphasis on the correspondence between the patterns of the narrative and the patterns of emotional reaction. The result is a reading of the plot that is comprehensive and coherent, both with regard to the overall arrangement of the incidents and the relationship among the incidents themselves; that incorporates and reflects a very definite sense of movement and development, from beginning to middle to end; and that is quite mindful of the close connection between narrative organization and emotional effect, with the narrative as a strategic whole consisting of a rather complex variety of interrelated and interdependent functions.

THE PLOT OF THE FOURTH GOSPEL: STRUCTURAL OUTLINE
THE JOURNEY(S) OF THE WORD

I. Narrative of Origins (1:1–18)

II. Narrative of the Public Life or Career (1:19–17:26)
   A. First Galilee/Jerusalem Cycle (1:19–3:36)
      1. First Narrative Section concerning John: Bethany beyond the Jordan (1:19–34)
      2. First Cycle (1:35–3:21)
         a. First Journey of Jesus to Galilee (1:35–2:12)
         b. First Journey of Jesus to Jerusalem (2:13–3:21)
      3. Second Narrative Section concerning John: Countryside of Judea (3:22–36)
   B. Second Galilee/Jerusalem Cycle (4:1–5:47)
      1. Second Journey of Jesus to Galilee (4:1–54)
      2. Second Journey of Jesus to Jerusalem (5:1–47)
   C. Third Galilee/Jerusalem Cycle (6:1–10:42)
      1. Third and Final Journey of Jesus to Galilee (6:1–7:9)
      2. Third Journey of Jesus to Jerusalem (7:10–10:39)
         a. First Cycle of Events (7:10–8:59)
         b. Second Cycle of Events (9:1–10:39)
      3. Third Narrative Section concerning John: Bethany beyond the Jordan (10:40–42)
   D. Fourth and Final Journey to Jerusalem (11:1–17:26)
      1. The Lazarus Cycle of Events: Journeys to Bethany (11:1–12:10)
         a. First Journey (11:1–54)
         b. Second Journey (11:55–12:11)
      2. Fourth Journey to Jerusalem (12:12–17:26)
         a. The Final Entry into Jerusalem (12:12–50)
         b. The Farewell Scene (13:1–17:26)
            (1) The Farewell Context (13:1–30)
            (2) The Farewell Discourse (13:31–17:26)

III. Narrative of Death and Lasting Significance (18:1–21:25)
   A. Preparatory Events (18:1–19:16)
      1. Introduction: The Arrest of Jesus by the Ruling Authorities (18:1–12)
      2. The Appearance of Jesus before the Jewish Authorities (18:13–27)
      3. The Appearance of Jesus before the Gentile Authorities (18:28–19:16)

B. The Narrative of Death and Lasting Significance
Proper (19:17–42)
1. The Death of Jesus (19:17–42)
2. The Resurrection Appearances (20:1–21:25)

NOTES

[1] I am presently at work on a three-volume study of the Fourth Gospel from a literary-rhetorical perspective for Fortress Press: the first volume, *The Farewell of the Word: A Johannine Call to Abide*, is due to appear in the spring of 1991; the second, *The Prayer of the Word: A Johannine Call to Unity*, is in the process of composition at this point; and the third volume, *The Life of the Word: A Johannine Call to Freedom*, is in the planning stages and will be the one where this initial reading of the plot of the Gospel will be further pursued and amplified.

[2] The latter is a task which I intend to pursue in a separate and forthcoming study on social location and biblical interpretation. Such a task ultimately represents what I would call an exercise in intercultural criticism.

[3] The different sections are titled as follows: "The Manifestation of the Divine Glory in Jesus" (1:1–2:12); "The New Order Inaugurated by the Coming of Jesus" (2:13–3:36); "New Life Made Available by the Coming of Jesus" (4:1-54); "The Life-Giving Word of Jesus and the Question of His Authority" (5:1-47); "Jesus is the Bread of Life" (6:1-71); "Jesus Supersedes the Law Because He is the Son of God" (7:1–8:59); "Jesus Enlightens Men to Know that He and the Father are One" (9:1–10:42); "Jesus is the Resurrection and the Life" (11:1-54); "Jesus Must Be Sacrificed before His Work is Accomplished" (11:55–12:50); "The Last Supper: Jesus and the Disciples. I" (13:1-38); "The Supper Discourses: Jesus and the Disciples. II" (14:1–16:33); "The Prayer of Jesus" (17:1-26); "The Trial and Death of Jesus" (18:1–19:42); "The Resurrection" (20:1-31).

[4] In fact, this motif of the journey plays a very important role as well in the plot of the other canonical gospels (Rhoads and Richie:63-72; Kingsbury:78-85; Matera:245, 250-51; Talbert:109-13). As such, the possibility of literary allusion by way of narrative situation (= the journey to Jerusalem) among the canonical gospels must be seriously considered; see my forthcoming "The Journey(s) of Jesus to Jerusalem: Plotting and Gospel Intertextuality," in *John and the Synoptics* (Colloquium Biblicum Lovaniense 39; ed. A. Denaux; Louvain: Louvain University Press).

[5] For a similar emphasis on the journeys of Jesus as central to the structure of the Gospel, see Rissi. However, I would point out the following differences in our respective readings of the Gospel: (a) instead of a twofold division of the Gospel (1:18–10:39; 10:40–20:31; chaps. 15–17 and 21 as later additions) based on the one motif of the journey, I argue for a threefold division following generic conventions; (b) the use of a mythological, cosmic journey—grounded in the threefold division itself—as an overall framework for the individual geographical journeys; (c) the grouping together of all four geographical journeys of Jesus to Jerusalem in a highly progressive sequence, with the last such journey as climactic and highly dramatic; (d) a much wider conception and delineation of the climactic fourth journey (Rissi: 10:40–12:41); (e) a wide recourse to a cluster of accompanying and subordinate motifs used repeatedly in the development of these geographical journeys; and (f) an explicit consideration of the various strategic concerns and aims in the use of this dominant motif of the journey.

WORKS CONSULTED

Abrams, M. H.
    1953   *The Mirror and the Lamp: Romantic Theory and the Critical Tradition*. London-Oxford-New York: Oxford University Press.
    1971   *A Glossary of Literary Terms*. 3rd ed. New York: Holt, Rinehart and Winston.

Alter, Robert.
    1981   *The Art of Biblical Narrative*. New York: Basic Books.

Aune, David E.
    1987   *The New Testament in Its Literary Environment*. Library of Early Christianity 8. Philadelphia: Westminster.

Brooks, Peter
    1985   *Reading for the Plot: Design and Intention in Narrative*. New York: Vintage.

Brown, Raymond E.
    1966–70   *The Gospel according to John*. 2 vols. The Anchor Bible 29, 29a. Garden City, N.Y.: Doubleday.

Caserio, Robert L.
    1979   *Plot, Story, and the Novel: From Dickens and Poe to the Modern Period*. Princeton: Princeton University Press.

Chatman, Seymour.
    1978   *Story and Discourse: Narrative Structure in Fiction and Film*. Ithaca and London: Cornell University Press.

Cox, Patricia.
    1983   *Biography in Late Antiquity: A Quest for the Holy Man*. Berkeley-Los Angeles-London: University of California Press.

Crane, R. S.
    1966   "The Concept of Plot." Pp. 233–43 in *Approaches to the Novel: Materials for a Poetics*. Rev. ed. Ed. R. Scholes. San Francisco: Chandler. Orig. published: 1952.

Culpepper, R. Alan.
    1983   *Anatomy of the Fourth Gospel: A Study in Literary Design*. Foundations & Facets: New Testament. Philadelphia: Fortress.

Egan, Kieran.
    1978   "What is a Plot?" *New Literary History* 9:455–73.

Fairweather, Janet.
    1974   "Fiction in the Biographies of Ancient Writers." *Ancient Society* 5:231–75.

Fortna, Robert T.
    1988   *The Fourth Gospel and Its Predecessor: From Narrative Source to Present Gospel.* Philadelphia: Fortress.

Freund, Elizabeth.
    1987   *The Return of the Reader: Reader-Response Criticism.* New Accents. London and New York: Methuen.

Friedman, Norman.
    1967   "Forms of the Plot." Pp. 145–66 in *The Theory of the Novel.* Ed. P. Stevick. New York: The Free Press; London: Collier-Macmillan, 1967. Originally published: 1955.

Frye, Northrop.
    1971   *Anatomy of Criticism: Four Essays.* Princeton: Princeton University Press.

Kawin, Bruce F.
    1972   *Telling It Again and Again: Repetition in Literature and Film.* Ithaca and London: Cornell University Press.

Kingsbury, J. D.
    1986   *Matthew as Story.* Philadelphia: Fortress.

Lindars, Barnabas.
    1979   *The Gospel of John.* London: Oliphants.

Malina, Bruce J.
    1981   *The New Testament World: Insights from Cultural Anthropology.* Atlanta: John Knox.

Martin, Wallace.
    1986   *Recent Theories of Narrative.* Ithaca and London: Cornell University Press.

Matera, Frank J.
    1987   "The Plot of Matthew's Gospel." *Catholic Biblical Quarterly* 49:233–53.

Miller, J. Hillis.
    1982   *Fiction and Repetition: Seven English Novels.* Cambridge: Harvard University Press.

Perrine, Lawrence.
1966   *Story and Structure*. New York: Harcourt, Brace and World.

Polman, G. H.
1974   "Chronological Biography and AKME in Plutarch." *Classical Philology* 69:169–77.

Rhoads, David and Donald Michie.
1982   *Mark as Story: An Introduction to the Narrative of a Gospel*. Philadelphia: Fortress.

Rissi, Matthias.
1983   "Der Aufbau des vierten Evangeliums." *New Testament Studies* 29:48–54.

Schnackenburg, Rudolf.
1965–75 *Das Johannesevangelium*. 3 vols. Herders Theologisches Kommentar zum Neuen Testament. Basel-Cologne-Vienna: Herder.

Scholes, Robert and Robert Kellogg.
1966   *The Nature of Narrative*. London-Oxford-New York: Oxford University Press.

Staley, Jeffrey L.
1988   *The Print's First Kiss: A Rhetorical Investigation of the Implied Reader in the Fourth Gospel*. SBL Dissertation Series 82. Atlanta: Scholars.

Talbert, Charles H.
1984   *Reading Luke: A Literary and Theological Commentary on the Third Gospel*. New York: Crossroad.

STUMBLING IN THE DARK, REACHING FOR THE LIGHT: READING CHARACTER IN JOHN 5 AND 9

Jeffrey L. Staley
University of Portland, OR

"Every character is a trap of a certain kind, one which the writer would like his readers to fall into" (Foldenyi:11).

ABSTRACT

R. A. Culpepper's *Anatomy of the Fourth Gospel* hinted at the similarity between the poetics of characterization in John and ancient Hebrew modes of characterization. In view of the recent work in ancient Hebrew narrative art by Robert Alter, Adele Berlin, Meir Sternberg, and Shimon Bar-Efrat this study shows how Culpepper's insight might be worked out in John 5 and 9.

Through a careful analysis of repetition and change in the narrator's language and the characters' speech patterns, strategically withheld information, narrative gaps, and ambiguous phraseology are highlighted. The interaction of these various narrative components gives a deeper understanding to characterization in the Fourth Gospel, showing that the succession of reading judgments must be accounted for in any analysis of Johannine characters.

1. INTRODUCTION

In R. A. Culpepper's analysis of characterization in the Fourth Gospel, he quotes Robert Scholes and Robert Kellogg where they are describing the difference between Greek and Hebraic characters. The paragraph is well-worn by biblical scholars:

> The heroes of the Old Testament were in a process of becoming, whereas the heroes of Greek narrative were in a state of being. Process in Greek narrative was confined to the action of a plot. And even so, the action exemplified unchanging, universal laws; while the agents of the action, the characters, became as the plot unfolded only more and more consistent ethical types. Abraham, Jacob, David, and Samson, on the other hand, are men whose personal development is the focus of interest (Scholes-Kellogg:169; Culpepper, 1983:103).

Building upon these observations, Culpepper notes that

> In John, the character of Jesus is static; it does not change. He only emerges more clearly as what he was from the beginning. Some of the minor characters, the Samaritan woman and the blind man in particular, undergo a signif-

icant change. To some extent, therefore, the Gospel of John draws from both Greek and Hebrew models of character development, but most of its characters appear to represent particular ethical types (1983:103).

A great deal has been written about the nature of ancient Hebrew narrative since Scholes and Kellogg's terse comparisons of twenty-five years ago and since Culpepper's suggestive comments now nearly ten years old.[1] Yet little has been done with Culpepper's observation regarding the "Hebrew model of character" in the Fourth Gospel beyond taking note of the same point he made.[2]

In light of Culpepper's insights, the purpose of this study is to explore in more depth how "the Hebrew models of character" and modes of characterization might enrich our reading of character in two particular miracle stories of the Fourth Gospel: the Sabbath-day healings of John 5:1–18 and 9:1–41. I have chosen these two stories for four reasons: First, the stories have a number of motifs in common that beg for comparison, and such repetition is an important feature of Hebrew poetics (Alter, 1981:88–113; Sternberg:365–440); second, I believe that by taking into account the role of direct discourse in Hebrew narrative, critical comments regarding the Johannine characters' conversations can be more carefully nuanced (Alter, 1981:63–87; Berlin:64–82; Sternberg:499–515; Bar-Efrat:218–237); third, I believe that the use of narration in characterization—while minimal in the Fourth Gospel—parallels that of Hebrew poetics in its subtlety (Alter, 1981:114–130; Berlin:57–64; Sternberg:190–222; Bar-Efrat:48–92); and finally, I believe that the central characters of these two stories invite readings that are especially open to the concerns of Reader Response Criticism—that is, ones that are sensitive to the successive unfolding judgments that take place during the reading experience.[3]

Among the many literary critics working with ancient Hebrew literature, Robert Alter, Adele Berlin, Meir Sternberg, and Shimon Bar-Efrat have made special efforts to describe the various kinds of characters which the biblical writers create, and they have tried to isolate the narrative modes of their characterization. With regard to the types of characters found in ancient Hebrew literature they all either explicitly or implicitly take issue with E. M. Forster's often quoted description of "flat" characters (68–78) as universally representative of Hebrew poetics (Scholes-Kellogg:164–166; Alter, 1981:114; Berlin:23, 37–38; Sternberg:191, 525; Bar-Efrat:90–92). Berlin, for example, finds three types of characters in Hebrew narrative (the "full-fledged character," the "type," and the "agent" (23–24, 31–32)), and coincidentally, Culpepper describes three types in the Fourth Gospel (the "protagonist," the "ficelles," and the "background characters" [1983:103–104]). There is, however, no one-to-one correspondence between Berlin's three types and Culpepper's three.

Rather than getting into an extended discussion of Johannine character types and attempting to classify either the bedridden man of John 5 or the blind man of John 9, I prefer to take my cue from Alter and Sternberg who eschew any straightforward typology of Hebrew characters. The two of them would seem to agree with Amelie Rorty who once developed an insightful, five-fold typology of character, and then concluded her study by saying, "The distinctions that I have drawn are forced; most philosophers and novelists blend the notions that I have distinguished. One would hardly find a pure case...." (319; see also Hochman:86–89).

If a typology of the Fourth Gospel's characters is not one of my aims, its modes of characterization and the interweaving of these modes certainly is. In his summary of characterization in ancient Hebrew narrative, Alter discusses its four modes—all of which appear in the Fourth Gospel: 1) the narrator's description of the character in terms of actions, appearance, or attitudes and intentions; 2) one character's comments on another; 3) the direct speech of the character; 4) inward speech (i.e., interior monologue; 1981:116–117; cf. Berlin:33–42; Sternberg:322–330, 342–348; Bar-Efrat:48–86). With regard to narration, Alter, Sternberg and Bar-Efrat argue that the ancient Hebraic narrators are reliable and omniscient, and are thus accorded descriptive certainty (1981:117; Sternberg:63–70; Bar-Efrat:13–45). The same holds true for the narrator of the Fourth Gospel (Culpepper, 1983:26–34). However, when describing characters, the Hebrew narrators tend to be laconic and highly selective in their use of those gifts (Alter, 1981:20, 126; Sternberg:180–185; Bar-Efrat:48–53). Again, Johannine poetics parallel this phenomenon (Staley:37–41, 95–98).

In comparison to narrators' descriptions of characters in ancient Hebrew narrative, the characters themselves often appear loquacious.[4] But ironically, Alter states that their words "may be more of a drawn shutter than an open window" (1981:117; see also, 1989:55; Berlin:64–65; Sternberg:346–364). From this observation Alter goes on to argue that in ancient Hebrew narrative the reader is therefore compelled "to get at character and motive through a process of inference from fragmentary data, often with crucial pieces of narrative exposition strategically withheld, and this leads to multiple or sometimes even wavering perspectives on the characters" (1981:126; see also Berlin:67; Sternberg:230–235). Alter thus gives special attention to the dynamic interplay between narration and dialogue and the subtle nuances of repetition (1981:63–113; see also Sternberg:365–375; 436–440). But it is especially Sternberg who concentrates upon analyzing the "crucial pieces of narrative exposition strategically withheld" (Alter, 1981:126); that is, the manipulation of ambiguity, suspense, curiosity, and surprise that make up a large part of Hebrew characterization (230–320; cf. Alter, 1981:12). Like a Palestinian peasant boy guiding his goats through the Judean wilderness, Alter, Berlin, Sternberg, and Bar-Efrat are masters at leading the reader through the sudden twists and sharp turns, the steep ridges and dizzying drop-offs that make up the art of ancient Hebrew characterization.

In view of these observations regarding ancient Hebrew narrative, my analysis of John 5 and 9 will attempt to show that the two miracle stories evince the same combination of rhetorical devices found so often in ancient Hebraic characterization: repetition and minute changes in direct speech and narration which play major roles in the formation of Johannine characters. As a consequence, Johannine characterization can sometimes be problematic, especially when one takes into account the dynamics of the reading process in the formation of the character.

2. READING CHARACTER IN JOHN 5

The two Johannine healings on the Sabbath have often been compared (Collins:41), and Culpepper himself lists 11 parallels in his analysis of the Johannine characters, most of which are easily recognized (1983:139). The setting is similar in both instances—pools in Jerusalem—and both unnamed characters are introduced as having long-term disabilities (a thirty-eight year infirmity and blindness from birth).[5] And because both men are healed on the Sabbath, the stories share the similar theological themes of work, sin, and the identity of Jesus. The parallels are so remarkable that at least one scholar has been led to see these two stories as complementary units in a giant chiasm which overlays the entire gospel (Deeks:107–128), and Brown and Culpepper see them as demarcating a major section of Johannine narrative (Brown:cxliv; Culpepper, 1990:139–140). Yet there are also significant differences between the two stories, not the least of which are that John 5 is a miracle story which will have important implications for the story's plot and Jesus' identity, whereas John 9 begins as a pronouncement story, turns into a miracle story, is three times as long as the story in John 5, and has virtually no plot function.

The miracle story structure of John 5:1–9 is straightforward and simple. Jesus goes up to Jerusalem to participate in a religious festival and while he is there, he sees a sick man lying beside a pool (5:1–6a). After a brief verbal exchange between the miracle worker and the sick man (5:6b–8), the man is healed (5:9a).[6] The only element that fleshes out the skeletal miracle story form is the conversation between Jesus and the sick man (5:6b–7).

Normally, after the hero has come on the scene and sized up the situation (e.g., "When Jesus saw this man lying there and realized that he had been there a long time . . ." [5:6a]), a miracle is performed. But in this story, rather than Jesus immediately effecting the cure, he asks the man, "Do you want to get well?" (5:6b). For the moment the question postpones the inevitable cure, whetting the reader's appetite for another impressive sign.[7] At the same time, it forces the reader to concentrate upon the peculiarities of the developing conversation.[8]

Initially, Jesus' question might seem to reinforce the obvious point in the story—a story which follows closely the pattern of thousands of other miracle stories. Of course the man wants to get well![9] The fact that the narrator had said that the man had been ill for thirty-eight years and that Jesus realized he had been there a long time begs for a solution to his problem. Yet the sick man does not give a straightforward reply to Jesus' question, such as, "Yes, I want to get well, can you help me?" Rather, he responds with a lengthy sentence; one fraught with innuendo: "Sir, I don't have anybody—whenever the water is stirred up—to put me into the pool. But while I'm on my way, someone else gets in before me."[10]

The indirect response of the bedridden man now forces the reader to reconsider the seemingly open-ended question of Jesus.[11] Could Jesus' question have had a different purpose than simply emphasizing the fact that this is a miracle story?[12] Does it imply a lack of determination on the man's part to get well (Brown:209; Culpepper, 1990:148)? Or could it be a sympathetic question, one which seeks to give public recognition to the man's disability? Perhaps it is bitingly sarcastic (cf. 3:10; 4:17b-18). And what should the reader make of the sick man's response? Is his statement a thinly veiled plea to Jesus to "be that man to put me in the pool"? Is it made to evoke sympathy from Jesus? Or is the man just complaining (Brown:209)? What is the illocutionary aspect of the sentences (Chatman:161-166)? Whatever their intended force, Jesus tells the sick man to begin to act on his own behalf. He says to him, "Get up, pick up your mat and keep walking" (*Egeire aron ton krabatton sou kai peripatei*, 5:8). There can be no second guessing the meaning of this statement by Jesus.

Immediately upon being healed—or perhaps as a means to being healed—the man picks up his pallet and walks, and so fulfills Jesus' command.[13] The narrator then adds a temporal notation previously omitted: "Now that day was a Sabbath" (5:9b).[14] What began as a relatively simple miracle story with a simple alignment of the reader's sympathies ("Nice work, Jesus!" "Way to go, sick man!") has now turned into something much more complex, with competing allegiances ("Wait a minute! Should Jesus have told the man to carry his mat?"). Healing the man is fine, but did Jesus choose the proper means to effect and illustrate the cure? And what will happen to the man who so innocently acted upon Jesus' Sabbath-breaking word?

In both John 5 and 9 the reader discovers that the healings were done on the Sabbath only after the miracle story has been narrated.[15] In this sense they are unique among the New Testament Sabbath day miracles. In every other case the miracle stories begin with someone (either the narrator or characters) noting that the day is a Sabbath (e.g., Matt. 12:9–14; Mark 1:21–28, 3:1–6; Luke 4:31–37, 6:6–11, 13:10–17, 14:1–6). But here, the narrator's belated reference to the Sabbath not only forces the reader to reevaluate the significance of the miracle—or rather the command of Jesus—but also forces the reader to reevaluate the characters involved in the story. Although Jesus has previously challenged certain Jewish religious scruples (purification rituals, 2:6–7; attitudes toward the temple, 2:13–22; attitudes toward Samaritans, 4:5–42), he has not actually broken Torah,[16] nor has he told anyone else to do so. However, now with the narrator's temporal note, the reader must re-view this seemingly innocuous action of Jesus. That Jesus should command the sick man to work on the Sabbath either in order to be healed or as a witness to his healing comes minimally as a surprise—if not as an outright shock to the reader.[17] And the sick man, whose initial sputtering, convoluted response to Jesus appeared sniveling and weak-kneed, in retrospect proves to be a daring and risk-taking individual, one who acts unquestioningly upon a stranger's Sabbath-breaking command.

As soon as the reader is clued in to the temporal setting of the miracle, the narrator introduces a third party to the story: "the Jews" (5:10).[18] But in contrast to Jesus and the sick man who know that a healing has taken place on the Sabbath precisely because the formerly sick man is carrying his mat, and in contrast to the reader who initially did not know that that day was a Sabbath, "the Jews" only know that "It is Sabbath, and it is not lawful for you to carry your mat" (5:10). There is no evidence that they know anything of the miracle which has just taken place.[19] The statement, "So the Jews kept saying to the man *who had been healed* . . ." (*tō tetherapeumenō*, 5:10a), is thus the point of view of the narrator, a perspective which Jesus and the reader also share (5:6, 9; cf. 13, 14). It is not the perspective of "the Jews" (cf. 5:12, 16), for in the remaining dialogue "the Jews" will continue to be concerned with "the one *who spoke*" the command (*ho eipōn soi*, 5:12), not with "the one *who made (someone) well*." The latter is the healed man's proclamation (*ho poiēsas me hygiē*, 5:11, 15) and the narrator's particular interest (*egeneto hygiēs*, 5:9; *tō tetherapeumenō*, 5:10; *ho iatheis*, 5:13).[20]

To "the Jews'" critical observation, "It is not lawful for you to carry your mat" (5:10), the healed man responds, "The man who made me well—he said to me, 'Pick up your mat and keep walking'" (5:11). "The Jews" do not ask him why he is carrying his mat, nor do they try to find out if someone else told him to carry it. Yet the healed man responds by proclaiming, "The one who made me well—he said to me. . . ." He does not mention his benefactor's name, but rather defines his benefactor only in terms of what he did, as "the one who made me well."[21] Now, at this point in the story the reader has no clue that the healed man doesn't know who his benefactor is; that will not be made known until 5:13.[22] Thus, his response to "the Jews'" observation, "It is not lawful," could simply be read as juxtaposing the legal authority of "the Jews" and the authority of a charismatic healer ("the one who made me well, he said. . .").[23] If this is so, then essentially the healed man's argument would be that the one who has the power to heal also has the power to abrogate Sabbath law (cf. 5:17, 19–23).[24]

"The Jews" then ask the healed man, "Who is the man, the one who told you to pick it up and walk?" (5:12). Clearly "the Jews" are not concerned with the man's testimonial, "The one who made me well," for they do not ask him, "Who made you well?" The possibility of a miraculous healing will not affect the infraction that confronts them: A man is carrying his bedding on the Sabbath and somebody put him up to it (Pancaro:15). But before the healed man has a chance to respond to "the Jews'" repeated question, the narrator intrudes and says, "The one who had been healed did not know who it was, for Jesus had slipped away—a crowd being in that place" (5:13).

What had just moments before appeared to be an important theological exchange between the religious élite and a formerly weak and timid man now empowered by Jesus' Sabbath command has been undermined by the narrator's remark. Had the healed man really devised a profound theological argument for replacing Torah with the words of a charismatic healer? Or was he simply revealing the fact that he didn't know his benefactor's name and was trying to put the blame for his actions on someone else by saying, "The one who made me well, he told me . . ." (Brown:209; Culpepper, 1983:138)? The healed man is not even granted the privilege of speaking the words, "I don't know" (cf. 9:12, 25), and he will not be permitted to speak for himself again.[25] It is almost as though the narrator were shielding him from his adversaries by whisking him away from the scene and then speaking on his behalf.[26] But is the narrator guarding the integrity of a character who has fought well and is now on the ropes, or is he protecting the reader from one of the gospel's least desirable models of faith?[27]

The story continues with Jesus' discovery of the healed man in the temple. It is not clear from the narrator's statement whether this was the place where the man's earlier confrontation with "the Jews" had taken place, but, for whatever reason, the man is there. Jesus, finding him there, says to him, "Look, you are well; don't continue to do wrong (*hamartane*),[28] or something worse may happen to you" (5:14). In response to this, the narrator draws the story to a close: "The man departed and announced (*anēngeilen*)[29] to the Jews that Jesus was the one who had made him well.[30] And for this reason the Jews began to stalk Jesus, because he was doing these things on the Sabbath" (5:15–16).

The account of Jesus' second meeting with the healed man again throws the reader's assessments of the two major characters into a quandary. Jesus' observation that the man is well echoes his initial question to the man (5:6) and seems to bring the miracle account to a fitting conclusion, but his injunction *"Mēketi hamartane"* (present imperative),[31] is surprising.[32] The only explicit character trait attributed to the healed man is couched in a prohibition and joined to a warning! But shouldn't the man's healing have been the evidence of forgiveness of sins? And hasn't he just stood up admirably well to the legal authorities? So what wrong or sin is the man presently guilty of? It must be a significant infraction, for Jesus takes the trouble to find him and warn him of a worse fate which could befall him.

The suddenness of Jesus' warning, his failure to flesh out the specifics of the man's "sin,"[33] and the narrator's disinterest in illuminating the reader, all have the effect of forcing the reader to fill this new gap by attempting to explain the healed man's character flaw.[34] Perhaps the healed man has been sinning somehow by flaunting his new found freedom from Torah in ways that the narrator fails to disclose—perhaps by parading with his mat around the temple courtyard.[35] Jesus had once told the healed man to pick up his mat and keep walking, and "the Jews" have just finished telling him that it is not lawful to do what he is doing. Could Jesus be telling the healed man that he is indeed "sinning" by continuing to do what he had previously asked him to do? Has Jesus gone back on his word? He's beginning to sound just like "the Jews!" Or better, is Jesus saying, "Enough is enough. You've had your fun, flaunting your freedom in the temple precincts, now put down your mat and get on with living?"

Jesus does not tell the healed man what his sin is, but perhaps the narrator gives the reader a clue to the meaning of Jesus' words. The narrator has said that Jesus finds the healed man in the temple (5:14). Maybe the healed man could be sinning simply by being in the temple—a religious site about which the reader already knows Jesus has expressed negative feelings (2:13–22; 4:21–24). But the narrator had also said that the healed man didn't know who Jesus was (5:13). Could Jesus' warning have been precipitated somehow by the healed man's previous response to "the Jews"? Perhaps he was "sinning" in not fully revealing the identity of his benefactor. What does Jesus' *"Mēketi hamartane"* mean in this context?

Whatever answer the reader might supply at this point, the phrase seems to raise more questions for the reader than it does for the character involved in the story. For the character, having quickly acted on Jesus' command once before, does so again (5:15).

It would appear, then, that the healed man understands Jesus' ambiguous "*Mēketi hamartane*" as somehow a response to his previous conversation with "the Jews," for he seems to return immediately to his interrogators with the new information, "Jesus [i.e., not just anybody] was the one who made me well." And since the narrator had earlier said that many of the people in Jerusalem had believed in Jesus precisely because of his signs (2:23; 3:1–2; 4:45), ironically, the healed man's intentions should be understood positively (cf. 11:45–46; 12:9–11, 17–18). Only the reader and Jesus know enough not to trust the level of belief in the Jerusalemites (2:24; 3:10; 4:1–3, 48). As a result of the healed man's proclamation, however, "the Jews" begin to stalk Jesus—because he was doing "these things" on the Sabbath.[36]

In view of this interpretation, one which seeks to take into account the reading process and the subtle nuances of repetition in narration and conversation, can one so easily categorize the character as one who "rats on" or "betrays" Jesus (Kysar:34; Smith:41; Countryman:41)? Is he really the "super ingrate" (Haenchen:1:247; cf. 259; Kysar:34), "ready to blame his violation of the Sabbath on his benefactor" (Culpepper, 1983:138; Brown:209)? Or is he simply a person who shows "persistent naivete" (Brown:209)? Such readings of the character are indeed possible in light of the narrator's and Jesus' earlier comments about the people of Jerusalem. But in view of the fact that neither the narrator nor Jesus condemns him—either explicitly or implicitly (cf. 2:24; 3:10; 4:1–3, 48)—a counter-reading is just as legitimate.[37] In his final narrated sentence, the healed man may unequivocally be making the case for the charismatic healer's authority over and above Torah authority—this time supplying the name of the healer in the hope that his interrogators will be impressed (2:23, 3:1–2; 4:45). Perhaps he is not a tattle-tale, but a character who serves in his own way, with his own theological argument, as a faithful witness to the sign performed.

In this reading of character, then, the healed man is no more a representative of those "whom even the signs cannot lead to authentic faith" (Culpepper, 1983:138) than the Samaritan woman. It should be remembered that her dramatic witness regarding the stranger who "Told me all that I ever did" (4:29, 39) was a question that expected a negative answer, "Surely this can't be the Christ can it?" (4:29). Both are imperfect witnesses, and in neither case does the narrator say "she/he believed" (*episteusen*).[38] The major difference between them is that the man lives in

Jerusalem and announces his good news to a city with a natural distrust of outside authority figures (1:19–24; 2:18–21), a city largely unable to trust wholly in Jesus (2:23–25) and whose leaders are a serious threat to him (4:1–3). The woman, on the other hand, lives far from Jerusalem in an area which "the Jews" don't control and where they cannot take deliberative actions against Jesus.

Finally, I would submit that no character in the Fourth Gospel fully grasps the narrator's perspective that "Jesus is the Christ, the Son of God" (20:31), except for the story's narrator, the beloved disciple (21:24–25). Culpepper is right in arguing that the individuality of the Johannine characters "is determined by their encounter with Jesus," and that the "characters represent a continuum of responses to Jesus, which exemplify misunderstandings the reader may share and responses one might make to the depiction of Jesus in the gospel" (1983:104). I would only add that the healed man of John 5—his act of faith and subsequent witness—has been unduly hobbled in the history of scholarship by a tendency to tie him too tightly to the plot (5:15–16; cf. 11:45–46) and Jesus' subsequent monologue (5:17–47). The result has been readings blind to any ambiguities of character.

3. READING CHARACTER IN JOHN 9

Unlike the bedridden man of John 5 who has rarely been the subject of independent study and is not one of the more memorable characters in the gospel, the blind man of John 9 is both well known and often has been the topic of extended research. Of course, much of the scholarly interest has not been so much generated by the man himself as it has been a result of the narrator's curious comments about the Pharisees' "synagogue ban" (9:22, 34–35; Martyn:37–62; Painter:31–61). But no less important have been those studies which direct readers to the dramatic elements in the story (Brown:376–377). These studies have noted the seven-fold scenes in the narrative (Martyn:24–36), the rising tempo of the Pharisees' accusations and the increasing insight of the blind man (Resseguie:299–303; Lieu:83–84), and the role of the blind man as *eirōn* (Duke:119–125). Following the leads of the latter studies, my analysis will attempt to show that sensitivity to the subtle changes in the repeated speech of the blind man's conversations and the narrator's descriptions (Alter 1981:63–113), and the author's manipulation of temporal order (Sternberg:230–320) can give a fuller portrait of the character than has been previously noted.

Although it seems to have gone unnoticed in the history of scholarship, the formal structure of John 9:1–5 is that of a pronouncement story, not a miracle story.[39] The scene is set when Jesus, "passing by," sees a man "blind from birth" (9:1). But rather than having the hero effect a cure as he has done numerous times in the past, Jesus' disciples force their way into the story and interject a theological question (9:2) which leads to a pronouncement by Jesus (9:3–5). From the very outset, however, the narrator teases the reader with the possibility of an ensuing miracle story and with the possibility of double meanings. It is, after all, a *blind man* who is the cause of the disciples' question, not some debatable activity of Jesus or his disciples (cf. Mark 2:13–28), and Jesus' seeing would seem to be of two kinds: 1) natural (seeing a blind man); 2) supernatural (realizing that the man has been blind *from birth*).[40] But the disciples' question shows that they, too, somehow know that the man was blind from birth,[41] and thus the pronouncement rather than the miracle will be the story's ultimate focus (Duke:118).

After Jesus' lengthy pronouncements (9:3–5) a miracle is swiftly narrated (9:6–7). Wordlessly, Jesus spits in the dust, makes clay, and anoints the man's eyes with the clay (the narrator uses the word *pēlon* twice).[42] In contrast to the bedridden man of John 5, Jesus does not ask the blind man anything nor does the man say anything to Jesus. Jesus is wholly the agent, the blind man is wholly the patient (O'Day:59). Jesus then gives a terse command, "Go, wash in the pool of Siloam" (9:7a), and disappears from the story. He will not speak again until he reveals his true identity to the healed man (9:35b–41).[43] After the narrator's interpretive note regarding the name of the pool, he describes the man's prompt action and its effect, "So he left and washed, and came back seeing" (9:7b). The blind man is no longer simply the occasion for the disciples' theological question and Jesus' revelatory remarks; he now takes on a living presence as one who acts upon the authoritative command of Jesus.

Unlike the bedridden man of John 5 whose plaintive voice caught the reader's ear prior to Jesus' miracle-producing words, this man is voiceless until he encounters those who once knew him as a beggar (9:8–12). And in contrast to the bedridden man who was immediately confronted by the hostile questions of authority figures, this man is given a chance to test his new-found voice on the curious and seemingly harmless questions of his neighbors and acquaintances.[44] His response to his inquisitive neighbors is almost an exact repetition of the narrator's description of the miracle, "The man, *the one named Jesus, made clay* and *anointed* my eyes, and *he said to me*, 'Go to Siloam and wash'; so I went and washed and gained my sight" (9:11). He knows quite well who it was who healed him (cf. 5:13) and the means by which the healing was done; but he is ignorant of his benefactor's present whereabouts (9:12).

But the story takes an ominous turn when the narrator says, "They took the formerly blind man to the Pharisees" (9:13). The reader knows that in the past, the Pharisees have been suspicious of Jesus (4:1; 7:32, 45–53; 8:13), so when the narrator goes on to add, "Now the day on which Jesus made clay and opened his eyes was a Sabbath" (9:14), a reevaluation of the neighbors' apparently guileless questions is in order.[45] In retrospect, perhaps there was an undercurrent of maliciousness lurking beneath them.[46]

Furthermore, if the blind man knew that he had been healed on the Sabbath, perhaps he should have been more careful in proclaiming the means by which the miracle had occurred. Yet by withholding the temporal notation until after the healed man's conversation with his neighbors, the reader's first assessment of the healed man and the neighbors cannot be construed negatively.[47] Both the reader and the healed man have been innocently caught in a web of words. The healed man has blurted out the name of his benefactor and the means of his cure to his trusted neighbors in a moment of radiant joy, and the reader had no idea that the day on which this all occurred was a Sabbath.

When the Pharisees appear on the scene, there is an unusual shift in the narrator's description of the healed man. Earlier, in the presence of those who had known him as a beggar, the narrator had described the healed man as "a beggar" (*prosaitēs*, 9:8). But now, in the presence of those who will refuse to recognize the miracle and the miracle-worker, the narrator describes him as "the one formerly blind" (*ton pote typhlon*, 9:13), or "the blind man" (*tō typhlō*, 9:17; *hos ēn typhlos*, 9:24). However, in the presence of his parents who recognize their son, the narrator will call him "the one who regained his sight" (9:18). The narrator's epithets betray an ideological perspective,[48] one which will lead the reader surreptitiously toward the pronouncement with which Jesus ends the story: Those with eyes to see do not have the ability to peer beneath the surface and find the person with true insight. Thus, from the perspective of the Pharisees, they never speak to anything more than an ignorant, "blind" person (9:41).

The Pharisees' first reaction to being confronted with the healed man is to ask the neighbors a question, and the Pharisees' query gives rise to the story's second gap. Their question is not what the reader might expect: "Why have your neighbors brought you here?" Instead, it is a question directed at the neighbors, one which presumes a miracle has occurred: "How did he regain his sight?" (9:15a; cf. 9:16–17).[49] It implies the neighbors had already repeated the healed man's story to the Pharisees. The healed man then responds to the Pharisees' question with a remarkably abbreviated account of what had happened to him (9:15b; cf. 17c, 25). In response to their question the healed man replies, "*He put* clay on my eyes, *I* washed, and *I see*" (9:15b).[50]

Although numerous commentators brush off the man's response as merely the author's attempt to shorten what otherwise would be a very redundant account,[51] Alter's and Sternberg's discussions of repetition in ancient Hebrew narrative open up other possible readings (Alter, 1981:97–113; Sternberg:365–427). In his opening statement, "He put clay on my eyes," the healed man does not mention his benefactor's name (9:15b)—although he had done so earlier (9:11). Could his omission of Jesus' name be due to the change in audience? Perhaps he doesn't want to disclose Jesus' identity.[52] This thesis gains further support when the reader comes to the man's next statement. The man does not use the narrator's word "make clay" (*poiein*) or "anoint" (*epichriein*) as he had earlier (9:11, cf. 9:6, 14; cf. 9:27), but instead, switches to the innocuous "put clay" (*epitithēnai*, 9:15). In so doing he successfully shields Jesus from two possible Sabbath violations.[53] Then, finally, as though to insure that there will not be the slightest possibility that one could accuse his benefactor of a Sabbath violation, he leaves out Jesus' command "Go and wash" (9:7, 11), and simply says, "I washed and I see."[54] In view of the extended repetitions of 9:7 and 11 and the change of audience, the remarkable brevity and different word choices in the healed man's response to the Pharisees should not go unnoticed. The man intends to protect his benefactor from his opponents' opening jabs, and he will keep his guard up throughout most of his interrogation—in spite of the pointed questions peppering him (9:26–27).

If the healed man's account of what had transpired earlier is a careful hedging, then the Pharisees' assumption that "the man can't be from God because he doesn't keep the Sabbath" (9:16) comes as a surprise. The healed man hasn't given them any data for coming to such a conclusion! The Pharisees' observation, then, like their opening question (9:15), cannot be based upon anything the healed man had told them. It, too, must be based upon the neighbors' remarks—those which the narrator had left unspoken.

After the healed man makes his first public declaration regarding Jesus (9:17), the narrator diverts the reader's attention away from the man for the moment and turns to "the Jews'" interrogation of his parents (9:18–23).[55] The dramatic shift is reminiscent of Jesus' dialogue with the Samaritan woman. There, immediately after Jesus had just revealed his identity to her (4:25–26), the narrator broke into the scene to announce the arrival of the disciples (4:27). Here, in a similar manner, the reader must also wait in suspense before hearing the Pharisees' reaction to the healed man's declaration, "He is a prophet" (9:17).

But the narrator's explanation of the parents' fear (9:22–23) opens up another narrative gap, one that forces the reader to reevaluate the healed man's earlier conversation with the Pharisees. It will also make the reader even more attentive to the healed man's future confessions. In retrospect, the parent's fear, coupled with "'the Jews'" determination to put out of the synagogue anyone who confessed Jesus to be the Christ (9:22), turns an unnecessary and rude conversation into a courtroom drama (Martyn:32). The narrator's slightly nuanced quotation of the parents' words, "He is of age, question him" (*eperōtēsate*, 9:23 for *erōtēsate*, 9:21) may also imply his perspective that this was a legal proceeding (Bauer et al.). How, indeed, will the Pharisees respond to the man's straightforward reply, "He is a prophet"? And will the healed man, like the Samaritan woman, move from perceiving that Jesus is a prophet to recognizing him as the Christ, thus ending up excluded from the synagogue (4:19, 29; cf. 1:19–21; 7:40–41, 45–52)?

After the dramatic interlude where his parents were called to testify (9:18–23),[56] the Pharisees ("the Jews") again question "the blind man" (9:24–34). The dialogue is reminiscent of 8:31–56, where the accusations of sin, lying, and dishonorable birth were raised. But ironically, the only "liar" in this scene is the healed man who responds to the questions, "What did he do to you? How did he open your eyes?" with, "I told you once and you didn't listen! Why do you want to hear the story again?" (9:27).[57] It is precisely because he didn't tell them the whole truth earlier that the Pharisees are becoming more and more exasperated and are still asking him the same questions! Finally, in this exchange the healed man attains his full stature as a character and opponent of the Pharisees, pummeling them with his own ripostes (9:30–32; Resseguie:299–300). Even without any directions from the narrator the irony of his questions and his biting sarcasm are obvious.[58] Amidst the debris of the hard-fought battle his benefactor will meet him again, and the healed man will show his true colors as he bows down and worships—not the Christ—but the Son of Man (9:35–38). The narrative closes when Jesus confronts the Pharisees with their own blindness (9:39–41).

As in the case of the bedridden man of John 5, careful attention to repetition, the interplay of narration and direct speech, and the dynamics of reading in John 9 have revealed hidden nuances in the Johannine art of characterization. The analysis of the healed man's speech (9:15) alerts the reader to his cleverness early on, and this will be confirmed by the end of the story (Brown:377). He is indeed a "quick-witted 'eiron'" (Duke:125) and a man of "dogged loyalty" (Countryman:65). But his quick-wittedness and dogged loyalty begin as early as his first encounter with the Pharisees (9:13–17), not just during the second interrogation (9:24–34). From the very beginning he tries to protect Jesus by refusing to tell the Pharisees that Jesus had made clay, anointed his eyes, and told him to wash in the Pool of Siloam. At the same time, the narrator's manipulation of the temporal order gradually unveils the neighbors' motives for questioning the man and bringing him to the Pharisees as something more than mere idle curiosity. Finally, the narrator's choice of epithets in the story is shown to be proleptic. The various descriptions of the healed man lead the reader to contemplate the Pharisees' blindness long before Jesus states it openly (9:39–41).

4. Conclusion

Reading these two miracle stories by paying close attention to the sequence of sentences and the gradual accumulation of information and responses reveals a correspondingly more complex portrait of the men whom Jesus healed on the Sabbath. In the first instance, blame for the persecution of Jesus cannot be put at the feet of the bedridden man. It was, after all, Jesus who healed him on the Sabbath and told him to carry the mat. In fact, his argument for the implicit authority of the charismatic healer is one which Jesus himself picks up later on and develops, albeit in a different manner (5:17, 19–21; cf. 7:21–23). Yet there are indeed ambiguities in the first man's response. For example, does he respond correctly to Jesus' injunction "*Mēketi hamartane*?" However, later when reading John 9, the first man's ambiguous behavior will become understandable. He has already broken the Sabbath when he encounters "the Jews." By way of contrast, the blind man does not do anything that even remotely could be considered unlawful (Pancaro:19). He simply washes his face on the Sabbath. Furthermore, he is seemingly safe so long as he does not acknowledge Jesus to be the Christ (something which, in fact, he never does).

Thus, there is an element of tragedy surrounding the first character: he is bound to his past. He broke the Sabbath, how can he rewrite history? The second character, on the other hand, is comical: he is liberated from his past. Is he the same man who used to sit and beg? Was he really blind? Can he wiggle his way out of the predicament in which his neighbors have put him? Together these two narratives express the double-edged, painful joy of Christian living as filtered through ancient Hebrew models of characterization: an experience that stumbles in the dark as it reaches for the light.

5. A Postscript

In their recent critiques of the application of Reader Response Criticism to the Bible, both Temma Berg and Stephen Moore challenge biblical reader-critics to reconceive their nascent "readers." From Berg's perspective, New Testament scholars' readings of biblical texts work—and also fail—precisely because they presume an understanding of reading unlike that of any real reader's reading experience. Their readings are painstakingly slow; there is no room for forgetfulness in them; they trudge on, without ever being interrupted (188, 195). My readings of the two Johannine miracles fit her criticisms perfectly. But while I will agree that my readings have been slow and laborious, I will steady them on the ground that they are light years faster than any other critical readings of the stories. All other readings have been predicated upon a paralyzed, immobile text; they sit, begging for insights from their unseen neighbors, but lack the courage to move beyond their shadowy porticos. They prefer the reassurance of the text's encircling grasp to the excitement of striding wild-eyed into the temple.

Moore, on the other hand, while recognizing that the biblical text is ideologically motivated and that its largest reading community shares those ideological concerns (125–126, 174–175), still finds New Testament reader-critics' readings to be overly cerebral and emotionally retarded (95–98; 107–108). His criticism, too, seems to knock the breath out of my readings at the very moment they attempt their first halting steps. I speak of problems that "beg for solutions"; of a reader who "reconsiders" seemingly direct questions; of characters who are "ignorant of things the reader knows." Whether from mountain or moor the view is the same: there apparently is a painful stumbling and stuttering in my readings, a blindness which fails to see the translucent holes beyond the opaque wholes. Can that blindness lead to insight? Does the bedridden reader ever really walk?

NOTES

[1] Erich Auerbach's 1953 essay "Odysseus' Scar" in *Mimesis: The Representation of Reality in Western Literature* prefigured Scholes and Kellogg's comparisons of Greek and Hebrew literature, but it is not quoted in Culpepper's chapter on character. Robert Alter's *The Art of Biblical Narrative* which appeared in 1981, is only mentioned twice in *Anatomy of the Fourth Gospel* and Adele Berlin's *Poetics and Interpretation of Biblical Narrative* appeared in 1983, the same year Culpepper's book was published. Subsequently, two major works have seen print in English: Meir Sternberg's *The Poetics of Biblical Narrative: Ideological Literature and the Drama of Reading* was published in 1985, and Shimon Bar-Efrat's second edition of *Narrative Art in the Bible* appeared in translation in 1989, five years after its Hebrew publication.

[2] For example, in his study of the characterization of Jesus in the Fourth Gospel, du Rand says that "one can agree with Culpepper that to some extent the Gospel of John draws from both Greek and Hebrew models of character development but that most of the Johannine characters are presented as definite ethical types" (25). But he does not attempt to delineate any aspects of the "Hebrew model."

³ For the role of the reader in the construction and evaluation of character, see especially Docherty (3-42); Sternberg (264-365); Hochman (138-167); Booth (227-291); and Phelan (83-162).

⁴ In the Fourth Gospel, only Jesus, "the Jews," the Samaritan woman, and the blind man could be similarly described.

⁵ Of unnamed characters in ancient Hebrew narrative, Sternberg has this to say, "Anonymity is the lot (and mark) of supernumeraries, type-characters, institutional figures, embodied plot devices. . . . To remain nameless is to remain faceless, with hardly a life of one's own. Accordingly, a character's emergence from anonymity may correlate with a rise in importance" (330). Quite nearly the opposite is the case in the Fourth Gospel. Here, the nameless mother of Jesus, the Samaritan woman, the blind man, and the beloved disciple are characters with more of "a life of their own" than named characters like a Judas, Nathaniel, Caiaphas, or a Philip.

⁶ Culpepper rightly notes, however, that this miracle story deviates markedly from the two previously narrated miracles in John 2:1-11 and 4:43-54 (1990:141-143).

⁷ By "reader" I mean an "implied reader," the kind of reader evoked by the rhetoric of the text. For a more detailed discussion of the theoretical underpinnings of the concept, see Staley:30-37.

⁸ I would agree with Haenchen at this point who says, Jesus' question is "not intended to determine whether the lame man has the desire to become well again (the Johannine Jesus is not trained to practice psychology)" (1:255), if he means by "intended" that the reader would not initially suspect a lack of desire on the part of the sick man. That is to say, Jesus does not ask him, *"Mē theleis hygiēs genesthai"* (cf. 3:4; 4:12, 29, 33), which would imply a negative response on the part of the bedridden man. The question is thus open-ended. However, I would want to allow for the reader's reevaluation of Jesus' question after the sick man's response.

⁹ Haenchen thought that the question by Jesus was "odd," but was one which "permit[ted] the reader to divine that a story of a healing [was] to follow" (1:255). I have difficulties with this solution to Jesus' question, since the reader has already read two other miracle stories in this book (2:1-11; 4:56-53) and should have no difficulty in figuring out from the setting (5:1-5) that a miracle is imminent. Jesus' question is "odd" precisely because the answer initially seems so transparent to the reader and Jesus (cf. 1:42, 47-48; 2:24; 4:17-19).

¹⁰ Alter argues that "In any given narrative event, and especially, at the beginning of any new story, the point at which dialogue first emerges will be worthy of special attention, and in most instances, the initial words spoken by a personage will be revelatory, perhaps more in manner than in matter, constituting an important moment in the exposition of character" (1981:74). Similarly, many Johannine commentators (not trained to write with Alter's poetic precision) have sensed that the bedridden man's opening words are somehow revelatory of his character.

¹¹ This type of dialogue is a common topic in discussions of Johannine style. Note, for example, Jesus' opening question in the gospel where he asks two disciples of John, "What are you looking for?" He asks this of two disciples who have just heard John exclaim, "Behold the Lamb of God!" John's two disciples then ask, "Rabbi, where are you staying?" to which Jesus responds, "Come and see." What usually has not been pointed out in these dialogues is the possible effect the unusual dialogue style might have upon the reader (see, for example, Giblin:191-211; Reinhartz:61-76). Sternberg's distinctions between surprise, suspense, and curiosity are helpful to review at this point (258-260). Here, the sick man's response provokes the reader's curiosity (283-284).

¹² For example, the verb *thelein* (5:6) will prove significant in Jesus' dramatic monologue (5:21, 35, 40).

¹³ The language of 5:8-9a is ambiguous. Is the narrator's phrase, "And immediately the man became well," temporally prior to the man's action of picking up his mat and

walking or is it merely logically prior? In Mark 2:1-12 the healing of the paralytic (e.g., "Your sins are forgiven," 2:5) is clearly temporally prior to his getting up and walking (2:9-12).

[14] To use Sternberg's term, this is a narrative "gap"; that is, "a lack of information about the world—an event, motive, causal link, character trait, plot structure, law of probability—contrived by a temporal displacement" (234-236; cf. Iser, 1974, 1978, and my assessment of his work, Staley:32-33). Somewhat facetiously one might almost say, "That which is now called 'gap' was formerly called 'aporia'" (cf. Haenchen:1:257).

[15] Brown and others discuss the "Sabbath motif" which is introduced "almost as an afterthought," primarily in terms of source critical issues (210; see also Fortna:113-117). My interest is in the rhetorical effect of the "afterthought," not its place of origin.

[16] Jeremiah 17:21; Brown:208; Yee:31-47. Pancaro also adds, that "Commanding something unlawful (what precisely is understood by this is not stated clearly, but the Sabbath was no doubt included) was punishable with death..." (15).

[17] Culpepper recognizes the surprise in the belated temporal notation when he says, "By withholding this information [i.e., that it was the Sabbath] and supplying it just at this point, the narrator forces the reader to review the healing from a new perspective which catches the reader by surprise" (1990:149). I would only want to add a note of specificity to his observation by saying that the reader is forced to reevaluate *the behavior of the characters* by the belated temporal notation. Sternberg calls this type of device "character-elevating" (165).

[18] For a full analysis of "the Jews" in this pericope, see Culpepper (1990:148-150).

[19] Contra Haenchen, who says, "It is astonishing that the Jews are unmoved by the miracle, either at this point or in what follows," (1:246-247; cf. Brown:208).

[20] The narrator, whose descriptions are usually quite limited, uses three different words to denote the formerly sick man. Interestingly, all three are passive verbal constructions with the agent left unidentified. The characters, on the other hand, are limited to the noun *hygiēs*. The narrator's interest is thus in Jesus' act of healing: the "giving of life" as *to poiein*, not in the man's activity of carrying his mat (see Haenchen:1:258). The *to poiein* of Jesus will also be an important point of emphasis in his dramatic monologue (5:21, 24-29, 39-40). The verb *airō* likewise occurs quite often in the miracle story (five times), but the narrator uses it only once, and not surprisingly it never occurs in Jesus' subsequent monologue.

[21] Brown says that "The fact that he had let his benefactor slip away without even asking his name is another instance of real dullness" (209; cf. Beasley-Murray:74; but cf. 4:29, 39!). Haenchen, on the other hand, asks, "[S]hould [Jesus] not perhaps have introduced himself to the lame man?" (1:247). At this point in the story, however, these commentators' judgments are presumptive. Such observations could only be made after reading the narrator's aside in 5:13.

[22] Here is another significant gap in the story, one which will make it more difficult for the reader to assess the narrator's evaluation of the healed man.

[23] Haenchen hints at this when he says, "The man who was healed responds, however, that the performer of miracles, who has just healed him, told him to [take up his pallet and walk around]" (1:257).

[24] For example, Vermes discusses the conflict between charismatics and Pharisees in the following manner, saying that "the one sphere in which supernatural proof was judged totally inadmissible was the definition of lawful conduct (halakhah). Nowhere is this better illustrated than in the legendary account of a doctrinal argument around the end of the first century AD between Rabbi Eliezer ben Hyrcanus and his colleagues. Having exhausted his arsenal of reasoning and still not convinced them, he performed a miracle, only to be told that there is no room for miracles in a legal debate" (81; see also Pancaro:15 [contra Bultmann:243]).

25 Even the healed man's final words to "the Jews" are put in indirect discourse (see below). Alter discusses such break-off points in dialogue as strategies that can be a type of "implicit commentary" (1981:125).

26 In speaking for the character, the narrator does not blame him for his failure to know his benefactor's name. The reason the narrator gives for the healed man's lack of knowledge is *"Jesus had slipped away,"* not, "The healed man ran off." Nor does the narrator say after 5:11, "This he said, not because he cared about Jesus, but because he did not know who had healed him." The Johannine narrator is well able to clarify the intent of characters' words when he wishes (see, for example, 12:5-6).

27 Culpepper says that he "represents those whom even the signs cannot lead to authentic faith" (1983:138; see also Collins:42-43).

28 This is the first occurrence of the verb *hamartanein* in the gospel, and the noun *hamartia* has only been used once thus far ("Look, the Lamb of God who takes away the sin of the world," 1:29).

29 The verb *anangellein* has only occurred at 4:25. It will appear again in 16:13, 14, 15. In these four instances characters use the word and always with a positive nuance.

30 Note here that the narrator does not say the healed man told "the Jews," "Jesus was the one who told him to carry his mat," but rather, "Jesus was the one who made him well" (cf. 5:11; also Pancaro:15). Alter's insightful discussion of how to read repetitions in direct speech and narrated speech is to the point: "When there is no divergence between a statement as it occurs in narration and as it recurs in dialogue, or vice versa, the repetition generally has the effect of giving a weight of emphasis to the specific terms which the speaker chooses for his speech" (1981:77-78). See further the comments below.

31 An aorist imperative would have meant, *"Don't start sinning (again),* or something worse will happen to you," implying that the act of healing was also an act of forgiving sins and that there was a causal connection between the illness and sin. But the present imperative would seem to imply that the man is still living in sin ("You've been sinning, now don't do it any more"), and thus perhaps that the initial healing was not related to any forgiveness of sins. Compare Luke 8:49; Eph. 4:28; and 1 Tim. 5:23 (in the textually suspect John 8:11 the phrase is preceded by *apo tou nyn,* giving the phrase *mēketi hamartane* an aoristic sense).

32 From the perspective of Reader Response Criticism, one cannot appeal to Jesus' *later* statement in 9:3 in order to argue that this *earlier* statement in 5:14 is surprising (Bultmann:243). One can only argue as Sternberg does, that surprise "catch[es] the reader off-guard due to a false impression given earlier" (259), and that "for the new information to perform its unsettling effect, the old must look settled" (309; cf. Schnackenburg:97; Haenchen:1:247). Here, the "false impression given earlier" is that of the healed man's innocence: The narrator, the healed man, and Jesus have all assumed it up to this point. Only "the Jews" have thought otherwise.

33 Compare, for example, the variety of scholarly attempts to explain Jesus' warning either in terms of 1) Jesus' own understanding of sin (Brown:208; Lindars:217; Hasitschka:285, 337); 2) the author's theology (Bultmann:243; Schnackenburg:97; Beasley-Murray:74), or 3) the healed man's life (e.g., "don't sin, as you did in the past, when you incurred a debilitating illness") (Collins:43; Haenchen:1:247); or, "don't continue in your sinful ways as you presently are doing" (Countryman:41); or, "you're healthy, but you should be concerned about your spiritual condition" (Lindars:217; Kysar:34; Culpepper, 1990:147).

34 The narrative gap is quickly passed over by commentators who wish to move on to the meatier, theological issues of the monologue (e.g., Schnackenburg:97; Countryman:40). But the narrative gap provoked by the text must not simply be eliminated as one hurries on to Jesus' monologue. True, the reader's gap-filling attempts cannot supply an ultimate answer to why Jesus tells the man, *"Mēketi hamartane"*—but this is precisely the point of *reading.* Through this gap (and the previous ones), the text

creates a reader who focuses upon earthly questions; one who delights in constructing plausible contexts for the character's words. Later on, in Jesus' monologue, the reader will be shown the inadequacies of those gap-filling attempts and will have been prepared to accept his conclusions.

35 Haenchen hints at something like this when he says, "If one examines verse 8 more closely, it then becomes apparent that Jesus does not give the man who is healed an order like he does in Mark 2:11: the man is not to go home, but is to parade around defiantly with his pallet. That is intended not only to serve as proof that the lame man was healed, but also that he thereby violated the sabbath in accordance with the order given him" (1:257). However, this unified reading is one which he later rejects (1:258).

36 Cf. 11:45-46. There, in response to the raising of Lazarus from the dead, some of "the Jews" who "believed in him . . . went to the Pharisees and told them the things that Jesus had done." Lindars catches the ambiguity of the narrator's conclusion (5:16) when he says, "the vagueness of the expression [these things] leaves it doubtful whether Jesus is to blame for causing someone else to break the Sabbath, or whether his own act of healing contravened it" (217).

37 Culpepper lists four factors why the character's final act should be interpreted negatively: "(1) The man's earlier responses have established the trait of seeking to pass responsibility from himself to others; (2) Jesus' warning in v. 14 underlines that he is a sinner; (3) we have seen formal contrasts between this passage and the first two signs, where individuals come to believe in Jesus; and (4) this pericope functions to establish the opposition to Jesus and explain some of the reasons for it" (1990:148). I believe that I have given strong arguments for an alternative reading to #1, and if they are reasonable, then the man's final report to "the Jews" can also be read as rectifying his "sin" (#2). Culpepper's third factor is important, and the formal contrasts in the rendering of the signs lead to many of the ambiguities in reading this character. It should be noted, however, that the narrator does not particularly value belief based upon seeing signs (2:23-24; 4:48; 6:25; 20:29; see particularly my reading of the first two signs [Staley:83-86]). Culpepper's fourth factor is dealt with below.

38 Culbertson makes the important observation, "Unbelievers in John's Gospel never admit to needing anything" (170). Both the Samaritan woman and the bedridden man admit their needs, although they do misunderstand how Jesus can fulfill them.

39 Even Bultmann misses this (329-333); see also Martyn, who describes the miracle story form (9:1, 6-7), skipping over the intervening verses (9:2-5) (25; Fortna:109-113). Pancaro, however, notes that the story "takes on the form (in its final moments) of a *Streitgespräch*" (17).

40 Compare, for example, 5:6 where the narrator used two verbs: "When Jesus saw [*idōn*] this man lying there, and knew [*gnous*] that he had already been there a long time. . . ." At the conclusion of this story Jesus will point out that there are indeed two kinds of sight—one that is open to new spiritual realities, and one that is blind to them (9:41).

41 Bultmann puts the issue this way, "Of course one may not ask how the disciples know that he was born blind" (330). In Sternberg's terms, Bultmann is saying that to ask this question is to be involved in "illegitimate gap-filling" (188).

42 Pancaro lists the kneading of mud as one of three Sabbath infractions in this story (the other two being the healing of a person whose life is not in danger and using a substance which was not normally used during the week to anoint eyes; 19-20; also Brown:373; Bultmann:332). But the kneading of mud is the only activity emphasized by the narrator (9:6, 14) and the healed man (9:11). Furthermore, the "how" of the miracle will be the central issue for the Pharisees (9:15, 19, 26).

43 Duke observes that this is Jesus' most prolonged absence in the entire gospel (119).

44 The questioners begin by talking about "the beggar" among themselves (note the third person *houtos*, 9:8-9), before finally addressing him directly (*sou hoi ophthalmoi*, 9:10).

45 Lindars accurately assesses the reader's perspective of the neighbors at this point when he says, "it is left to the reader to guess why this was done," i.e., why they took him to the Pharisees (345).

46 O'Day realizes that "the neighbors are not so guileless" as the healed man (62), and Kysar theorizes that the religious authorities "are brought into this matter because the healing has taken place on the Sabbath, and so must determine whether or not the Sabbath regulations have been violated" (49). Neither Lindars nor Beasley-Murray, however, sees any connection between the neighbors bringing the healed man to the Pharisees and the narrator's notation that it was a Sabbath (Lindars:345; Beasley-Murray:156).

47 Pancaro asks the important question, "Why did Jn wait until v. 14 to mention this fact?," i.e., the fact that it was a Sabbath (18). But his answer relates the gap to the miracle's symbolism of baptism—the importance of which lies in the man's (post-baptismal) witness to his neighbors (26). See my earlier discussion of narrative gaps, n. 14.

48 Sternberg's discussion of the role of epithets in ancient Hebrew narrative is helpful for the analysis of John 9. He says they are usually "proleptic" (337), for they "shape the sequence of our expectations (as foreshadowing device[s]) because [they are] bound to shape the sequence of events (as developmental factor[s]). . . . [They] appear as cause[s] that signal some effect yet unborn in the world, but already presence[s] to be reckoned with in the reading" (338).

49 By placing this initial question in indirect discourse and by having the Pharisees discuss the healed man's response among themselves (9:16-17), the author puts some distance between the central character and his opponents. Thus, the reader and the character are shielded from the Pharisees' probing, barbed questions. Even after the Pharisees finally ask a question in direct discourse ("What do you have to say about him, since 'he opened your eyes?'"), and the man answers, "He is a prophet" (9:17), the narrator immediately intrudes by announcing the calling of the man's parents (9:18).

50 Most commentators have been content to assume that the author somehow gives a summary account of the healing through the voice of the character (i.e, a narrative gap occurs in the healed man's shortened account). In this reading, the reader should assume that, in fact, the healed man "told all" to the Pharisees—the author just hasn't told all. Based upon a different understanding of narrative (Staley:27-30), I would argue that the neighbors must have repeated the man's story to the Pharisees, and thus that is the place where the narrative gap occurs (see below, the discussion of the healed man's words).

51 Haenchen says, "The narrative becomes shorter with each repetition—the reader knows it and should not be bored with the repetition" (2:39; see also Schnackenburg:247-248). Resseguie describes the man in this scene as one who "still lacks color: to the questions of the authorities he responds with short, declarative sentences" (300). Only O'Day comes close to the real significance of the healed man's brief answer when she says, "Nothing more is offered than the minimum required to answer the Pharisees' question" (63).

52 O'Day astutely observes that "As much as Jesus is talked about in the interrogations of verses 8-34, Jesus' name is never named [by a character] after verse 11. . . . There are many reasons for this reluctance to name Jesus' name. The Pharisees do not name the name of Jesus because to do so would give credence and standing to the one who bears the name. The man born blind does not name the name because the significance of the name will only dawn on him as the narrative advances. The man's parents do not name the name because they are afraid to do so (v. 23)" (56). O'Day's observa-

tions are insightful. However, I would object to her reason for the blind man's deference. He does indeed identify Jesus by name to his neighbors (9:11). Only after he meets the Pharisees does he refuse to name his benefactor.

[53] *"Putting clay"* on one's body was not necessarily work, but *"making clay"* and anointing certainly were (Pancaro:19-20).

[54] Schnackenburg argues that the choice of the narrator's verb "he opened" (*aneōksen*, 9:14) is "deliberate, since it brings Jesus into prominence as healer and sabbath-breaker" (247). When the man speaks, however, he uses the plain "I see" (*blepō*, 9:15), which does not necessarily assume that the person who "put clay on his eyes" had any curative powers.

[55] As many commentators have noted, in this scene the narrator calls those who interrogate the man's parents "the Jews" rather than "the Pharisees" as he had earlier (9:13, 15-16; cf. 9:40). The phenomenon is not unusual in the gospel (cf. 1:19, 24; 7:32-35; 8:13, 22), but no perfect answer to the peculiarity has been found. Generally speaking, "the Jews" are found on the scene whenever antagonism toward Jesus reaches a breaking point (e.g., 5:16-17; 6:41, 52; 7:10-15, 35; 8:21-59; 10:19-39; 11:31-54; 18:31-19:22; see Culpepper, 1983:125-132). Here, as elsewhere, the epithet may warn the reader that banners are being unfurled. Battle lines are being drawn tighter, the opposition is closing ranks.

[56] See especially O' Day's insightful discussion of this scene (64-65).

[57] Beasley-Murray makes a strong case for understanding the earlier command "Give glory to God," as "a command to the man to confess his sin, i.e., the sin of lying as to his blindness and subsequent healing by Jesus...." (158).

[58] Bultmann says, "By pretending that he believes them really to be in earnest, he treats the insincerity of the inquiry with the greatest possible irony" (336; Duke:121-123).

WORKS CONSULTED

Alter, Robert
    1981   *The Art of Biblical Narrative*. New York: Basic Books.
    1989   *The Pleasure of Reading in an Ideological Age*. New York: Simon and Schuster.

Auerbach, Erich
    1953   *Mimesis. The Representation of Reality in Western Literature.* Princeton: Princeton University Press.

Bar-Efrat, Shimon
    1989   *Narrative Art in the Bible*. Bible and Literature Series 17. Sheffield: Almond.

Bauer, Walter, Arndt, W., Gingrich, F., Danker, F.
    1979   *A Greek-English Lexicon of the New Testament and other Early Christian Literature*. Chicago: University of Chicago Press.

Beasley-Murray, George R.
    1987   *John*. Word Commentary 36. Waco, TX: Word.

Berg, Temma
　1989　"Reading in/to Mark." *Semeia* 48:187–206.

Berlin, Adele
　1983　*Poetics and Interpretation of Biblical Narrative.* Bible and Literature Series 9. Sheffield: Almond.

Booth, Wayne C.
　1988　*The Company We Keep: An Ethics of Fiction.* Berkeley: University of California Press.

Brown, Raymond E.
　1966　*The Gospel According to John.* Anchor Bible Series 29. Garden City, NY: Doubleday.

Bultmann, Rudolf
　1971　*The Gospel of John: A Commentary.* Trans. G. R. Beasley-Murray, et al. Philadelphia: Westminster.

Chatman, Seymour
　1978　*Story and Discourse: Narrative Structure in Fiction and Film.* Ithaca: Cornell University Press.

Collins, Raymond F.
　1976　"The Representative Figures in the Fourth Gospel." *The Downside Review* 94:26–46; 95:118–132.

Countryman, L. William
　1987　*The Mystical Way in the Fourth Gospel: Crossing Over into God.* Philadelphia: Fortress.

Culbertson, Diana
　1989　*The Poetics of Revelation: Recognition and the Narrative Tradition.* Studies in American Biblical Hermeneutics 4. Macon, GA: Mercer University Press.

Culpepper, R. Alan
　1983　*Anatomy of the Fourth Gospel.* Philadelphia: Fortress.
　1990　"Un exemple de commentaire fondé sur la critique narrative: Jean 5,1–18." Pp. 136–152 in *La Communauté Johannique et son Histoire.* Ed. Jean-Michel Poffet and Jean Zumstein. Geneva: Labor et Fides.

Deeks, David
　1968–69 "The Structure of the Fourth Gospel." *New Testament Studies* 27:107–128.

Docherty, Thomas
1983   *Reading (Absent) Character: Towards a Theory of Characterization in Fiction.* Oxford: Oxford University Press.

Duke, Paul D.
1985   *Irony in the Fourth Gospel.* Atlanta: John Knox.

du Rand, J.
1985   "The Characterization of Jesus as Depicted in the Narrative of the Fourth Gospel." *Neotestamentica* 19:18–36.

Foldenyi, Laszlo F.
1989   "Novel and Individuality." *Neophilologus* 73:1–13.

Forster, E. M.
1927   *Aspects of the Novel.* New York: Harcourt, Brace & World.

Fortna, Robert T.
1988   *The Fourth Gospel and Its Predecessor: From Narrative Source to Present Gospel.* Philadelphia: Fortress.

Giblin, C. H.
1979–80 "Suggestion, Negative Response and Positive Action in St. John's Portrayal of Jesus." *New Testament Studies* 26:191–211.

Haenchen, Ernst
1984   *The Gospel of John.* 2 vols. Ed. Ulrich Busse. Trans. Robert W. Funk. Philadelphia: Fortress.

Hasitschka, Martin
1989   *Befreiung von Sünde nach dem Johannesevangelium: Eine bibeltheologische Untersuchung.* Innsbrucker theologische Studien 27. Innsbruck: Tyrolia-Verlag.

Hochman, Baruch
1985   *Character in Literature.* Ithaca, NY: Cornell University Press.

Iser, Wolfgang
1974   *The Implied Reader: Patterns of Communication in Prose Fiction from Bunyan to Beckett.* Baltimore: The Johns Hopkins University Press.
1978   *The Act of Reading: A Theory of Aesthetic Response.* Baltimore: The Johns Hopkins University Press.

Kysar, Robert
1984   *John's Story of Jesus.* Philadelphia: Fortress.

Lieu, Judith
    1988   "Blindness in the Johannine Tradition." *New Testament Studies* 34:83–95.

Martyn, J. Louis
    1979   *History and Theology in the Fourth Gospel.* Revised ed. Nashville: Abingdon.

Moore, Steven
    1989   *Literary Criticism and the Gospels: The Theoretical Challenge.* New Haven: Yale University Press.

O'Day, Gail
    1987   *The Word Disclosed: John's Story and Narrative Preaching.* St. Louis: CPB.

Pancaro, Severino
    1975   *The Law in the Fourth Gospel: The Torah and the Gospel of Moses and Jesus, Judaism and Christianity According to John.* Supplements to Novum Testamentum 42. Leiden: E. J. Brill.

Painter, John
    1986   "John 9 and the Interpretation of the Fourth Gospel." *Journal for the Study of the New Testament* 32:596–608.

Phelan, James
    1989   *Reading People, Reading Plots: Character, Progression, and the Interpretation of Narrative.* Chicago and London: University of Chicago Press.

Reinhartz, Adele
    1989   "Great Expectations: A Reader-Oriented Approach to Johannine Christology and Eschatology." *Journal of Literature and Theology* 3:61–76.

Resseguie, James L.
    1982   "John 9: A Literary-Critical Analysis." Pp. 295–303 in *Literary Interpretations of Biblical Narratives.* Vol. II. Ed. Kenneth R. R. Gros Louis. Nashville: Abingdon.

Rorty, Amelie Oskenberg
    1976   "A Literary Postscript: Characters, Persons, Selves, Individuals." Pp. 301–323 in *The Identity of Persons.* Ed. Amelie O. Rorty. Berkeley: University of California Press.

Schnackenburg, Rudolf
   1980   *The Gospel According to St. John.* Vol. 2. Trans. Cecily Hastings, et al. New York: Seabury Press.

Scholes, Robert and Kellogg, Robert
   1966   *The Nature of Narrative.* New York: Oxford University Press.

Smith, D. Moody
   1986   *John.* Proclamation Commentaries. 2nd edition. Philadelphia: Fortress.

Staley, Jeffrey L.
   1988   *The Print's First Kiss: A Rhetorical Investigation of the Implied Reader in the Fourth Gospel.* SBL Dissertation Series 82. Atlanta: Scholars.

Sternberg, Meir
   1985   *The Poetics of Biblical Narrative: Ideological Literature and the Drama of Reading.* Bloomington: Indiana University Press.

Vermes, Geza
   1981   *Jesus the Jew: A Historian's Reading of the Gospels.* Philadelphia: Fortress.

Yee, Gale A.
   1989   *Jewish Feasts and the Gospel of John.* Wilmington: Michael Glazier.

JOHANNINE METAPHOR—MEANING AND FUNCTION: A LITERARY CASE STUDY OF JOHN 10:1–8

Robert Kysar
The Lutheran Theological Seminary at Philadelphia

ABSTRACT

The images on the lips of Jesus in the fourth gospel are most often drastically distinguished from his parables in the synoptics, but there is little agreement regarding the genre of the Johannine images. This study proposes that the function of the Johannine metaphors is similar to those recently claimed to be characteristic of the synoptic parables. The genre of the images in John 10:1–18 is examined in terms of their function in the structure of the passage. A reader response criticism is utilized to discover the strategies employed by the implied author's use of the images and the way in which they are formed into a whole in the passage. The result of the investigation is that with deliberate and skillful strategies the implied author has created a single, integral structure that is carefully designed to lead the reader through a series of true, poetic metaphors (diaphors). The features of those metaphors are the participatory, shocking, paradoxical, contrastive, and decisional qualities of their impact on the reader's experience. Along with other less significant comparisons, these qualities are shared with the metaphorical parables of Jesus in the synoptic gospels.

INTRODUCTION

In the past several decades a great deal has been written on the nature and function of the parables of Jesus in the synoptic gospels.[1] A new appreciation for their literary character has been achieved thanks to the abundant attention they have received. It is curious that the literary qualities of the Johannine metaphors on the lips of Jesus have received far less attention. One might speculate as to the reasons for this apparent lack of interest in Johannine metaphor. Perhaps it is rooted in the now dated presupposition that the Gospel of John affords no avenue to the historical Jesus, while the synoptic parables are often claimed to represent his original genius.[2] Or, maybe it arises from the presupposition that the fourth evangelist's symbolism is purely and simply a theological vehicle, contrived for that purpose alone.[3] Possibly, too, it is merely the case that the fourth gospel is seldom the beneficiary of the newer scholarly interests until those fresh methodologies have been well tested on the synoptic proving ground.[4] Whatever the reason for this neglect, it is time to open a long overdue discussion of the literary qualities of the Johannine metaphors.

This paper purports to do little more than that, namely, to initiate a discussion and arouse a new interest in the subject. My thesis is that from the perspective of the reader the Johannine metaphors function in a manner not dissimilar to those functions assigned the parables of Jesus in the synoptic gospels except that they are marked with peculiar Johannine characteristics and purpose. It is not the intent of this paper to make any claims regarding the authentic voice of Jesus in the Johannine metaphors. Such a question is far too complex and distinct from the literary analysis I have in mind.[5] But I do purport to make a case for the originality of the metaphors, their character as poetic symbols, and their use in the implied author's literary scheme.

To make this preliminary probe it is necessary to select a sample case of metaphor in the fourth gospel. John 10:1–18 comes to mind for several reasons. The first is that it is a passage in which some clear parabolic features are present, i.e., the use of vehicles from daily life to illuminate a significant reality for Christian belief. Another reason for choosing this passage is, of course, its problematic features. Some discussion of those features will follow, but suffice it for now to say simply that it appears to be an instance in which metaphors are mixed in a confusing way.

Specifically, the objective of this paper is to investigate the interrelated concerns of the structure, integrity, and genre of the images found in 10:1–18.

My methodology is admittedly elementary and eclectic. I would like to bring little more than the tools of observation and query to this sampling of Johannine metaphor. I want to ask what happens to one as she or he reads this passage with care and sensitivity. My effort is, then, an attempt to inquire after the response of the reader to the passage as it stands without recourse to the classical critical questions which have informed its interpretation in the past. This investigation, therefore, is conceived as an elemental form of reader response criticism. It is synchronic in that it brackets the historical questions of setting, sources, redaction, and the intent of the "real author." It is intratextual in its initial interests at least and concerned primarily with the strategies and the rhetoric of the text. There is also implicit attention to the temporal quality of the text as it is experienced by the implied reader.[6] What is attempted is the effort to produce a reading of the passage that might arise from an intimate participation in the text in which the reader allows him or herself to become vulnerable to its influence. In such an enterprise the text is experienced more as an event than as an object (Moore:20). This, it seems to me, might be the place to start a new conversation regarding the metaphors of the fourth gospel.

Two additional methodological observations are appropriate. The first is to venture into the fog-covered field of the locus of meaning. Without any attempt to peer through that fog, I declare myself still committed to a modified essentialistic or realistic appraisal of the role of the text. The text is not entirely a creation of the reader but has an integrity of its own—a givenness. But meaning is not mined out of the text, as one would dig for worms on a damp summer morning, as much as it is constructed through imaginative intercourse with the text. Meaning is the result of reading, but that reading is in response to the demands of the text. I am assuming that the text does something to the reader. Specifically, it occasions a unique experience. A concern for *how* the text does what it does is the professed method with which I begin. This does not necessitate believing that meaning is set in the objectivity of the text but only that it is the consequence of an engagement with the text. The subject-object dichotomy between reader and text is transcended insofar as meaning is possible only as the text and the reader become one reality. The reader enters the world of the text to become one with it, bringing his or her own subjectivity into it, or pulling the text out of its objectivity into the reader's own consciousness. But the text is more than the creation of the reader's imagination. In the momentary union of subject and object the text is enabled to do its work within the world of the reader's subjectivity. Mine is a modified essentialist position—modified by the absolute dependence on the reader for meaningfulness.

The second methodological observation is to alert the reader to shifts in the methods among the constituent parts of this essay. After a brief summary of the historical critical views of the passage, there follows an analysis of the surface structure of the verses. Methodologically this section attempts to summarize what the reader experiences in terms of the way the passage flows but also to epitomize what is evoked from the vulnerable reader in the course of participating in this structure. The third part of the paper discusses the reader's sense of dealing with an integral unit in the passage and how the text evokes that sense of unity in the reader's mind. The fourth section deals with how the reader experiences the images of the passage and what that means for the genre of those images. Here it is necessary momentarily to abandon a purely intrinsic, intratextual approach when we ask how the genre of the images compares with those encountered in the parables of Jesus found in the synoptic gospels. Still, even here I have attempted to keep a reader focus in the discussion.

1. THE STRUCTURE, INTEGRITY, AND GENRE OF JOHN 10:1-18
IN CONTEMPORARY COHANNINE SCHOLARSHIP[7]

The formal *structure* of John 10:1-18 gives us clues to the way in which the images of the passage are used and their meaning. But the precise understanding of the structure varies considerably among contemporary commentators. Most common is the assumption that there are two main parts, verses 1-5 and 7b-18 with verses 6-7a serving as a transition between the two. The relationship between verses 1-5 and 7-18 is conceived in a number of different ways. Most commentators, however, see the latter part as some sort of exposition of the former. Raymond E. Brown's analysis suffices as an example of such a view. According to Brown, verses 1-5 contain first the parable of the gate (vv. 1-3a) and then the parable of the shepherd (vv. 3b-5), the two comprising "twin parables." Verses 7-18 are "allegorical explanations" of those parables. Verses 7-10 explain the parable of the gate and verses 11-16 the parable of the shepherd.[8]

The tendency, then, is to see a shift in the nature of the metaphorical language between these two halves, with only the first having the character of parable in any proper sense of the word. Whatever the character of the metaphorical language of the second half of the passage, it is implicitly demeaned by speaking of it as allegory, interpretation, expansion, or some such term.[9] Commentators generally tend to see the passage in two major halves, each employing a different genre, the second of which departs significantly from the first.[10]

Not surprisingly, then, the *integrity* of the passage is often questioned in contemporary Johannine research. Bultmann understood the passage as a composite of at least four independent units (1971:363-375). Brown contends that "a simple parabolic expression has been applied by the evangelist to a later church situation...."[11] Lindars agrees with the analysis of J. A. T. Robinson that in verses 1-5 two originally distinct parables have been meshed (Lindars, 1972:354-355; Robinson, 1962:69). Barrett suggests that the passage contains numerous pieces which have been reworked by the evangelist (368). Dodd (1963:383) immortalized his analysis of the passage when he described it as "the wreckage of two parables fused into one, the fusion having partly destroyed the original form of both."[12]

Commentators are divided over the question of the relationship of verses 17-18 to earlier parts of the passage. A good number of them, however, understand these verses to stand separate from and independent of the images of verses 1-16. Bultmann insists that 17-18 leave "aside for the most part the metaphors in the parable" (1971:380). Brown speaks of them as "a short commentary on the phrase in v. 15, 'I lay down my life,' rather than on any element of the pastoral symbolism" (1966:399; cf. Haenchen:49). "The allegory is now almost abandoned, as Jesus expands the point made in verse 15," writes Lindars (1972:363; cf. Haenchen:49). Others, however, are inclined to view verses 17–18 as integral to the whole passage and stress the relationship of this christological statement to the symbolism of the discourse.[13] As a whole, however, they are not able to agree on the integrity of the entirety of 10:1–18.

In general scholars have tended to see within the complexity of the passage evidence of tradition and redaction and theorize that the fusion of the two have produced the disunity of the whole. Consequently Bultmann's impression that there is "confusion of the various images" (1971:359) is widely shared,[14] even when such a severe judgment is withheld.[15] Scholars have tended not to find an integrity to the passage, however gentle their expression of such a discovery may be.

When the issue of the *genre* of the component parts of the passage is pressed, there is little agreement among commentators. It is widely agreed that the use of *paroimia* in verse 6 has roots in the Hebrew *mashal* and that the latter word is represented in both the New Testament words, *paroimia* and *parabolē*.[16] Some insist that verses 1–5 are truly parabolic, (e.g., Brown, 1966:390; Bultmann, 1971:370, n. 4; and Dodd:383) while others deny that that is the case,[17] and others seem uncertain.[18] Generally, one must conclude, the labeling of the genre is done without recourse to clear distinctions among various kinds of metaphorical language and arises almost exclusively from an effort to understand *paroimia* in terms of its Hebraic roots. Little or no attempt is made to ask how the images of the passage function for the reader.[19]

The foregoing discussion is sufficient to illustrate some of the difficulties of the passage for contemporary interpreters. It is not unfair to draw three general conclusions from a survey of the contemporary interpretation of John 10:1–18: (1) The structure of the passage is comprised of two main parts with a shift in the kind of metaphorical language employed between the two. (2) The passage lacks a basic unity and probably reflects the presence of both tradition and redaction. (3) The genre of the parts is varied and evasive. The lack of agreement among commentators and the occasional vagueness of their remarks about it are sufficient to warrant a new look at the passage in terms of its literary features. The inadequacies of what has become the traditional historical-critical methodology are evident enough in the study of John 10:1–18. Whether or not a strictly literary approach entirely overcomes those deficiencies remains to be seen.

2. A Literary Reading of the Structure of John 10:1–18

My own view is that the passage is composed of four interlocking "human images"[20] with an expansion of the last of those images, followed by an explicitly "theological image." All five of the images are contrastive in form, in each case posing a positive image (A) over against a negative one (B). The structure of the passage appears thus:

THE IMAGE OF ENTERING THE SHEEPFOLD (VV. 1–3A)

1   *"Truly, truly I say to you,*
    B   he who does not enter the sheepfold by the door
        but climbs in by another way,
        that man is a thief and a robber;
2   A   but he who enters by the door is the shepherd of
        the sheep.
3   To him the gatekeeper opens";

THE IMAGE OF WHAT THE SHEPHERD DOES AND WHAT THE SHEEP DO (VV. 3B–5)

    A   "the sheep hear his voice,
        and he calls his own sheep by name
        and leads them out.
4   When he has brought out all his own,
        he goes before them,
            and the sheep follow him,
            for they know his voice.
5   B   A stranger they will not follow,
        but they will flee from him,
            for they do not know the voice of
            strangers."

THE NARRATOR'S COMMENT AND TRANSITION (VV. 6–7A)

6   "These figures Jesus used with them,
        but they did not understand what he was
            saying to them.
7   So Jesus again said to them,"

THE IMAGE OF THE DOOR TO THE SHEEP (VV. 7B–10)

    "Truly, truly, I say to you
    A   I am the door of the sheep.

8   B   All who came before me are thieves and
            robbers;
                but the sheep did not heed them.
9   A   **I am the door;**
            if any one enters by me,
                he/she will be saved
                    and will go in and out
                    and find pasture.
10 B   The thief comes
            only to steal and kill and destroy;
    A   I came
            that they may have life,
            and have it abundantly."

THE IMAGE OF THE GOOD SHEPHERD (VV. 11–15)

11 A   "**I am the good shepherd.**
            The good shepherd lays down his life for
                the sheep.
12 B   The one who is a hireling
            and not a shepherd,
                whose own the sheep are not,
                    sees the wolf coming
                    and leaves the sheep
                    and flees;
                and the wolf snatches them
                    and scatters them.
13   He/she flees
            because he/she is a hireling
                and cares nothing for the sheep.
14 A   **I am the good shepherd;**
            I know my own
                and my own know me,
15   as the Father knows me
                and I know the Father;
            and I lay down my life for the sheep."

AN EXPANSION OF THE IMAGE OF THE GOOD SHEPHERD (V. 16)

16   "And I have other sheep,
        that are not of this fold;
    I must bring them also,
        and they will heed my voice.
    So there shall be one flock, one shepherd."

A THEOLOGICAL IMAGE (VV. 17–18)

17   A   "For this reason the Father loves me,
           because I lay down my life
              that I may take it again.
18   B   No one takes it from me,
     A   but I lay it down of my own accord.
         I have power to lay it down,
            and I have power to take it again;
        this charge I have received from my Father."[21]

Three characteristics emerge from this analysis. The first regards *the way in which the contrasts appear and are varied*. In the first image the pattern is B/A; in the second A/B; in the third A/B/A/B/A; in the fourth A/B/A; and in the theological image A/B/A. In each case, except the second, the image concludes with the positive (A). The series begins with a negative image, continuing the polemic quality of the context of the passage found in chapter 9 and specifically 9:40–41. The first two images are symmetrically formed with a B/A/A/B pattern. It is after the negative conclusion of the second image that the narratorial comment in verses 6–7a addresses the reader. The entire series of images begins with the negative and concludes with the positive. The variation of the pattern keeps the reader off guard and surprised. But the concluding positive statement of each (but the second) of the images and the entire series continuously emphasizes the affirmative in the reader's mind. This alternation between the positive and the negative tends to continue the same variation begun in chapter 9. However, the general impact of the affirmative tone of the whole of 10:1–18 moves the reader away from the polemical conclusion of the previous narrative (chapter 9).

The reader is kept off guard by the variation of the affirmative and negative comparisons. However, the second characteristic of the passage is that the reader is also challenged by *the rapid transitions among the images*. The transition between the first image of entering the sheepfold and the complex image of what the sheep and shepherd do is abrupt and without signal or warning. First Jesus is the one who enters the door (v.

1), then the door itself (v. 7). While the narrator imposes an explanatory transition at verses 6–7a, the image of Jesus as the door of the sheep (v. 7b) gives way unexpectedly to that of the good shepherd (v. 11) without any metaphoric or narratorial preparation. The reader is led from a discussion of how unauthorized as opposed to authorized persons enter the sheepfold to the behavior of the sheep and shepherd, on to the consideration of the door to the sheepfold, to the good shepherd, and finally to the relationship of the Father and Son. All of this in the course of eighteen verses (cf. Kysar, 1986:164–165).

The expansion of the image of the good shepherd found in verse 16 moves the reader swiftly to consideration of another dimension of the previous image (vv. 11–15). The metaphorical language of the previous images is sustained ("sheep," "fold," "voice," "flock," and "shepherd"), but the image is expanded. This single verse, however, does more than expand the image of the good shepherd. Readers are subtly made aware of the fact that here they come to some conclusion of the human images in which they have been moving. The language of the image (which in terms of content is an expansion of the fourth image, as commentators have observed) serves to draw the first four images together. (See the discussion of the integrity of the passage below.)

Likewise, the theological image in verses 17–18 continues the readers in the world of sheep and shepherds ("because I lay down my life", v. 17), but now leading them into a new imaginary realm. This conclusion does not summarize the "meaning" of the previous images. They are left to stand on their own without theological abstraction. Rather the theological language offers a new image, which one might label divine relationship. That is to say, the metaphorical language is continued in the theological statements regarding the relationship between the divine Parent and child. The "logic" of the implied author at verses 17–18 is no longer confusing when one realizes that the verses are not an attempt to summarize the preceding images but are a continuation of imagery which drags the reader into still another picture world.

A final characteristic of the passage emerges: John 10:1–18 is not without *aids to reading*, the first of which are betrayed by a consideration of its surface structure. Each image begins with a key word which facilitates the reader's shift of imagination (however abrupt the shift may be). The participle, *ho eiserchomenos*, announces the central focus of the first image. "The sheep" in verse 3b redirects the reader's attention to the subject of the second image. The "I am" sayings of verses 7 and 11 aid the reader's attention. "The Father" in verse 17 hints that the object of the imagery has now changed from the human realm to the divine. The implied author has effectively led the reader through the seeming maze of imagery of the passage.

In conclusion, from the perspective of the reader and her or his response, the structure of the passage moves consistently and artistically, if unanticipatedly through four consecutive images and even through the theological image. The narrator's comment at verses 6–7a is less a division between two main parts as it is an aid to reading the images. The division effected by the comment invites the reader on to further word pictures. The commentary at verses 6–7a should be seen in terms of its function to aid the reader's center of attention as well as an indication that some sort of change of genre is about to occur.

3. A LITERARY READING OF THE INTEGRITY OF JOHN 10:1–18

When viewed intratextually, there is a remarkable unity in the passage, in spite of commentators' reservations concerning the issue. That unity is evidenced both in the total passage and within its component parts.

Each of the subunits has an integrity of its own while at the same time being bonded to others. The first image is internally united by the words "door" (*thura*) and "entering" (*eiserchomai*). It is furthermore formed as a complete antithetical parallelism, so that the reader is led from the negative to the positive. The image of the behavior of the sheep and the shepherd is bound together by the theme of the voice (*phonē*) in verses 3b, 4, and 5, as well as with "hear his voice" in verse 3b and "do not know the voice of strangers" in verse 5. The word "voice" thus forms closures around the pair of contrasting images of the familiar voice of the shepherd and the alien voice of the stranger.

Yet the first two images are interlocked in several ways. Most obvious is the fact that both invite the visualization of sheep and sheepfold, as well as legitimate and illegitimate personnel caring for the sheep. But they are further tied together by the persona of the "thief/robber" in the first and the "stranger(s)" in the second, the two identifications creating bookends around the pair of images.

The unity of the image of the door to the sheep is attained by repetition of the "I am" sayings at verses 7 and 9, as well as the theme of coming (*ēlthon* in v. 8 and 10b and *erchetai* in v. 10a). Add to those occurrences the use of entering (*eiselthē* in v. 9), and going in and out (*eiseleusetai* and *exeleusetai* in v. 9) and the reading is saturated with representations of motion. As a consequence, the reader is caught up in a world of movement. Moreover, three "I statements" unite the passage (vv. 7, 9, 10), adding a tone of personal immediacy to the two images.

The image of the good shepherd repeats the "I am" saying in verses 11 and 14, again forming the opening and closing of the subunit between which is sandwiched the representation of the hireling. The allusion to giving up life for the sake of the sheep occurs twice (vv. 11 and 15). In addition, the pair of expressions *idia* (v. 12) and *ta ema* (twice in v. 14) unifies the passage while at the same time further fostering a tone of intimacy.

The image of the good shepherd is linked to its predecessor thematically through the figures of the thief/robber in the first and the hireling in the second. Linguistically the two images are linked through the recurrence of the "I" sayings. The third and fourth images are each formed around "I am" expressions. The "I am" is repeated in each (vv. 7b, 9 and 11, 12). Consequently, the reader subtly gains a sense of the unity of the two images through their formal similarity. The "I" sayings also bind the images of the door and the shepherd with one another through their emotional tone of personal immediacy. The movement characteristic of the image of the door to the sheep is continued in that of the good shepherd ("lays down," v. 11, "coming," "leaves," and "scatters," v. 12, and "flees," vv. 12 and 13). The reader continues to inhabit a world filled with motion in time and space.

The expansion of the image of the good shepherd in verse 16 is hardly read as anything more than a further dimension of the fourth image. This is due in part to the use of the words, "sheep," "shepherd," and "fold." Formally the verse pulls images from the previous units together to create a new whole. The word, "other" (*alla*) directs the reader to another perspective of the good shepherd. However, the word "sheep" welds all four of the images together. The word, "voice," joins this image with the second and "heed" (*akouō*) links this verse with both the second and third images. "Shepherd" not only ties this verse closely with the fourth but also recalls the first of the images (v. 2). Finally, "fold" (*aulē*, v. 16) provides closure to the beginning of the human images in verse 1. Consequently, verse 16 serves a double function. It expands the imagery of the good shepherd, but it also brings to a closure the imagery drawn from the human realm of sheep, sheepfolds, shepherds, and strangers in the midst of the sheep.

That verses 17–18 constitute a new subunit is evident both from the shift of language and by their own integrity as a pericope. A new and single image arises in these verses. They are, furthermore, bracketed with the word, "Father," which introduces the new image at verse 17a and concludes it at 18b. One might conclude that the theological language of verses 17–18 is intrusive in the passage or even that they belong outside the unity of verses 1–16. This is so only if the reader is bound to the human realm, exclusive of the divine. The invitation of the four human images, however, has been precisely to tantalize the reader with the possibility that the human dimension betrays the presence of the divine. Hence, the four human images have teased the reader into the consideration of the divine represented by the human. Now in the conclusion of the passage the imagery shifts to the divine, and the relationship of Jesus and God is explicitly addressed in a new imagery. That shift is anticipated in the previous verses not only by the function of the figures to break open the human realm to reveal the divine presence in the human but also by the seemingly misplaced verse 15. The appearance of that verse in the midst of the fourth image anticipates and prepares the reader for the theological image of verses 17–18.

While I have chosen to speak of verses 17–18 as a "theological image," that label has limited usefulness. While the content of the verses has to do with a theological dimension—the relationship of Jesus to God—the language, like the preceding images, is imaginative. The reader is asked to picture that relationship as one between a parent and a child. It evokes images of the parent's command (*entolē*) for the child and the parent's love of the child who obeys even the most demanding of parental requests. Even more fundamental to the imagery of the verses 17–18 is the human experience of relationship. Relationship is something the reader knows from intercourse with others. The verses solicit the reader's reflection on christology in terms of the experience of relationship. In light of these considerations, the concluding image is theological but theology done with an anthropological metaphor.[22]

The concluding theological image then continues the imaginative character of the entire passage while passing beyond the pictures used in the four human images. It pushes the reader along into a new frame of reference. While doing so, it brings to a conclusion the use of the first person pronouns of the passage and distinctly articulates the christological subject of the previous images.

As disparate as the images may seem ("mixing of the metaphors"), the five images are packaged as a whole. Obviously their unity involves the metaphorical vehicle of sheep, shepherds, and dangerous persons. But beyond the obvious the contrastive form joins the five. The "amen, amen" formula holds the first pair of images together with the second. The images change swiftly and imaginatively, but not without the guidance of the author. The move is from the human images to the theological image of verses 17–18, but not without consistency and preparation.

The narrator's comment in verses 6–7a seems at first disruptive in the structure of the passage, but on further consideration it is seen to add significantly to the movement of the discourse. The narrator declares that the "figures" were not understood and verse 7 continues, "So (*oun*) Jesus again said to them . . . " In the figures which precede these verses the metaphors are implicit and in those which follow they are explicit. Distinct from the figures in verses 1–5, those in 7–15 include *eimi*. Thus the figures in the first section are implicitly metaphorical but in the second explicitly metaphorical.[23] Commentators are correct in their identification of verses 6–7a as transitional. However, the reader response confirms that the transition is not as radical nor as intrusive as sometimes claimed. Far from a distracting intrusion in the passage the narrator's comment prepares the reader to be led more deeply into the universe of the escalating images.

Verses 6–7a prepare the reader for the increasingly intimate character (the personal immediacy) of the succeeding images that function to draw him or her closer to Jesus in the discourse. The reader experiences a crescendo of the first person pronoun as she or he is led through verses 7b–18. Verse 7b begins with the first of four "I am" statements, and the first use of "me" is encountered immediately in verse 8 (*pro emou*). Thereafter the first person pronoun occurs with increasing frequency, its acceleration enhanced by the liberal use of the "me" and "my" from verse 14 on. (In the English the reader counts sixteen uses of "I" and ten occurrences of "me" or "my" in vv. 7b–18.) The third person pronoun recurs in verse 11, recalling its dominance in verses 1–5, but then is used only of the antagonist figure of the hireling (v. 12). In the experience of this gradual enlargement of the role of the first person the reader's sense of the power of the immediate presence of the speaker is intensified (Funk, 1982), climbing incrementally to the theological image of verses 17–18 which invites the reader to imagine the identity of that speaker.

The omniscient narrator (who knows the hearers do not understand) provides another clue to the strategy of the passage. Verses 6–7a supply the middle member of three interlocking statements of the absence of understanding among the hearers. Thereby the verses anchor the whole of 10:1–18 in its context. In 9:40–41 immediately preceding our passage the "Pharisees" struggle to understand the meaning of Jesus' words regarding seeing and blindness. In 10:19–20 the narrator reports that the words of Jesus provoke "a division among the Jews."

Commentators are correct then in their insistence that verses 6–7a mark a transition. However, the insistence that the verses signal a transition from parable to allegory (or some other transition beyond the simple difference between implicit and explicit metaphor) is less than satisfactory, as we shall see. That the verses indicate the shift from tradition to a redactional explanation is even less satisfying, since such a view does not take seriously enough the integrity of the entire passage. A reader response to verses 6–7a dictates that the comment functions as an authorial guide into the next set of images. There is indeed a transition at this point in the passage, but two things argue against verses 6–7a as demarcating a major division in the passage. The first is the unity of the whole series of images which makes unnecessary any explanation for a major shift at verses 6–7a. The second argument against viewing the narrator's comment as a break in the passage is a fundamental similarity in the functional nature of the images before and after verses 6–7a. Granted there is a transition from implicit to explicit metaphor at this juncture, but I shall argue below that the images before and after verses 6–7a all have a common character. The genre of the images must now be considered.

4. A Literary Reading of the Genre of John 10:1–18

An appreciative reading of the genre of the passage involves some grasp of the function played by each of the images. But before attempting to determine the precise genre of the images, it is necessary to investigate the strategy of their use. If genre arises from function, the reader needs to become conscious of how the implied author leads the reader through the complex of images. I am concerned at this point to explore further how the implied author has employed the set of images to lead the implied reader toward some desired destination. The reader has been asked to construct meaning in and among the images as they invade her or his consciousness. But an even more complex strategy is at work.

The Strategy of the Use of the Images

Jeffrey L. Staley has argued that the narrative of the Gospel of John in general tends to draw the implied reader "into the bosom of the implied author" (Staley:91). This strategy is accomplished in our passage only with considerable tension. The tension exists between the implied reader's astonishment at the series of metaphors, on the one hand, and, on the other hand, her or his pleasure in not entirely sharing the lack of understanding characteristic of the hearers alluded to in verse 6 and identified as "Pharisees" in 9:40 and some of the "Jews" in 10:19.

On the one hand, the implied reader experiences a distancing from Jesus and the narrator as a consequence of this passage. The abrupt series of images works to confuse the implied reader. First, the reader thinks she or he understands the metaphor, but then the metaphor changes, and the reader is left behind, struggling to keep up with the temporal flow of the discourse. Verse 6 warns the reader that the danger of not understanding the images is real and threatening. The reader stands on the brink of becoming identified with those who lack the insights to grasp the meaning of the images—on the precipice of identification with unbelief. In a sense the reader becomes a victim of the implied author at this point. "The victimization of the implied reader" is a frequent strategy in the fourth gospel. It is a strategy that forces the reader, if only momentarily, out of his or her status as an insider into that of an outsider.[24] In this case the entrapment of the reader is accomplished by allowing him or her to believe that she or he understands the image, only to be confronted with the next image which challenges the first understanding. The reader comes to the passage with some confidence, equipped with the previous narrative (most especially the prologue, 1:1–18). So the reading pilgrim of the narrative has been led to feel that she or he has the crucial key to comprehend the enigmatic words of Jesus and is thereby dissociated with the misunderstanding and unbelief of the characters in the narrative. But in the case of the successive images of our passage, confidence in that comprehension and dissociation is called into question.

Hence, the implied author creates a situation of suspense. Will the reader succumb to misunderstanding? A sense of conflict is evoked by the enigmatic images. It is a conflict that drives the reader on in search of the resolution of the conflict. The reader is put off guard by the images and urged on by them toward clarification. Unlike elsewhere in the narrative the implied author or narrator does not immediately unlock the meaning of Jesus' words (e.g., 2:21–25). On the other hand, the setting of the passage clearly suggests that it is the outsiders—the Pharisees and the unbelieving Jews—who fail to grasp the sense of the images. The reader gains a pleasure from knowing (to some degree) the clue to the images that the characters in the narrative do not have. The reader is victimized by the images, but not alienated. She or he possesses enough understanding to continue on in the journey of reading with confidence that the narrator will be faithful in bringing him or her to harmonious understanding with the teller of the story, even as that allusive figure has done previously.

Therefore, the images create a tension between the reader's failure to understand and his or her complete identification with the opponents of Jesus. While not debilitating the reader, the implied author keeps the reader off-balance by challenging any smugness and annihilating any complacency. This strategy keeps the reader close to the narrator—clinging to the coattails of the story teller—if not in the narrator's bosom. It functions to lead the reader further into the narrative in search for resolution without utterly destroying the relationship which the narrator has established with the implied reader.

The reader's apprehension of the images is, therefore, an *affective* experience as well as a *cognitive* one. It is not simply cognitive confusion that is elicited by the series of images in our passage (although that is surely part of the strategy), but an emotional instability as well. The sense of being thrown off balance, of being cast into the realm of uncertainty, of being dangerously close to the antagonists of the narrative summons forth an affective response in the reader (Moore:96).

The implied author employs an effective strategy in the use of this series of images—one that propels the reader on in the narrative. The passage is far more potent than is sometimes realized.

The Genre of the Images

But the genre itself of the images is important to the strategy of the text. Therefore, we need to ask further what the precise nature of those figures is. How shall they be categorized? The discussion underway is a test of the hypothesis that genre arises more out of the function an image performs for the reader than its nature abstracted from the text in which it is found. That is to say, the determination of the precise nature of the images in John 10:1–18 cannot be ascertained in isolation from the task they perform in the strategy of the passage. Hence, we must ask if the effort to label the images of verses 1–5 as parable and those of 7–15 as allegory (or the lot of them as allegories) makes any sense in terms of the function they play in the reading of the passage. What genre best describes the images when their function for the reader is considered? In effect one might say this experiment intends to ask whether images can ever be helpfully defined "essentialistically" at all or whether "functional" (that is, reader response) definitions are not both more descriptive and helpful.

The implied author has treated the reader to a series of rapidly changing images, asking the reader to shift visions abruptly and unexpectedly, drawing four distinct comparisons from one metaphorical field, a fifth from another realm, and in the process bombarding the reader with provocative pictures. The first observation pertinent to the genre of the images is the simple fact that the reader is asked implicitly or explicitly to make a *comparison* in each of the figures of the passage. The reader is asked to compare Jesus with the entry to the sheepfold, with the shepherd who tends and cares for the sheep, and with the obedient child of a loving parent. Comparison is invited between life under the care of Jesus with life in the sheepfold under the care of a responsible and devoted shepherd. In contrast the threats besetting the reader are compared to illegitimate persons who enter the sheepfold—a thief, a robber, and a hireling who do not care whether the sheep are scattered and killed.

But what is the character of these comparisons? Our response is hampered by disagreement about the correct use of words such as "image," "simile," and "metaphor."[25] The question I want to ask is whether or not we have in these Johannine figures something like what contemporary scholars have claimed is the metaphorical character of at least some of the parables of Jesus. Do the images function for the reader in a way that is comparable to the synoptic parables?

It is the identification of parable and metaphor, Bernard Brandon Scott suggests, that has set off new appreciation for the synoptic parables.[26] That new appreciation roots in understanding the metaphor as more than an illustration or simple teaching device. The parabolic metaphors are—in the classification of Philip Wheelwright—tensive language used "diaphorically" (Wheelwright:78–79; cf. Scott, 1989:61). This is to say that the metaphor is indispensable to the truth it conveys. Truth is "in and through" the image itself. It is not a "throw-away" instrument (an "epiphor") to communicate a truth knowable independent of the metaphor itself. "Parable as metaphor demands the parable never be done away with . . . We cannot state what a parable means, for it has no meaning separate from itself" (Scott, 1989:15). John Dominic Crossan has advanced this understanding of poetic metaphor by further distinguishing between the two kinds of metaphors. The poetic metaphor is not chosen as a means of expression, Crossan writes, but rather the truth received is the metaphor itself, so that no discursive summary of that truth can be extracted from the metaphor.

> The thesis is that metaphor can also articulate a referent so new or so alien to consciousness that this referent can only be grasped within the metaphor itself. The metaphor here contains a new possibility of world and of language so that any information one might obtain from it can only be received *after* one has participated through the metaphor in its new and alien referential world . . . this primacy of participation over and before information is most profoundly relevant (Crossan, 1973:13; cf. McFague, 1975:49).

Consequently one must speak of two types of metaphor: those in which information is first received which allows one to participate in the metaphor and those "in which participation precedes information so that the function of metaphor is to create participation in the metaphor's referent" (Crossan, 1973:14; cf. Funk, 1982:34). A "true metaphor," Crossan insists, is of the second kind. Jesus used such metaphors to break open the world of his listeners with a new world (Crossan, 1973:27).[27] Robert Funk has claimed that a metaphor,

> because of the juxtaposition of two discrete and not entirely comparable entities, produces an impact upon the imagination and induces a vision of that which cannot be conveyed by prosaic or discursive speech (Funk, 1966:136).

On the basis of a reader response experience of them are we able to say that the images of John 10:1–18 are such poetic metaphors? Are they "true metaphors" or more prosaic comparisons? The latter has often been thought to be the case. Johannine scholarship has referred to such figures as these as *mashal*[28] or as "allegories."[29] There has been a concern to distinguish the figures used in the fourth gospel from those of the synoptic parables, rightly attempting to protect the distinctiveness of both the Johannine and the synoptic portrayals of the message of Jesus.

Still, it is clear that in the images in John 10:1–18 there is a remarkable and even startling series of comparisons. When the commentator tries to summarize the meaning of the figures, the results are puny and sometimes almost comical. The figures defy our attempts to translate them into discursive language. They carry their own truth which resists generalization. They evoke from the reader a participation which in turns nourishes a "knowing" far different from the illustrative metaphor, which is dispensed with once it has served its purpose. The figures invite the reader into the flock of Jesus, there to share an intimacy with the shepherd and to benefit from protection from the threatening forces around her or him.[30] This *participatory* feature is characteristic of each of the images individually but of the entire series as well. That is, the mosaic of images draws the reader in, constantly provoking with each abrupt move to a new figure (Kysar, 1980:215–216). The series of images forms a single experience in which the reader is lured into the picture world as a member of the sheepfold and confronted with the decision as to whether his or her world can survive the onslaught of this new world dominated by the image of the sheepfold and the shepherd/son. That participatory experience resists any effort to be reduced to discursive language.

The series of images shares the *shock* of true metaphorical language.[31] The poetic metaphor startles the imagination by the comparison it offers and thereby opens a new and unanticipated possibility of truth. "In the metaphor," writes Wilder, "we have an image with a certain shock to the imagination which directly conveys visions of what is signified . . . " (Wilder, 1964:80). The series of metaphors in John 10:1–18 produces that shock, that splitting of the ordinary reality which allows the possibility of the new.[32] This is part of what Alan Culpepper has called the "deformation of language" in the fourth gospel, the use of the familiar in unfamiliar ways.[33]

But beyond this there is something more in the Johannine metaphors of this passage which shares a functional resemblance to the metaphorical parables. If the parables attributed to Jesus in the first three gospels are often characterized by shock or surprise in the use of certain vehicles, such appears in our passage.[34] But part of the experience of that shock is the *irresolvable paradox* characteristic of the synoptic parables (Crossan, 1980:58). If that is indeed the response to the parables, it is clearly also one shared by the reader of John 10:1-18. The images of the passage spark a paradoxical response to the portrayal of the divine in the mundane images of shepherd, sheepfold, and child. Paradoxical, too, is reaction to the feature so often labeled as the "mixture of metaphors." The reader is driven to imagine Jesus as the door to the sheepfold as well as shepherd of the sheep himself. If the reader is faithful, however, the shepherd-door must also be visualized as the son of a parent. But more significantly, the paradox of the images is the ambivalent posture into which the reader is innocently led by the metaphors—that of insider and outsider, protagonist and antagonist, companion and alien to the narrator.[35]

The participatory, shocking, and paradoxical qualities of the images of John 10:1-8 suggest that they are experienced as no mere similes or teaching vehicles. They are rather *"true metaphors" with poetic power* to initiate a new kind of experience. The implied author creates a new reality with these metaphors, a reality impossible without them.[36] Indeed, the entire Gospel of John might be considered an extended metaphor in which the author is trying less to communicate some universal truths through individual narratives and speeches than create a reader experience of a world at the center of which stands the Christ figure. The individual metaphors of 10:1-18 become part of a whole metaphorical reality. A new world of meaning is revealed in the language of the gospel. Typical of this gospel, however, that new universe of meaning is Christ himself.

However, the metaphors of John 10:1-18 serve a *contrastive* role, posing opposites, utilizing bipolar images. This oppositional nature of the metaphors in John 10:1-18 (e.g., the good shepherd opposed to the hireling) reminds one of certain synoptic parables in which such a feature is betrayed (cf. e.g., Luke 18:9-14; Matthew 7:24-27; Luke 6:47-49; Dodd:383). But the setting of the images of John 10:1-18 in the entirety of the narrative of the fourth gospel gives them a role for the reader which is distinct from the synoptic parables. Not unlike the so-called dualism or bipolarity of the fourth gospel, the metaphors of 10:1-18 function in the reader's imagination to distinguish two realities. They pose the alternatives in polar opposites, much as does the light/darkness theme of the gospel. The implied author imposes a duality upon the reader, insisting by the imagery that there are two and only two realities, one true and one false, one life-giving and one life-threatening. Consequently, the reader is forced to respond to the two options without any alternatives. Participating in the images of the sheepfold with its good shepherd and menacing strangers, the implied reader must evaluate experience in terms of shepherd or thief/robber/hireling. Do I want to live in the world of the sheepfold of Jesus or another? The metaphors smash the complacency of or the resignation to the reader's world with another world possibility.

This suggests that the metaphors of the Gospel of John share a role in the broader compass of the document, contributing to the either/or strategy of the implied author.

This polar contrastive feature suggests the *decisional* character of the metaphors in our passage which in turn echoes the eschatological urgency of the synoptic parables.[37] In the first three of the gospels that urgency is related to the new age that is dawning in the ministry of Jesus and his disciples; it is part of the kerygmatic content of the message attributed to Jesus concerning the rule of God. The metaphors before us in John 10:1–18 betray a similar kind of urgency, if cast in a very different context. These metaphors force upon the reader the necessity of response to the claims of Jesus. The issue at stake is nothing less than the "life" of the reader. Shall the reader embrace the claim of Jesus or allow existence to be threatened by the thieves/robbers/strangers? The decision thrust upon the reader is simply, shall I choose life or death, light or darkness? The Johannine metaphors do evoke a sense of urgency, however different the eschatological setting might be.[38]

In summary, the comparisons asked of the reader in John 10:1–18 function as poetic metaphors (diaphors) by virtue of their demand for participation before knowing, their shocking impact, and their thrust of the reader into irresolvable paradox. Moreover, like the true metaphorical parables of the synoptics they elicit contrastive images and provoke decision.

But certain other similarities between the metaphors of our passage and the synoptic parables merit mention. We momentarily abandon our reader response orientation to note these resemblances. It is frequently observed that the *pairing* of parables in the synoptic tradition is a common feature (cf. e.g., Luke 14:28–32; 15:3–10; cf. Brown, 1966:393). The passage under investigation pairs images (vv. 1–5 and 7–15), but carries that assemblage further to produce a complex of metaphors. The *metaphorical field* of farming, sowing and harvesting is prominent in the synoptic parables, as is that of a master leaving servants in charge during his absence (e.g., Mark 4:3–8 and parallels; Matthew 24:45–51 and Luke 12:42–46).[39] In John 10:1–18 we witness two other metaphorical fields, in this case the field of sheep, shepherds and dangerous persons, as well as that of the parent-child relationship. It is well known and often emphasized that the authentic parables of Jesus have a *realism* about them. They speak of the mundane, daily reality of their hearers, lifting up the most common activity or occurrence. As Amos Wilder claims, "One can even speak of their secularity" (Wilder, 1964:81 and 1982:90). If that is true, it is surely correct to speak of the secularity of sheep and shepherds and the threat posed to the flock by the intruders. Or further, the secularity of the relationship of parent and child is evident. The figures of John 10:1–18 draw on common realities of the first century world and use an ordinary common sense knowledge as the occasion for new meaning.[40]

The effort to analyze the genre of the images of the passage has led to the conclusion that they function as poetic or true metaphors (diaphors), rather than simple vehicles of truth (epiphors). I have contended on the basis of a reader response to the passage that these images share the characteristics claimed for at least certain of the synoptic parables, including their participatory character, their shocking effect, their paradox-inducing consequence, their contrastive feature, and their decisional quality. In terms of their function for the reader the images are poetic metaphors and as such they share much with the parables attributed to Jesus in the synoptic gospels quite aside from the question of how and to what degree they invite allegorization on the part of the reader. Less important for our investigation is the fact that, like the synoptic parables, the metaphors in our passage exhibit the practice of pairing, the employment of metaphorical fields, and the application of the secular to open the sacred.

5. CONCLUSION

Notwithstanding the tendencies of the commentaries, John 10:1–18 appears to the reader as five interrelated images, flowing one after the other with abruptness and unexpectedness but with skillful guidance in the text. The passage functions as a single whole in both content and form, in spite of attempts to fragment it and find divisions on the basis of either content or form. The functional genre of the images (i.e., the reader experience), I suggest, is that of poetic or true metaphor quite apart from the question of where they provoke simple comparison and where they stimulate allegorizing.[41] The passage shares much with the literary quality of some of the parables attributed to Jesus in the synoptic gospels, so that the sharp distinction between the Johannine metaphors and the synoptic parables is to be seriously qualified. This is not to deny a difference between the metaphorical function of a story parable and the images of John 10:1–18.[42] It is to argue, however, that in terms of a reader response both may and do perform as true or poetic metaphor.

This experiment has purported to be no more than a "literary case study" in Johannine metaphor. Whether or not the conclusions regarding John 10:1–18 are typical of Johannine metaphor in general requires further investigation. The findings of our study, however, are significant enough to merit a new and different kind of probe of the vast reservoir of imagery in the fourth gospel—one that takes as its focus the literary function of those metaphors within the scope of a reader response criticism.

This initial study has been set within the context of a dialogue with the contemporary historical critical investigations of the fourth gospel, particularly as we find that method employed in the standard commentaries on the document. Such a dialogical setting has proven to be a way by which reader-centered attention to the text might be defined in distinction from the historical focus of traditional critical scholarship. Indeed, every attempt at a new methodology needs to work dialogically with the prevailing methods. But this author does not conceive the relationship between the methodology attempted above and the historical critical methods as mutually exclusive. What I have attempted begs the questions of sources, redaction, and most especially the intent of the "real author." My interpretation of the passage addresses only the shape of the text as it stands and this reader's response to it. The historical critical questions may still be appropriate, but on another level or in a different mode. It is hoped that a new literary criticism of the fourth gospel can serve as a corrective to the traditional historical critical approach and take its place alongside those methodologies as a equal partner, allowing us still more tools with which to investigate this rich and intriguing gospel.

NOTES

[1] For a summary of the developments cf. Perrin:chap. 3. A more thorough bibliographical survey is found in Kissinger.

[2] E.g., Wilder, 1964:90 and Breech:217 among others. Scott has claimed that the burden of proof is on those "who would claim a parable is not from Jesus" (1986:8).

[3] E.g., Léon-Dufour. In her excellent study of revelation and irony in the fourth gospel Gail O'Day proposes a more useful perspective. She writes, "The revelatory dynamic of the Fourth Gospel rests in the interplay between revelation *en paroimiais* and revelation *parresia*, and in the transformation of categories and assumptions that takes place through the juxtaposition of those two modes" (O'Day:109). O'Day's work marks one of the important and initial efforts to take the literary qualities of the fourth gospel seriously, especially as they relate to the theological message of the document.

[4] Gratefully, the gap between the applications of new methodologies in synoptic and Johannine studies has been narrowed due to the appearance of an increasing number of investigations of the fourth gospel from a literary perspective. This movement in its contemporary form perhaps began with Olsson. But its primary impetus in American scholarship arose from the publication of Culpepper. That seminal work has been followed by a stream of studies from a literary critical perspective, including Duke, O'Day, Staley, and less directly Moore. Cf. Mack:87-88. A number of structural studies have been done. Exemplary of such is Patte, 1983. Cf. Girard:79-110 and Patte, 1990. Semiotic studies are represented in the work of Colloud and Genuyt, 1985 and 1987. An American semiotic investigation is Boers. The present *Semeia* volume hopes to close the gap still further between the advances made in synoptic studies and those in Johannine research.

[5] Such claims for some of the metaphors attributed to Jesus in the Gospel of John have, of course, been made. Among the most notable and influential of such efforts are Dodd:366-387 and Robinson, 1962:67-75 and 1985:chap. VII. Both Dodd and Robinson

make excessive claims, it seems to me, for the historical reliability of the fourth evangelist's representation of Jesus' teachings. Cf. Sturch, 1978 and Lindars, 1970.

⁶ For definitions of the terms "implied author," "implied reader," and "narrator" in the following discussion, cf. Culpepper:15-18, 205-211, and Staley:27-47. Cf. Moore:46. Moore later states, "To read any text is necessarily to engage, in and through its rhetoric (however overt or subtle), a projection of the reader that that text requires. This projection is proffered as a *role*, one which can be taken on or rejected but which can not be circumvented . . . . Indeed, if the hypothetical reader (or hearer) is thought of as one exposed to the text for the first time, then we have a working definition of reader-response criticism in the New Testament context" (72).

⁷ The most recent and helpful bibliographies on the passage are found in Beasley-Murray:162-163 and Haenchen:43-44.

⁸ Brown, 1966:390-396. Cf. Schneider:220-225. Bultmann calls 7-10 and 14-18 interpretations of the parables in verses 1-5 (1971:363-375). Lindars prefers to speak of verses 7-18 as expansions and developments of the parables in verses 1-5 (1972:354-355). For Beasley-Murray verses 7-18 are "a meditation on the parable" (167). Schnackenburg refers to the component parts of verses 7-15 as "extensions of the imagery outlined in the *paroimia*" (294). The parables of verses 1-5 are "exploited" by the evangelist in verses 7-18, according to Dodd:385.

⁹ Robinson (1962) suggests that verses 7-18 are the result of the church's allegorization of the original parable in verses 1-5 and typical of the tendency in the early church to interpret the parables of Jesus allegorically. For a different interpretation cf. Meyer:232-235.

¹⁰ The view that the passage has suffered serious disarrangement has been proposed. Examples include: Bultmann, 1971:358-360; Bernard:xxiv; Macgregor:232ff. A careful analysis of Bultmann's proposal is found in Smith:163-166. Such disarrangement theories are widely rejected today, as a perusal of recent commentaries shows.

¹¹ Brown, 1966:396. Bruce suggests that verses 7-9 comprise "a short parable" inserted into a longer one, verses 1-5 and 10-17, hence accounting for the sudden shift to the consideration of Jesus himself as the door (225).

¹² A dissenting voice to the assumption that verses 1-5 are the composite of two separate parables is heard in Beasley-Murray (167), who cites in support Becker:325.

¹³ Cf. e.g. Schnackenburg (299) who denies that verses 16-18 are redactional and claims that they "develop the idea of the good shepherd's offering of his life." Dodd seems to regard 7-18 as a single unit (384, n. 2), as does Beasley-Murray who understands verses 17-18 as the conclusion of the "meditation on the parable" found in verses 1-6 (171).

¹⁴ Cf. Smith:29. Urban C. von Wahlde suggests that 10:15b-16 betrays "a level of theology more appropriate to the later editions [of the gospel]" (125).

¹⁵ E.g., Barrett (367): "Meaning assigned to sheep seems to vary." The thought of the passage then "moves in spirals rather than straight lines." For an argument favoring the unity of verses 1-18 cf. Tragan.

¹⁶ E.g., Brown, 1966:390 and Beasley-Murray:164. For a discussion of the problem of the genre of 10:1-18 cf. Busse:520-521.

¹⁷ In my commentary I labeled all the images of verses 1-18 allegories while admitting that the term is not the most descriptive of what appears in the passage (Kysar, 1986:159). Schnackenburg insists that the passage is neither parable nor allegory but "a figurative device of a mixed kind, a parable with symbolic features . . . a way of speaking that is *sui generis*" (284-285). Haenchen argues that it is "a dark saying or figure of speech with a hidden meaning" (47). Cf. Barrett:367 and Bauer:613.

¹⁸ Lindars calls the whole passage an "allegory" (1972:352) but then says, "It is not so much an allegory as a discourse in monologue form" (354). Regarding verses 1-5 he concludes that they are "to some extent allegorized" because their features are "not simply drawn from life" (354). He then titles verses 7-18, "The Allegory" (357).

[19] Dewey has correctly pointed out that the word, *paroimia*, in John covers a wide range of literary forms including parable, metaphor, allegory and proverb (82). Cf. Simonis:74-85.

[20] I have chosen to use the word, "image," here in a neutral way, so as not to prejudge the genre of the pictures used in the passage. The genre, I mean to suggest, is understood only after the structure and unity or disunity of the passage is considered. Genre arises from function. "Human" is used as a way of distinguishing the images having to do with Jesus' relationship with humans as opposed to the "theological image" in verses 17-18, which directs attention to the relationship between Jesus and God.

[21] For another and different analysis of the structure of the passage cf. Simonis:20-22 and his concluding chart. While Simonis' analysis is helpful, it overlooks a number of important features for our project.

[22] This effort to elucidate the theological language of verses 17-18 as image or metaphor is indebted in part to the work of McFague, esp. 1982. Cf. McFague, 1987:31-40.

[23] Cf. Frye:56. Caird speaks of the same distinction as the difference between simile and metaphor. "If a comparison is explicit we call it a simile . . . . If it is implicit we call it a metaphor" (144).

[24] Staley:97-98 and 116. Staley describes "reader victimization" or "entrapment" in this way: "It first presents the reader with the narrative 'facts' in such a way that the reader is induced to commit the character's or narrator's errors, then it forces the reader to recognize his or her misjudgments by supplying or implying the corrective perspective" (95-96). Moore argues "that the recipients of the Fourth Gospel are the ultimate victims of its irony" (168).

[25] Compare for instance Caird:144 and Frye:56. Cf. Culpepper:182.

[26] Scott, 1981:13. Cf. Kjärgaard, who argues that both the similes and parables of the synoptic gospels are in fact metaphors in the true sense.

[27] Wilder expresses a similar idea: "Now we know that a true metaphor or symbol is more than a sign, it is a bearer of the reality to which it refers. The hearer not only learns about that reality, he participates in it. He is invaded by it" (1964:92). Cf. Tillich, 1955:189-197 and 1951:I, 239-241.

[28] Brown, 1966:390. Cf. Scott's discussion of *mashal* and parable (1989:7-62).

[29] No better example exists than the comment of this author in comparing the synoptic and Johannine representations of Jesus: "The story parable is entirely missing. There are comparisons made, but they take on the form of elaborate allegories and lose the simplicity which their counterparts in the Synoptics have" (Kysar, 1976:8). Cf. Kysar, 1986:158-159.

[30] Evidence of this is found in the way the image of the "good shepherd" functions in popular Christian mentality. While many Christian believers will speak of Jesus as the good shepherd, few would be able to express in discursive language what they mean by that identification. The metaphor is its own truth, and it defies translation into propositional terms. The lay mentality may better grasp the nature of the metaphor than do scholarly enterprises!

[31] The startling quality of the images suggests Robert Alter's distinction among conventional, intensive and innovative images. He uses as examples of innovative images the poetry of Job and makes several observations pertinent to our discussion. First, he observes how on occasion there is a "rapid flow of innovative figures" in Job. Such is surely the case as well in John 10:1-18. Second, he suggests that the force of the innovative image "colors our perception of its referent." Referring to the innovative metaphors of the Song of Songs, he writes, "imagery is given such full and free play . . . that the lines of semantic subordination blur, and it becomes a little uncertain what is illustration and what is referent" (Alter:189-190, 192-193). Those descriptions of innovative imagery could justifiably be made of John 10:1-18.

³² Brown speaks of what I have called shock as the "puzzlement" of the Johannine discourses. "Puzzlement is the way in which the readers/hearers are brought to recognize, however incompletely, who this Jesus is . . . " (1989:63). Scott writes, "Jesus' discourse changes or challenges the implied structural network of associations" (1989:61). My suggestion is that the images in John 10:1-18 are shocking precisely because they violate the assumed system of associations.

³³ Culpepper:198. Culpepper shares the expression with Beardslee:11. This literary insight is comparable to Malina's sociological suggestion that the language of the fourth gospel is "antilanguage," that is, the use of a culture's language by an antisocial group. Among the features of antilanguage is its relexicalization of vocabulary (Malina:11-17).

³⁴ E.g., the use of the shepherd. Kenneth E. Bailey points out, "flesh and blood shepherds who in the first century wandered around after sheep were clearly *am ha-aretz* and unclean" (147).

³⁵ Such is not an infrequent feature of the Johannine rhetoric. Moore argues briefly but convincingly that Johannine irony "collapse[s] in paradox" (163).

³⁶ Cf. McKnight's discussion of the values of deconstruction for biblical criticism (93-94).

³⁷ In the words of Joachim Jeremias, "The hour of fulfillment is come, that is the urgent note that sounds through them all" (230). Cf. Via:182ff.

³⁸ In a sense then Robinson is correct in insisting that the parables of verses 1-5 have an eschatological urgency of their own, which he conceives of in terms of the "realized eschatology" of the fourth gospel (1962:74). I prefer to think of the eschatological urgency of the passage and of the entire Johannine gospel as "existential" rather than temporal. Whether that emphasis constitutes a Johannine demythologizing of the early Christian eschatology as Bultmann argued is another question (1955:pt. III).

³⁹ Caird speaks of "metaphor systems" in which groups of metaphors are "linked together by their common origin in a single area of human observation, experience or activity, which has generated its own peculiar sublanguage or jargon . . . " (155).

⁴⁰ Richard concludes his study of expressions of double meaning in the fourth gospel by saying, "Ultimately John's vision is ambiguous . . . . John's readers are constantly challenged to consider both the earthly and the heavenly" (107).

⁴¹ The distinction between simple comparison and allegory is at best a thin one, as Caird demonstrates (165-167). The same argument is made in Klauck. When the metaphor functions poetically in the way we have described, the difference between singular comparison and allegory dissolves entirely, for both may perform as true metaphor. This is not to deny, however, the distinction between allegory and allegorizing.

⁴² Still, another avenue to be explored is the nature of some Johannine metaphors as "condensed stories" and the relationship between their abbreviated story character and that of the synoptic story parables. It may be that the distinction between johannine metaphor and synoptic story parable is not as sharp as has sometimes been assumed.

WORKS CONSULTED

Alter, Robert
    1985   *The Art of Biblical Poetry*. New York: Basic Books.

Bailey, Kenneth E.
    1976   *Poet and Peasant*. Grand Rapids, MI: Eerdmans.

Barrett, C. K.
    1978   *The Gospel According to St. John*. 2nd edition. Philadelphia: Westminster.

Bauer, Walter, et al.
    1979   *A Greek-English Lexicon of the New Testament and Other Early Christian Literature*. 2nd edition. Chicago: University of Chicago.

Beardslee, William A.
    1970   *Literary Criticism of the New Testament*. Guides to Biblical Scholarship, NT Series. Philadelphia: Fortress.

Beasley-Murray, George R.
    1987   *John*. Word Biblical Commentary 36. Waco, TX: Word.

Becker, J.
    1979–81   *Das Evangelium des Johannes*. 2 vols. Ökumenische Taschenbuch-Kommentar zum Neuen Testament 4:1, 2. Gütersloh: G. Mohn.

Bernard, J. H.
    1928   *Gospel According to St. John*. Vol. I. Edinburgh: T. and T. Clark.

Boers, Hendrikus
    1988   *Neither on This Mountain Nor in Jerusalem: A Study of John 4*. Atlanta: Scholars.

Breech, James
    1984   *The Silence of Jesus: The Authentic Voice of Jesus*. Philadelphia: Fortress.

Brown, Raymond E.
    1966   *The Gospel According to John, I–XII*. Anchor Bible 29. Garden City, NY: Doubleday.
    1989   "The Johannine World for Preachers." *Interpretation* 43:58–65.

Bruce, F. F.
    1983   *The Gospel of John*. Grand Rapids, MI: Eerdmans.

Bultmann, Rudolf
    1955   *Theology of the New Testament*. 2 vols. New York: Charles Scribner's.
    1971   *The Gospel of John*. Oxford: Blackwell.

Busse, Ulrich
    1987   "Offene Fragen zu Joh 10." *NTS* 33:520–521.

Caird, George B.
    1980   *The Language and Imagery of the Bible*. Philadelphia: Westminster.

Colloud, J. and Genuyt, F.
    1985   *Le discours d'adieu. Jean 13–17. Analyse sémiotique*. Lyon: Centre pour l'Analyse du Discours Religieux.
    1987   *L'Evangile de Jean (II). Lecture sémiotique des chapîtres 7 à 12*. Dossiers du Centre Thomas More. L'Arbresle: Centre Thomas More.

Crossan, John Dominic
    1973   *In Parables: The Challenge of the Historical Jesus*. New York: Harper.
    1980   *Cliffs of Fall: Paradox and Polyvalence in the Parables of Jesus*. New York: Seabury.

Culpepper, R. Alan
    1983   *Anatomy of the Fourth Gospel: A Study in Literary Design*. Foundations and Facets: New Testament. Philadelphia: Fortress.

Dewey, Kim E.
    1980   "PAROIMIAI in the Gospel of John." *Semeia* 17:81–100.

Dodd, C. H.
    1963   *Historical Tradition in the Fourth Gospel*. Cambridge: University.

Duke, Paul D.
    1985   *Irony in the Fourth Gospel*. Atlanta: John Knox.

Frye, Northrop
    1982   *The Great Code: The Bible and Literature*. New York: Harcourt Brace Jovanovich.

Funk, Robert W.
1966   *Language, Hermeneutic, and the Word of God.* New York: Harper.
1982   *Parables and Presence: Forms of the New Testament Tradition.* Philadelphia: Fortress.

Girard, M.
1982   "L'unité de composition de Jean 6, au regard de l'analyse structurel." *Église et Théologie* 13:79–110.

Haenchen, Ernst
1984   *John 2.* Hermeneia. Philadelphia: Fortress.

Jeremias, Joachim
1963   *The Parables of Jesus.* Rev. edition. New York: Charles Scribner's.

Kissinger, Warren S.
1979   *The Parables of Jesus.* American Theological Library Association Bibliography Series 4. Metuchen, NJ: Scarecrow.

Kjärgaard, M. S.
1986   *Metaphor and Parable. A Systematic Analysis of the Specific Structure and Cognitive Function of the Synoptic Similes and Parables qua Metaphors.* Acta Theologica Danica 19. Leiden: Brill.

Klauck, H.-J.
1978   *Allegorie und Allegorese in synoptischen Gleichnistexten.* Neutestamentliche Abhandlungen, Neue Folge 13. Münster: Aschendorff.

Kysar, Robert
1976   *John, the Maverick Gospel.* Atlanta: John Knox.
1980   "The Promises and Perils of Preaching on the Gospel of John." *Dialog* 19:215–216.
1986   *John.* Augsburg New Testament Commentaries. Minneapolis: Augsburg.

Léon-Dufour, Xavier
1981   "Towards a Symbolic Reading of the Fourth Gospel." *NTS* 27:439–456.

Lindars, Barnabas
1970   "Two Parables in John." *NTS* 16:318–329.
1972   *The Gospel of John.* New Century Bible. London: Oliphants.

Macgregor, G. H. C.
   n.d. *The Gospel of John.* Moffatt New Testament Commentary. New York: Harper.

Mack, Burton L.
   1990 *Rhetoric and the New Testament.* Guides to Biblical Scholarship, NT Series. Minneapolis: Fortress.

Malina, Bruce J.
   1985 "The Gospel of John in Sociolinguistic Perspective." Pp. 1–23 in *Center for Hermeneutical Studies in Hellenistic and Modern Culture. Colloquy 48.* Ed. Herman C. Waetjen, Berkeley, CA: Graduate Theological Union and University of California, Berkeley.

McFague, Sallie.
   1975 *Speaking in Parables.* Philadelphia: Fortress.
   1982 *Metaphorical Theology.* Philadelphia: Fortress.
   1987 *Models of God.* Philadelphia: Fortress.

McKnight, Edgar V.
   1985 *The Bible and the Reader: An Introduction to Literary Criticism.* Philadelphia: Fortress.

Meyer, Paul W.
   1956 "A Note on John 10:1–18." *JBL* 75:232–235.

Moore, Stephen D.
   1989 *Literary Criticism and the Gospels.* New Haven: Yale University.

O'Day, Gail
   1986 *Revelation in the Fourth Gospel.* Philadelphia: Fortress.

Olsson, Birger
   1974 *Structure and Meaning in the Fourth Gospel. A Text-Linguistic Analysis of John 2:1–11 and 4:1–42.* ConBNT 6. Lund: Gleerup.

Patte, Daniel
   1990 *Structural Exegesis for New Testament Critics.* Guides to Biblical Scholarship, NT Series. Minneapolis: Fortress.
   1983 *Narrative and Discourse in Structural Exegesis: John 6 and 1 Thessalonians.* Ed. Daniel Patte. *Semeia* 26. Atlanta: Scholars.

Perrin, Norman
   1976 *Jesus and the Language of the Kingdom.* Philadelphia: Fortress.

Richard, E.
    1985   "Expressions of Double Meaning and Their Function in the Gospel of John." *NTS* 31:96–112.

Robinson, John A. T.
    1985   *The Priority of John*. London: SCM.
    1962   "The Parable of the Shepherd (John 10:1–5)." Pp. 76–93 in *Twelve New Testament Studies*. Naperville, IL: Allenson.

Schnackenburg, Rudolf
    1980   *The Gospel According to St. John*. Vol. II. New York: Seabury.

Schneider, J.
    1947   "Zur Komposition von Joh 10." *ConNT* 11:220–225.

Scott, Bernard Brandon
    1981   *Jesus, Symbol-Maker for the Kingdom*. Philadelphia: Fortress.
    1986   "Essaying the Rock: The Authenticity of the Jesus Parable Tradition." *Foundations and Facets Forum* 2,1:3–53
    1989   *Hear Then the Parables: A Commentary on the Parables of Jesus*. Minneapolis: Fortress.

Simonis, A. J.
    1967   *Die Hirtenrede im Johannes-Evangelium. Versuch einer Analyse von Johannes 10, 1–18 nach Entstehung, Hintergrund und Inhalb*. AnBib 29. Rome: Biblical Institute.

Smith, D. Moody
    1965   *The Composition and Order of the Fourth Gospel: Bultmann's Literary Theory*. New Haven: Yale.

Staley, Jeffrey Lloyd
    1988   *The Print's First Kiss: A Rhetorical Investigation of the Implied Reader in the Fourth Gospel*. SBL Dissertation Series 82. Atlanta: Scholars.

Sturch, R. L.
    1978   "Jeremias and John: Parables in the Fourth Gospel." *Expository Times* 89:235–238.

Tillich, Paul
    1951   *Systematic Theology*. Vol. I. Chicago: University of Chicago.
    1955   "Religious Symbols and Our Knowledge of God." *The Christian Scholar* 38:189–197.

Tragan, P.-R.
    1980   *La parabole du "Pasteur" et ses explications: Jean 10, 1–18. La genèse, les milieux littéraires*. Studia Anselmiana 67. Rome: Editrice Anselmiana.

Via, Dan Otto, Jr.
    1967   *The Parables: Their Literary and Existential Dimension*. Philadelphia: Fortress.

von Wahlde, Urban C.
    1989   *The Earliest Version of John's Gospel: Recovering the Gospel of Signs*. Wilmington, DE: Glazier.

Wheelwright, Philip
    1962   *Metaphor and Reality*. Bloomington, IN: Indiana University.

Wilder, Amos
    1964   *The Language of the Gospel: Early Christian Rhetoric*. New York: Harper.
    1982   *Jesus' Parables and the War of Myths: Essays on Imagination in the Scriptures*. Philadelphia: Fortress.

PUTTING LIFE BACK INTO THE LAZARUS STORY AND ITS READING: THE NARRATIVE RHETORIC OF JOHN 11 AS THE NARRATION OF FAITH

Wilhelm Wuellner
Pacific School of Religion

ABSTRACT

Part I introduces the analytical and interpretive tools of modern rhetorical criticism for a study of the Lazarus narrative as argument. Special attention is paid to five interrelated issues: the rhetorical units determinative of this story, its intentionality, its argumentative structure, its style, and its argumentative coherence. Part II addresses some broader questions relating to theories and practices of modern rhetorical criticism; the dialectic between modern and postmodern rhetorical criticism; the question whether rhetorical criticism is a method at all, or more than, even other than a method; and a brief outlook on the relation of rhetorical criticism to stylistics, literary criticism, and to social and communication theories.

1. INTRODUCTION

The thesis I want to promote is this: appearances to the contrary, the Lazarus narrative does not seek to narrate the raising of Lazarus as one of the "many other signs which Jesus performed in the presence of the disciples" (John 20:30), both explicit and implicit in John. Rather, the Lazarus narrative is written for the purpose of enhancing, confirming the readers' belief in Jesus as the Christ, as the Son of God, and thereby enhancing, confirming the readers' "having life in His name." I want to demonstrate why, and how, and with what results, the analytical and interpretive tools of modern rhetorical criticism (Wuellner, 1987; Lambrecht) help us in appreciating the difficult, but necessary and unending task of both narrating faith and of entering into some critical commitments engendered in the varying cultural and institutional contexts in which we experience the reading of the narration of faith.

The Threefold Scope of this Study

A rhetorical reading works on three levels: (a) the author and the produced text; (b) the reader interacting with the text, thereby bringing the text to life, as orchestra and audience do when both together make up the "performance"; and (c) the scholarly critic, nowadays fully aware of the ambiguous legacy of the modern sciences in a post-modern era.

On the first level we need to note that what the author through his voice, the narrator, produced in the Lazarus story as an artifact is more than a mere *literary* artifact. The story's syntactical, textual (literary and rhetorical) constraints constitute *one* part (of the *three* parts) of the distinctively Johannine narrative world, which is narrated with consummate skill and profound intentionality. *This* part of the narrative rhetoric may be called the rhetoric in John, for it pertains to the literary and linguistic devices which are *internal* to the text (Descamp; Vouga). Culpepper speaks of the narrative's "anatomy," Moore speaks of the narrative "mechanics." These textual constraints, produced by the author and the narrator, do not, however, generate by themselves either semantic meaning or pragmatic effect; they facilitate the *reader* to produce meaning. We are used to spending most of our time and energy on this first level. We will see immediately, however, that, and how, the other two levels get involved unavoidably (Becker:65–72 on the integration of methods).

The rhetorical critic has no principal objection to an analysis of the linguistic and literary conventions and patterns in a given text. The rhetorical critic is open to the concern for the literary genre(s) employed in a given text, which in our case would be the much discussed genre of ancient miracle stories (Funk). The rhetorical critic is open to narrative techniques and styles, along with ideas and theologies, which are characteristic of both the (Jewish, Hellenistic, Gnostic, Synoptic and Apocryphal gospel) traditions and sources used *and* the alleged stages of the composition from the original "John" to its final form, including manuscript variants. Indeed, the rhetorical critic is very much concerned with the effect which a chosen medium has on the style choices for the intended persuasiveness of the hearing or reading. Here we face the recent discussion of orality *versus* literacy (Kelber, 1983). But even if every instance of repetition or *inclusio* were reducible to underlying primary (or nowadays secondary) orality (see Achtemeier:19–27 for New Testament examples), the rhetorician's focus remains on the argumentative, i.e., persuasive function of the discernible techniques.

The second level is concerned with what readers (whether as the original readers of the Johannine community, *or all subsequent readers*, past, present, and future) *experience* in the ever changing, never static reading of John's narrative rhetoric. Here we focus on the *functional* dimension which is no longer unilaterally textual, but is bilateral (for a critique of the exclusively functional and formal approach, see Becker:7–21). It could be called the rhetoric of John. To speak, with Kennedy (159), of "the power of [the] texts as unitary messages" is to speak to this second dimension. Booth (1988) speaks of a text's power as the reading experiences of a variety of evaluative responses during and after reading. The power of the Lazarus story is, rhetorically speaking, largely a function of its argumentative force; our evaluative responses to its argumentation (belief as conviction and persuasion, versus unbelief), especially *after* reading, are more than mere appraisals; they are commitments (to accept or reject; to tolerate all or some of it). Such reading response and responsibility is always ultimately a corporate, cultural experience, and never mainly a private, individualistic one; and it is an ongoing, never ending process, specific to its cultural context and its media-choice (Miller's materiality of reading).

It is primarily in the performance of the text that we begin to appreciate the rhetoric *of* John. The text is then no longer merely or mainly an object to be analyzed, or a subject (like a speaker/author) to be understood. The experience of the Lazarus story (heard, read, or sung; seen in script or in some performing arts; on television or on computer screens) is then no longer an activity with "only one consciousness, one subject." The performance, even as shared scholarship activity, turns the encounter with the text, even the most critical, into a "dialogic relation [requiring] two consciousnesses and two subjects" (Bakhtin:125).

The third level of the rhetorically critical reading of the Lazarus story focuses on the rhetoric of rhetorical theory and of rhetorical criticism itself. What the scholarly critical readers both give and receive in their critical deliberations about the producer, the product, and the consumer of the Johannine rhetoric in, and of, John 11 is in itself a profoundly rhetorical activity. We exegetical scholars seek to be both convincing and persuasive in what we share concerning our findings, oftentimes with fellow-scholars exclusively. This is the rhetoric, and not just the hermeneutic, of the scholarship of "critical understanding" (Booth, 1979; Wuellner, 1989b). Scholarship informed and inspired by third-world liberation theology or by feminist criticism has made us conscious of the rhetoric (and ethics) of scholarship (Fiorenza) and the ethics of reading (Phelan, 1988; Miller).

2. THE NARRATIVE RHETORIC OF THE JOHANNINE LAZARUS STORY

a. Narrative as Argument and as Rhetorical Unit(s)

We start with the conceptualization of story, and its narration, as argument, and with the premise that story, and its narration, with its narrative "mechanism" of "concealing, revealing, and reveiling" (Kelber, 1988b), can be viewed as a conflict of value positions (Fisher; also Phelan, 1989 for a set of principles and methods for analyzing narrative as rhetoric). Narratives, especially religious ones, are rhetorical transactions with ideological effects or consequences for any given reading experience (Phelan, 1988:138). Value conflicts are exemplified in the Lazarus story in at least three instances: (1) at the story's beginning and end in the opposition by the Judean religious authorities (10:39 and 11:45–57); (2) in the agitation of the worried or protesting disciples (11:7–16); (3) in the form of first the private reproof by Martha (11:21), then the public reproof by Mary (11:31).

As a rhetorical unit the Lazarus story has its certain beginning and uncertain ending. The beginning comes in two steps: one is the closure of the preceding portion of John's narrative, ending in Jesus's forced hiding (10:39–42). A similar overlap of two episodes in John can be found in 11:54–57, which is both closure of the Lazarus episode and the overture to another episode at Bethany and the triumphal entry in John 12 (Tsuchido:610, n. 10). Together with the following opening of the Lazarus story proper, the two conflict-settings set the mood for the actual beginning of the Lazarus narrative (11:1–6) in the request for help by emissary from the two sisters (11:1–3). The request is motivated by the code of loving friendship (see 11:11, "our friend"; 11:35, "how he loved him"), but the code gets violated by the deliberate delay. (On the deixis of "two days" [11:6] and its intertextuality code [Hosea 6:1–2], see Guilding:151).

This opening "setting" is fraught with tragedy because it forces Jesus and his partners out of hiding back into the public and hostile arena. This pattern of hiding or withdrawing and then reappearing in public view despite the known danger from opponents extends the conflict-setting: it partly continues the previous conflicts, but partly generates new conflict. Both settings are located in a named and unnamed Bethany, with Bethany reappearing in 12:1 as deixis of a charged place along with a deixis of charged time which also marks the closing scene in 11:54–57.

The story has its uncertain ending with Jesus' return to forced hiding (vv. 54–57). The literary code invoked with this framing action of hiding from persecution, in both beginning and ending sections of the Lazarus story, may well be the persecution of Elijah and his hiding (e.g., 1 Kgs 19:3; for other textual allusions, see Guilding:143–153). As clearly definable rhetorical unit the Lazarus story contains within itself smaller rhetorical units (e.g., 11:5–16), but is contained in turn within other rhetorical units preceding (what led to the forced hiding, and, as 11:37 signals, the healing of the blind man in John 9) and rhetorical units following (as signalled by the narrator in 11:2, the anointing of Jesus for his own burial in John 12). This intertwining of rhetorical units is "building up a structure which embraces the whole (narrative)" (Kennedy 1984:34). More on this below (section e) on "argumentative coherence."

Within the story and its plot we distinguish between (1) events we experience with the eyes, heart, and mind of one or the other of the characters *in* the story, and (2) experiencing the story or plot events from the perspective of the third person-narrator *outside* the story. This difference in experiencing the narrative is "crucial" for narratologist Chatman (258; also Staley:21–49). What is real for the conflict setting of the story's characters as the story of Jesus raising Lazarus becomes real in yet two further senses when the narrator makes us aware that the surface plot involves two other plots: the glorification through death of Jesus and of the disciples respectively.

b. Intentionality or Rhetorical Situation

The intentionality of the narrative as argument is manifest in the introduction of a conflict of values which comes early in the argumentation by dissociation. It is the argumentative dissociation of the *reality* of God's glory from the *appearance* of sickness and death for believers in God (11:4).

Argumentation by dissociation is "always prompted by the desire to remove an incompatibility arising out of the confrontation of one proposition with others, whether one is dealing with norms, facts, or truths" (Perelman:413). To narrate (or argue) dissociatively (Perelman:411–459) is done "on behalf of another outlook and another criterion of reality" (Perelman:436).

To bring death and glory in conjunction thus functions like an *oxymoron*. The plausibility of divine glory to be generated by death is as paradoxical at the outset (v. 4) as it remains till the end when Lazarus, with the two funerary signs and symbols of death (v. 44: body bound in linen wrappings; face covered with face-cloth), moves about and waits to be freed from them, as Jesus will be shown freed from them (20:6–7). The *reality* of Lazarus' new life remains, narratively and thus argumentatively, for the reader accessible only in the *appearance* of symbols of death.

The narrative rhetoric of the Lazarus story is constituted by this desire and need of resolving the incompatibilities arising out of the confrontations of conflicting codes, facts, or truths. The narrative situation is also the Lazarus story's rhetorical situation. Its "credibility" is paradoxical, i.e., implausible, incredible, and contrary to all "common sense," regardless of how we, or the narrative's culture, define the norms and values of "common sense."

c. Disposition or Rhetorical Structure

The structure and disposition of the story, as argument for the plausibility of the value and action it calls for, show up in the following plot structure as argumentation. The argument's exordium states the case at hand twice: once in 10:39-42 by introducing the split jury over the validity of the claim made by, and for, Jesus as God's agent (Harvey on "agent" as cultural code; Matsunaga on John's *theos*-christology), with "many believing" [that "the father and I are one"], but others forcing Jesus and the believers into hiding. The "case" is stated again clearly in almost propositional form in 11:4, a verse generally recognized as expressive of John's distinctive theology.

The narrative unfolds as argumentation for the plausibility of this implausible paradox, but also as persuasion for a certain commitment on the part of its readers (on the important distinction, as well as interrelation, between persuading and convincing, see Perelman:26-31). The aim of the narrative is to "move" the characters *in* the story, and the reader *of* the story, to be convinced *and* persuaded, i.e., to "believe," by way of acceptance of "another outlook and another criterion of reality." The witness to Jesus, as later on the response to the gospel preached by the apostles, is "told" and "shown" to be "unreliable" (2:24), if it rests solely on the "theory" (i.e., the five-sensory perception) of the signs done by Jesus, and expected to be done by the disciples. The reliability has to rest on something more, indeed on something *other* than, what can be "seen" about God's work and God's glory. We shall return to this important distinction which generates the argumentative and narrative dissociation.

In the second scene of purely verbal or mental events in vv. 7-16 the disciples voice their fear and apprehension associated with the enforced move out of the place of hiding back into public view. And this public exposure comes at the worst possible place, the very gates of Jerusalem, and at the worst possible time, the week before Passover! (On spatial and temporal deixis in John's narration, see also below section e.5). The agitated disciples address Jesus in v. 8; in v. 16 they speak to each other. This first narrative development in vv. 7-16 brings characters *in* the story, and readers *outside* of the story, to a first awareness of the irony in the linkage between the three interlocking stories, of which two get narrated, the story of Lazarus' death and of Jesus' death (as interlinked as the deaths of Joshua and Eleazar in Josh 24; see Guilding:150-1), but the story of the disciples' death, equally unheroic, gets only fore-"told" (as in John 21:18-19), but is not "shown."

In the third scene (vv. 17-27) we have the following elements that make for dissociative argumentation: (1) the first repetition since v. 14 that Lazarus is dead and entombed (v. 17); (2) the emotionally charged communal funeral party in the deceased's house; (3) the continuing appeal to the explicit God code (sometimes implicit, e.g., v. 4; v. 37); (4) the oxymoron of "though dying, yet living" (v. 25); and (5) the separate, yet interacting roles of Lazarus' two sisters.

In the fourth scene (vv. 28–37) we witness a paradoxical narrative move: on the one hand a movement *outward* from private/personal to public/communal dimensions; on the other hand a simultaneous movement *inward*, as the narrator focuses on Mary's grief (vv. 31 and 33), and on her reproach of Jesus, identical with Martha's (vv. 21 and 32); then the focus on Jesus' own deep emotional/spiritual agitation (vv. 33, 35, and 38; on the literary code involved, see Guilding:148–9); and even, or especially, on the comments by members of the Jerusalem funeral party—at least half of which must have been women!—about Jesus' affection for the deceased (v. 36). The disciples are a conspicuous non-entity in this and the following scene.

The focus on the expressed and shared grief and anger highlights two important aspects: (1) The bond between rhetoric and the emotive, imaginative, and unconscious side of human nature, both individual and corporate. Persuasion "moves" the reader (*of* the narrative, as well as characters *inside* the story) only when *pathos* is added to *ethos* and *logos*. The integration of *eros* and *thanatos*, so essential and indispensable to personal and corporate "individuation" and maturity, requires "original pain work" (Bradshaw:66–80). (2) The link between the study of rhetoric and psychology (Wuellner, 1989b:25, n. 114), still largely ignored, and by exegetes preoccupied with cognitive theology largely contested, leads me to plea here for some consideration of rehabilitating psychological exegesis (Rollins) along with rehabilitating rhetorical criticism. But it must be said emphatically that rhetorical criticism is neither reducible to psychological, *nor* to sociological analysis. It is always more than both, but never less than either.

In the fifth scene (vv. 38–44) paradoxes abound: the stone is to the tomb what bandages and facial cloth are for the corpse; the command to remove invites dissociative narration and narrative argumentation by dissociation. A further paradox: all eyes are drawn to the opening of the cave once the cover stone is removed (v. 41a), looking *down*, while Jesus simultaneously lifts *up* his eyes—with the "eyes" of the reader following, looking *up*! A cross-eyed moment (if you pardon the pun!): simultaneously drawn to look down and up!

Moreover, at the very climax and seeming denouement of the story, after the dead man has emerged even while still fully wrapped in response to the cry "Come Out!" (on its literary code [Isaiah 49:8–9], see Schneiders:55), there opens up a startling "gap" which the reader is to fill, or rather, *not* to fill. We are neither shown, nor told, that (let alone how, or by whom) Lazarus got untied and "let go." We are left completely in the dark about the reactions of the two sisters, or of the disciples, not to speak of the reactions of Lazarus himself. The unfinished task of untying Lazarus becomes the readers' task of untying the text (Young). This challenge to readers to untie this text is not only unfinished; due to the rhetoric of the narration of faith, it is an unfinishable task.

In the sixth scene (vv. 45–53), the first of two follow-up scenes, the linkage between Lazarus' death and Jesus' death is keeping the lingering paradox alive, including the return to shown and told irony. The public and communal dimension of the plot and its desired but evading resolution continues.

In the seventh and final scene (vv. 54–57) the resolution is suspended; the ending is not the end; with Jesus temporarily back in hiding, the disciples briefly return on the stage without comment. Yet their action is fraught with ambiguity: they follow Jesus into a place near the wilderness, a "shown" move that foreshadows the "told" move in 21:18–19 of being "brought to a place where you do not want to go" (on the deixis of the name "Ephraim" in connection with the linked pairs Joshua/Jesus and Eleazar/Lazarus, see Guilding:150). In this hidden place it is Jesus who is said to be staying, or abiding, with the disciples, not the other way around. Some of the characters *in* the story are shown, or told, to have come to be convinced and persuaded (they "believed in him" v. 45), but others are not. Others still, like the disciples or Lazarus' sisters, though presumably witnessing the event, remain unreported as to their belief or outlook following this narrative argumentation.

Through the rhetorical disposition or argumentative structuring of the narrative—especially the moves from inside out, and outside in; from private to public, and from openness to hiding—we have become aware of not one (Lazarus' death), not two (Jesus' and Lazarus' deaths), but three stories altogether (Lazarus', Jesus', and the disciples' God-glorifying deaths) embedded in the surface plot structure. It is the story of the narration of faith as conviction and persuasion concerning values tested and contested about God being present in Jesus as God's ambassador, and the disciples as Jesus' ambassadors. These two stories (of Jesus' and the disciples' death as occasion for the revelation of God's glory) embedded in the Lazarus story will become clearer as we explore an area which, more than any other, has been, and remains, identified with rhetoric.

d. Style or Rhetorical Techniques

The task is long overdue to break with our deeply entrenched, centuries-old convention of (1) simply listing the stylistic features to be found in a given text or author, e.g. John's predilection for *hina*-clauses, or his use of metaphors; or (2) categorizing stylistic features in terms of the classical textbooks of rhetoric or stylistics (Lausberg, 1960; Nida et al.). This convention of scholarship goes back as far as Augustine's *De Doctrina Christiana*, Book 4, and characterizes even those admirable early efforts at highlighting the style of individual New Testament authors in their respective distinctiveness. One of the earliest examples is to be found in Matthias Flacius Illyricus' *Clavis Scripturae* (1567), the originator of scholarly hermeneutics with its now recognized roots in rhetoric (Wuellner, 1989b:11–13).

What we find in the Lazarus story are stylistic means that are richly textured and appropriate to achieving the desired ends of gaining or stabilizing plausibility for the oxymoron of glorification through death—first, and on the surface, in the death of Lazarus, but simultaneously also in the God-glorifying death of Jesus, and ultimately also through the disciples' deaths. The typological or symbolic, even allegorical character of the events narrated in John moves the reader, facilitated by the stylistic means of the narration (beginning with the opening phonetic assonance in 11:1), to be committed to the realization that a servant is not greater than the master, nor the one who is commissioned greater than the commissioner (13:15–16). Let me illustrate by making reference to a few of the many stylistic means employed in the Lazarus story.

1. Take the series of **internal monologues**, or narration of mental events (as distinct from physical or verbal events) that shape the surface of the narrative (Cohn:58–98 on quoted monologue; Savran:49–51 on quoted thought; Lausberg, 1969:410 on mental speech as "affective figure"). In 10:41 and 11:4 "saying" equals "thinking/affirming." These two instances of internal monologue do for the exordium of the argumentation what 11:9–10 does for the first argument, namely, Jesus' interaction with his disciples. The same goes for vv. 41–42, the prayer, in the resumed argument with Martha (11:38–42); vv. 47–48 (the chief priests and Pharisees' musings) in the second to last argument, the reaction of the unconvinced jury (11:46–53); and v. 56, the musing Temple crowd at Passover time, in the final argument (11:54–57). The narrative world of the characters *inside* the narrative world and also the world of the reader *outside* of the story (as well as the world of the person listening to or reading this scholarly exegetical exposé of the Lazarus story) are all permeated by such internal monologues. These inner reflections, which the narrator shares with the reader, lay the ground work for the story to remain ultimately unresolved, i.e., with no closure or denouement, and thereby generating new narrative momentum for resuming the unfinished, if not indeed unfinishable, narrative.

2. Let me turn to another stylistic means: the choice of the *katachresis/abusio* trope in 11:4. The glorification of God in bringing dead Lazarus to life brings simultaneously the living Jesus to his "glorious" death. The ensuing first argumentative development (vv. 5–16) offers a verbal action with his disciples (vv. 7–16), and the physical action of (once more) coming out of hiding (v. 17), as several times before (e.g. 5:13; 6:15; 7:1–13; 9:12?), and returning to the public sphere, the cultural, political sphere of life and death. This first argument is characterized by the use of the trope of irony by Jesus and underscored by the narrator's comment (11:13). Thomas' concluding appeal (11:16) strikes a note which is both ironic and non-ironic (Schneiders:50). The conflict of values is obvious; the resolution of the conflict is not only not obvious, it is downright unacceptable, given the contingency of the disciples' certain death (e.g. Peter's in 21:18–19 as means of glorifying God), following Jesus' own death as the hour of divine glory.

3. What then do we make of the stylistic feature of **irony**? Kenneth Burke spoke of irony as one of the "four master tropes" (1945:503–517), and characterized it as a form of "literary mysticism" (1950:324–328). Irony is one of the distinctive rhetorical devices used in John 11, indeed throughout John (O'Day:11–32). A student of the function of irony in John characterizes its power as "so forcefully engag[ing] us in what we read . . . [that] it jolts us with incongruity or nudges us with meaning or a value or a commitment . . . irony is like the Incarnation itself" (Duke:155).

These observations appear to give support to the position held by Culler and Jameson about irony as a rhetorical means of *undoing* meaning or producing uncertainty in the face of conventional certainty (e.g., the hopelessness in death), rather than Wayne Booth's view of irony as means of *producing* meaning. But Booth also observed that "every irony inevitably builds a community of believers even as it excludes" (1974:28), which equally or more so may apply, when irony gets "collapsed in paradox" or "the hierarchical structure of Johannine irony [gets annulled]" (Moore:159–163, entitled "The Failure of Johannine Irony").

4. The stylistic means of **repetitions** mark the second and third argumentative sequences (vv. 17–27, dialogue with Martha; vv. 28–37, the encounter with Mary). Sternberg (365–440) makes a case for the structure of repetition and the strategies of redundancy in the biblical art of narrative persuasion. The oxymoron in v. 25 (believers shall live though they die) keeps the focus of the *argumentative* situation, established in v. 4, on the *verbal* (inter)actions between Jesus and the believer, both inside and outside of the narrative world, rather than focusing on the miracle itself. The *katachresis*, created by the verbal event in v. 4, continues into the climax of the plot: the expected narrative denouement, though bringing

Lazarus to life and bringing us to await his getting unshrouded (vv. 38–45), also introduces the expected, because foretold, intensification of efforts of bringing Jesus to his own glorifying death (11:46–57) and getting Jesus shrouded in the Jewish burial custom (19:39–40, narrated with hyperbole, if not parody). But how, or by whom, he got unshrouded (20:6–7) is also not narrated.

Paradoxically, it is not Lazarus's resurrection, but his death which brings about the (implausible) glorification of God, just as Jesus brings God's glorification to fullest expression and completion on the cross, not on Easter, as the disciples are reminded by being shown "his hands and his side" (20:20, 25, 27). Likewise, Peter glorifies God by death (21:18–19) which is made plausible with the familiar *topos* choice of grain bearing much fruit only after first dying (12:24–26, which has Pauline and Synoptic parallels).

5. Lastly but not least, there are the **deictic** and **modal** features which "are used to construct contexts of utterance and of reference" (Fowler:90; for the Greek New Testament, see Porter:75–109). These contexts can range from the sublime emotional or religious to the historical, social, and cultural (on spatial and temporal deixis, see also section c above).

These linguistic features are not unimportant for the rhetoric of narration. It has long and frequently been noted that John's style is marked by the use of personal and demonstrative pronouns which frequently have their deictic function. The use of *hina*-clauses with their modal function has often been noted as to the certainty, or possibility, or necessity of the *narrative* propositions. And we could, and should, go on with the role of interrogative modals (more than half of them used in John 11 are Jesus'); with aspectual choices, such as the use of the "historical" present (11:23–24.44); the modal nature of the future "tense" (11:22–26); and numerous others. Snyman and Porter have outlined new ways of dealing with these features in contrast to the still largely prevailing approaches even in updated New Testament Greek Grammars (Nida).

It is not enough simply to register the presence of these stylistic features, to rate them statistically, or to trace their cultural provenance and trajectory (see Festugière, Ruckstuhl, Schnackenburg, Schweizer—to name only a few of the most often quoted scholars in the field of Johannine stylistics). What is needed is a perception of the *functional* roles which each and every one of the employed stylistic means play in facilitating the readers' perception of their commitment to be evoked by their reading (the pragmatic component of syntax semantics in Porter). In Perelman's words (168) the concern for "the techniques of persuasive discourse" should not so much focus on the study of "the problem of figures [of speech or thought]" as it should focus on showing *"how* and *in what respects the use of particular figures is explained by the requirements of argumentation"* (Perelman's emphasis).

e. Argumentative Coherence

To look for unity or overarching meaning, as hermeneutical exegetes are prone to do (e.g., Beker on contingency and coherence of the gospel; see also Bridges), is quite different from the concern of the rhetorical critic for *argumentative* coherence. Daniel Patte's proposal based on Greimas's semiotics provides a critical alternative. Coherence in the rhetorical sense has two aspects: there is (1) coherence as property of the Johannine narrative—with its textual configurations, textual ruptures, protagonist interacting with antagonists (Marchadour:67ff. speaks of "la logique narrative"). (2) There is coherence as perceived or generated by the reader and the critic, especially in narratives like the Lazarus story, full of jolts, ruptures, and inconsistencies (including the absence of any telling or showing of who subsequently did untie the resurrected Lazarus, or of any reactions by the disciples, Mary or Martha, let alone reactions by Lazarus).

Jesus provides a coherence of his own by continuing the pattern of hiding followed by choices of public disclosure three more times following John 11: (1) The disclosure at the Bethany anointing (for burial!), the triumphal entry into Jerusalem and subsequent public teaching (12:1–36), followed by another departure into hiding (12:36b). (2) The in-door activities, beginning with the footwashing, Judas' betrayal which would force his hand, and the farewell discourse about "going [to a place] where you cannot come" (first announced in 7:34, then 13:33), followed by the voluntary arrest (18:6–8). (3) The semi-incognito appearances prior to his ascent to the Father (as presumed gardener [20:11–18]; as bread and fish-serving host on the beach in Galilee [21:1–14]) and subsequent hiddenness "till I come."

The coherence of the narrative strategy of John 11 can be seen in such seemingly incoherent appearances as (1) the textual gaps, like those just outlined; (2) the textual surplus features, such as the seemingly superfluous adverbial or adnominal qualifiers in 11:1–2, 11:18, or the details of the body and face wrappings in 11:44, to name only a few; and (3) the thematization and [uncertain] closure, and with it the intended allusion to other texts (for Old Testament "codes" in John, see Guilding; Lausberg, 1979; Roth; Van der Hoek) as clues for God's continuing action in, and disruption of, history, and of representatives of God's own people habitually responding to God's agent ambiguously. Religious (especially biblical) discourse has a coherence all its own (Keller), as Sternberg has shown about the role of rhetoric in "the drama of reading."

The rhetorical critic also speaks of coherence, but does so largely in opposition to the prevailing trend among modern biblical narrative critics who work with a view of the gospel narratives as characterized by "wholeness and internal consistency." Moore calls this view "traditional, humanistic, 'comfortable.'" But the rhetorical critic, with resources other than the familiar ones from traditional literary criticism, highlights the fact that, despite the discernible "will for coherence and the striving for design" (the focus of traditional composition criticism and redaction criticism), the Johannine narrative has its own measure of "anomalies, impossible combinations, and internal contradictions" (Moore:53) as ways and means of victimizing the implied reader in John (Staley:105–7, for parts of John 11). This is the coherence of the Johannine narrative that is generated and sustained by a "tension between what the evangelist might be said to control" and what he is "unable to control" (Moore:54).

The subversive effect of this rhetorical coherence of the Lazarus story gets recognized both *while* reading John 11, as well as *before* reading John 11, either due to the experience, or remembrance, of texts like John 1–10 (and its marked intertextuality with Christian and Jewish texts); or due to experiences which readers/interpreters bring with themselves of morbid or moribund (social, institutional) structures outside of the text, as third-world readings or feminist criticism have shown (see also Kelber, 1988a; Moore).

3. CONCLUSION

Among several questions arising from our analysis I would like to single out the following three:

(a) Can the reader, moving on from John 11 to John 14, make any sense of the promise that "greater works than these [you] must do" (14:12; see Dietzfelbinger)? Our rhetorical reading suggests that the answer is, yes, provided the power of the text we read as the narration of faith is experienced as the narrating of the living God who manifests the powers of life in the midst of every living generation. The reading of such rhetorical narration as the Lazarus story "moves" us to evoke life, in ourselves and in others where we and others only see death; evoke hope where others resign in hopelessness; evoke wholeness, *shalom*, justice, and freedom, where others see fragmentation and despair.

(b) Why does narrating faith here, as elsewhere in Scripture, evoke simultaneously the narrating of unbelief, not the kind attributed to godless unbelievers, but the puzzling kind found among members of God's people? Our rhetorical reading suggests as answer that the experience of faith, even in the act of reading, is an "assurance of things hoped for, and a conviction of things *not* seen" (Heb 11:1). As such, faith is never static; like love, it has to be constantly renewed and deepened, and in that process will/shall be transformed. All parties in the Lazarus story are believers in God, yet only some are convinced of things even when seen (let alone *unseen*), while some do not believe, even though they are recognizably religious. To narrate faith invites us, as readers, to face the latent unbelief both inside of ourselves and outside in persons, in social and cultural conventions, and in institutional (even, or especially, religious institutional) settings.

(c) Does the rhetorical strategy of "reader victimization," which Staley identified as determinative of the whole of John's narrative (John 1–21), serve the reader's "move onward and upward in his journey of faith" (Staley:116)? The rhetorical interpretation shows that the answer must be "yes" and "no." Staley knows that not all of John's narration of faith is reducible to "a rhetoric of reader victimization" (116-7). But in the reading, where faith speaks to faith, the implied reader, that is the rhetorically "invented" reader, experiences the narration of faith equal to the disciples' own experience of having *God* cognitively and volitionally "revealed" to them (John 1:18; on the crucial role of 1:18, see Lausberg, 1982).

This happens in such convincing and persuasive ("moving") ways that they, too, like their master as God's emissary, have "streams of living water flow from [their] innermost being" (7:38; 20:21-23 [the Johannine "commission"]) and so affect the lives of others. But like the characters in the narrative, the readers will have their empowering reading experience tested and contested by prevailing cultural (including gender and race) identities and by institutional power structures. Rhetorical criticism is also political and ideological criticism.

To untie the Lazarus text is to enter into a transformation and identity which is, by its nature, in conflict with the old, but in harmony with the new. As with "the difference between theology and spirituality" (Schneiders:53), so with the difference between the prevailing preoccupation with Johannine theology and Johannine narrative rhetoric: it is the difference between cognitive reflection on revelation and personal as well as corporate and institutional commitment to, and engagement of the imagination in, the unfolding truth. All persuasion aims at commitment (Perelman:59–62). All reading of narrative rhetoric involves responsibility (Booth, 1988), and with it the challenges of not only the ethics of interpretation (Fiorenza), but also the politics of interpretation (Mitchell).

WORKS CONSULTED

Achtemeier, Paul J.
1990 "*Omne verbum sonat*: The New Testament and the Oral Environment of Late Antiquity." *JBL* 109:3–27.

Bakhtin, Mikhail M.
1981 *The Dialogic Imagination.* Ed. M. Holquist. Slavic Series 1. Austin, TX: University of Texas Press.

Becker, Jürgen
1986 "Das Johannesevangelium im Streit der Methoden (1980–1984)." *Theologische Rundschau* 51:1–78.

Beker, J. Christiaan
1980 *Paul the Apostle: The Triumph of God in Life and Thought.* Philadelphia: Fortress.

Booth, Wayne C.
1974 *A Rhetoric of Irony.* Chicago and London: University of Chicago Press.
1979 *Critical Understanding: The Powers and Limits of Pluralism.* Chicago and London: University of Chicago Press.
1988 *The Company We Keep: An Ethics of Fiction.* Berkeley-Los Angeles-London: University of California Press.

Bradshaw, John
1990 *Homecoming. Reclaiming and Championing Your Inner Child.* New York: Bantam Books.

Bridges, James J.
1988 "Structure and History in John 11: A Methodological Study Comparing Structural and Historical Critical Approaches." Ph.D. Dissertation, Graduate Theological Union, Berkeley, CA.

Brinton, Alan
1981 "Situation in the Theory of Rhetoric." *Philosophy and Rhetoric* 14:234–248.

Burke, Kenneth
1945 *A Grammar of Motives.* Berkeley: University of California Press.
1950 *A Rhetoric of Motives.* Berkeley-Los Angeles-London: University of California Press.

Chatman, Seymour
1989 "The 'Rhetoric' 'of' 'Fiction.'" Pp. 40–56 in *Narrative. Form, Ethics, Ideology*. Ed. J. Phelan. Columbus: Ohio State University Press.

Cohn, Dorrit
1978 *Transparent Minds*. Princeton: Princeton University Press.

Culpepper, R. Alan
1983 *Anatomy of the Fourth Gospel: A Study in Literary Design*. New Testament Foundations and Facets. Philadelphia: Fortress.

Descamps A.-L. et al.
1981 *Genèse et structure d'un texte du Nouveau Testament: Étude interdisciplinaire du chapitre XI de l'Évangile de Jean*. Bibliothèque des Cahiers de l'Institut de Linguistique de Louvain 5/20. Paris: Cerf.

Dietzfelbinger, C.
1989 "Die grösseren Werke (Joh 14.12f.)." *NTS* 35:27–47.

Duke, Paul D.
1985 *Irony in the Fourth Gospel*. Atlanta: John Knox.

Festugière, A.-J.
1974 *Observations stylistiques sur L'Évangile de S. Jean*. Études et commentaires 84. Paris: Klincksieck.

Fiorenza, Elizabeth S.
1988 "The Ethics of Interpretation: De-Centering Biblical Scholarship." *JBL* 107:3–17.

Fisher, W. R.
1987 *Human Communication as Narration: Toward a Philosophy of Reason, Value, and Action*. Columbia, SC: University of South Carolina Press.

Fowler, Roger
1986 *Linguistic Criticism*. Oxford: Oxford University Press.

Funk, Robert W., ed.
1978 *Early Christian Miracle Stories*. Semeia 11. Atlanta: Scholars.

Guilding, A.
1960   *The Fourth Gospel and Jewish Worship: A Study of the Relation of St. John's Gospel to the Ancient Jewish Lectionary System.* Oxford: Oxford University Press.

Harvey, Anthony E.
1987   "Christ as Agent." Pp. 239–50 in *The Glory of Christ in the New Testament: Studies in Christology in Memory of George Bradford Caird.* Ed. L. D. Hurst and N. T. Wright. Oxford: Oxford University Press.

Kelber, Werner H.
1983   *The Oral and the Written Gospel: The Hermeneutics of Speaking and Writing in the Synoptic Tradition, Mark, Paul, and Q.* Philadephia: Fortress.
1988   "Gospel Narrative and Critical Theory." *Biblical Theology Bulletin* 18:130–136.
1988b   "Narrative and Disclosure: Mechanisms of Concealing, Revealing, and Reveiling." *Semeia* 43:1–20.

Keller, Joseph
1985   "The Coherence of Religious Discourse." *Anglican Theological Review* 67:349–360.

Kennedy, George A.
1984   *New Testament Interpretation through Rhetorical Criticism.* Chapel Hill and London: University of North Carolina Press.

Lambrecht, Jan
1989   "Rhetorical Criticism and the New Testament." *Bijdragen* 50:239–253.

Lausberg, Heinrich
1960   *Handbuch der literarischen Rhetorik.* Munich: Hueber.
1979   "Minuscula philologica (V): Jesaja 55,10–11 im Evangelium nach Johannes." *Nachrichten der Akademie der Wissenschaften in Göttingen. I. Philologisch-Historische Klasse* 7. Göttingen: Vandenhoeck & Ruprecht.
1982   "Minuscula philologica VII: Das Epiphonem des Johannes-Prologs (J 1,18)." *Nachrichten der Akademie der Wissenschaften in Göttingen. I. Philologisch-Historische Klasse* 7. Göttingen: Vandenhoeck & Ruprecht.

Mack, Burton L.
1989   *Rhetoric and the New Testament*. Guides to Biblical Scholarship. Minneapolis: Augsburg Fortress.

Marchadour, Alain
1988   *Lazare: Histoire d'un récit. Récits d'une histoire*. Paris: Cerf.

Matsunaga, Kikuo
1990   "The Self-Identification of Christianity with Special Reference to the Twelfth of the Eighteen Benedictions." In *Eusebius, Christianity, and Judaism*. Ed. H.W. Attridge and G. Hata. Detroit, MI: Wayne State University Press.

Miller, J. Hillis
1989   "Is There an Ethics of Reading?" Pp. 79–101 in *Reading Narrative: Form, Ethics, Ideology*. Ed. J. Phelan. Columbus: Ohio State University Press.

Mitchell, W. J. T., ed.
1983   *The Politics of Interpretation*. Chicago and London: University of Chicago Press.

Moore, Stephen D.
1989   *Literary Criticism and the Gospels: The Theoretical Challenge*. New Haven and London: Yale University Press.

Nida, E. A. et al.
1983   *Style and Discourse with Special Reference to the Text of the Greek New Testament*. Cape Town: Bible Society.

O'Day, Gail R.
1986   *Revelation in the Fourth Gospel: Narrative Mode and Theological Claim*. Philadelphia: Fortress.

Patte, Daniel
1990   *The Religious Dimensions of Biblical Texts*. Semeia Studies. Atlanta: Scholars Press.

Perelman, C. and L. Olbrechts-Tyteca.
1969   *The New Rhetoric: A Treatise on Argumentation*. Trans. J. Wilkinson and P. Wever. Notre Dame and London: University of Notre Dame Press.

Phelan, James, ed.
1988   *Reading Narrative: Form, Ethics, Ideology*. Columbus, Ohio: Ohio State University Press.

1989   *Reading People, Reading Plots: Character, Progression, and the Interpretation of Narrative.* Chicago: University of Chicago Press.

Porter, Stanley E.
1989   *Verbal Aspect in the Greek of the New Testament, with Reference to Tense and Mood.* Studies in Biblical Greek 1. New York-Bern-Frankfurt-Paris: Peter Lang.

Rabinowitz, Peter J.
1987   *Before Reading. Narrative Conventions and the Politics of Interpretation.* Ithaca and London: Cornell University Press.

Rollins, Wayne
1985   "Jung on Scripture and Hermeneutics: Retrospect and Prospect." Pp. 81–94 in *Essays on Jung and the Study of Religion.* Ed. Luther H. Martin and James Goss. Lanham, MD: University Press of America.

Roth, Wolfgang
1987   "Scripture Coding in the Fourth Gospel." *Papers of the Chicago Society of Biblical Research* 32:6–29.

Schneiders, Sandra M.
1987   "Death in the Community of Eternal Life: History, Theology, and Spirituality in John 11." *Interpretation* 41:44–56.

Snyman, Andries H.
1988   "On Studying the Figures (*schemata*) in the New Testament." *Biblica* 69:93–107.

Staley, Jeffrey Lloyd
1988   *The Print's First Kiss: A Rhetorical Investigation of the Implied Reader in the Fourth Gospel.* SBLDS 82. Atlanta: Scholars.

Sternberg, Meir
1985   *The Poetics of Biblical Narrative: Ideological Literature and the Drama of Reading.* Bloomington: Indiana University Press.

Tsuchido, Kiyoshi
1984   "Tradition and Redaction in John 12.1–43." *NTS* 30:609–619.

Van der Hoek, G.W.
1987   "The Function of Ps 82 in the Fourth Gospel and History of the Johannine Community: A Comparative Midrash Study."

Ph.D. Dissertation, Claremont Graduate School, Claremont, CA.

Vouga, Francois
1977　*Le cadre historique et l'intention théologique de Jean.* Paris: Beauchesne.

Wuellner, Wilhelm
1987　"Where is Rhetorical Criticism Taking Us?" *CBQ* 49:448–463.
1989a　"The Rhetorical Structure of Luke 12 in its Wider Context." *Neotestamentica* 22:283–310.
1989b　*Hermeneutics and Rhetorics.* Scriptura 3. Stellenbosch: Centre for Hermeneutical Studies.
1989c　"Is There an Encoded Reader Fallacy?" *Semeia* 48:41–54.

Young, R., ed.
1981　*Untying the Text: A Post-Structuralist Reader.* London: Routledge & Kegan Paul.

THE JOHANNINE *HYPODEIGMA:* A READING OF JOHN 13

R. Alan Culpepper
Baylor University

ABSTRACT

The aim of this paper is to propose a reading of John 13 as a cohesive segment of the Gospel. Because John 13 poses serious interpretive problems for the reader and difficulties in finding a consistent logic in the text, commentators have generally concluded that the text must be dissected into strata of sources and redaction to make sense of it. The reading proposed here is an effort to understand John 13 in its present state while neither denying the likelihood that it is the product of a protracted compositional process nor accepting the premise that the text can only be read in light of attempts to reconstruct its redactional history.

The underlying question we shall address is the process by which we read and interpret the text. How does this text guide the reader in the construction of its meaning, and what responses does it elicit from the reader? In *Anatomy of the Fourth Gospel* I concluded that the plot of the Gospel develops the conflict between belief and unbelief as responses to Jesus' central role as the revealer. In a series of repetitive episodes the Gospel narrative explores various responses to Jesus. It exposes the errors of unbelief and its attendant misunderstandings, all the while guiding the reader toward a response of faith (John 20:30–31). The Gospel of John, therefore, is a dynamic, performative text. It engages the reader, elicits responses, and then critiques deficient responses as the reader works through the episodes of the narrative sequentially and seeks to make sense of its theologically loaded language, its *double entendres,* its imagery and symbolism, and its pervasive ironies. The present essay, consequently, is an effort both to read John 13 in its narrative context and to recognize how it elicits responses from those who seek to read it.

1. OVERVIEW: THEME, NARRATIVE STRATEGY, AND SEGMENTATION

John 13 highlights the recurring theme of knowledge and ignorance.[1] The chapter reports what Jesus knew and the actions that followed from that knowledge. The disciples, especially Peter and Judas, do not share

Jesus' knowledge, and their ignorance leads to denial and betrayal. The disciples are a foil for Jesus (and the reader) because they do not understand, and their ignorance leads to disastrous consequences, which by implication the reader can avoid only by being more perceptive and more responsive to Jesus' revelation than the disciples were. The following interpretation of John 13 will demonstrate how this narrative strategy is developed.

Before turning to the individual segments of the text, a brief overview of the whole will orient the reader. John 13 is composed of several distinct units:

vv. 1–5: Introduction

vv. 6–11: The First Conversation with Peter

vv. 12–17: Jesus' Exhortation to the Disciples

vv. 18–20: The Forecast of Betrayal

vv. 21–30: Jesus and Judas

vv. 31–38: The Second Conversation with Peter

Questions introduce two of these units (vv. 6, 12) and figure prominently in the others (v. 25, indirectly v. 33, and vv. 36–38). Most commentaries have defined the unit as 13:1–30, with vv. 31–38 comprising the introduction to the farewell discourse. Others have treated either 13:1–20 or 13:1–38 as the basic unit. Although vv. 21–30 introduce new elements that are not directly related to the footwashing, these verses are also integral to John 13 because they describe Judas' departure, which is referred to in vv. 2 and 11. Similarly, vv. 31–38 relate to themes introduced earlier in chapter 13: Jesus' departure, the pattern of action that follows from obedience to Jesus, and the effects of Peter's lack of understanding. Again, we need not deny the connections between vv. 31–38 and the discourse that follows, but here we will be primarily interested in the ways in which these verses culminate the narrative of John 13.[2]

2. INTRODUCTION (VV. 1–5)

The first five verses introduce the scene by reporting its setting and locating Jesus' action in the context of his own unique knowledge. Jesus' action for his own is also set in contrast to the Devil's action in relation to Judas. The piling up of participial clauses in these verses is often pointed out as a difficulty that suggests that we have here the conflation of two sources of material (Boismard; Schnackenburg:10–12, 14; Segovia:39–42. See also Richter; Thyen; Wojciechowski).[3]

The extended description of the setting of this scene points to its significance within the Gospel. Interpreters generally agree that 13:1 marks the most significant transition in the Gospel, introducing not only the scene of the footwashing but the entire second half of the Gospel. The first element of the setting to which the reader's attention is called is its temporal setting. Two systems of time have been highlighted earlier in the narrative: the calendar of Jewish festivals (2:13, 23; 4:45; 5:1; etc.) and the approach of Jesus' hour (2:4; 4:21, 23; 7:30; 8:20; 12:23, 27). In John, therefore, we have the time of the *Ioudaioi* ("Jews," "Judeans," or "Judean authorities") and the hour that is set for Jesus by his Father. Here, for the first time, these two systems of time are set in relation to one another in the same verse.

The first verbal form in this unit is the participle, *eidōs* ("When Jesus knew"), the verb that is central to the dynamic of the entire unit.[4] The narrator, the voice which tells the story and reports the action without any dialogue throughout vv. 1–5, now provides an inside view of the mind of Jesus. The narrator tells us what Jesus knew at that moment: that his hour had come. The narrator does not explain whether this knowledge was mediated directly from the Father, or whether Jesus realized that his hour had come as a result of his experience at Lazarus' tomb, his entry into Jerusalem, or the coming of the Greeks. Indeed, Jesus' knowledge as the incarnate *logos* has been a vital part of John's characterization of Jesus from the beginning of the Gospel:

Jesus knows Nathanael before Philip called him (1:48);

he knows all things, even what is in the hearts of others (2:24–25);

he knows that the testimony about him is true (5:32);

he knows what he is about to do (6:6);

he knows when his disciples grumble about him (6:61);

he knows those who do not believe in him and he knows who his betrayer will be (6:64);

he knows the one who sent him (7:29; 8:55);

he knows from whence he came and where he was going (8:14);

he knows that the Father always hears him (11:42);

he knows that the Father's command is eternal life (12:50).

The significance of Jesus' hour is considerably extended and interpreted by John 13:1. Earlier references have told the reader only that Jesus' hour had not yet come (2:4; 7:30; 8:20), and then that "the hour has come for the Son of man to be glorified" (12:23), and that Jesus had come for this hour (12:27). John 13:1 now adds that Jesus' hour is the time of his departure from this world and his return to the Father.

The last phrase of v. 1 is open to different interpretations. "His own" are now clearly his disciples rather than Israel (cf. 1:11; 10:3, 4, 12). The phrase *eis telos*, however, can be taken either qualitatively ("perfectly," "completely"; favored by Schnackenburg:16),[5] temporally ("to the end"; favored by Barrett:438), or both (Brown:550; Lindars:448). The action that demonstrates his love may be either the footwashing or Jesus' approaching death, at which he exclaims, "It is finished!" (*tetelestai*; 19:30). The *double entendre* serves the vital function of linking the footwashing to Jesus' death and interpreting Jesus' action as the culmination of his love for his own. Moreover, Jesus' action (both the footwashing and his voluntary death) follows from his knowledge that the hour of his departure and return to the Father had come.

V. 1, therefore, sets the agenda for the footwashing and the farewell discourse which follow:

(a) "Jesus knew" (Jesus as revealer)
(b) "that his hour had come" (Jesus' hour, his death)
(c) "to depart out of this world to the Father,"
    (Jesus' death as departure and exaltation)
(d) "having loved his own," (Jesus' relation to the disciples)
(e) "he loved them to the end"
    (Jesus' death as a manifestation of his love).[6]

V. 2 serves as a counterpoint to v. 1. The reader may assume that this verse is reporting more of what Jesus knew at that time, but that is not stated. The identity of the betrayer has already been referred to earlier in John (6:64, 70, 71; 12:4). Jesus' preparation for his death is now matched by the Devil's preparation for his betrayal. The meaning of v. 2 is problematic both because it involves a Semitic idiom, "to put in mind" or make up one's mind (Job 22:22; 1 Sam 29:10). It also seems to stand in tension with v. 27, which reports that *"after the morsel*, Satan entered into him [Judas]." An alternative translation recognizes the idiom and resolves the tension with v. 27: "The devil had already made up his mind that Judas should betray him [Jesus]" (Barrett:439).[7] The narrator's comment in v. 2, therefore, contrasts the mind of the devil with what we have just been told about the mind of Jesus.

V. 3 again places Jesus' knowledge in the foreground. Jesus knows that the Father has given all things "into his hands" (cf. 3:35). V. 3 also reasserts Jesus' knowledge of his origin and return to the Father, the knowledge which exerts such a controlling influence on the Johannine Jesus. The reader cannot really know who Jesus is unless Jesus is understood in terms of his "whence" and his "whither."

The extended participial clauses in vv. 1–3 weave together the setting and the report of what Jesus knew. They also locate the footwashing in relation to Jesus' knowledge. The piling up of participial clauses gives the introduction "a most solemn effect" (Lindars:448). The delay in the action of the scene caused by the extended introduction is prolonged by the detailed description in v. 4 of Jesus' preparations, discarding his garments and wrapping the towel about himself. V. 4, therefore, begins the action but builds suspense. Its language also has thematic significance. In chapters 10 and 11 the same verb (*tithēsin*, "laid aside") was used for the Good Shepherd laying down his life (10:11, 15, 17, 18) and for the burial of Lazarus (11:34). Similarly, when Jesus takes up his garments again after washing the disciples' feet, the verb is *elaben* ("had taken"), which was also used in Jesus' affirmation that he can take up his life again (10:17, 18). The description of Jesus' laying aside his garments may therefore already suggest the connection between the footwashing and Jesus' death (this use of *tithēmi* is also noted by Dunn:248).

V. 5 reports the footwashing simply and briefly. The use of water is emphasized and links this scene to the theme of water and cleansing earlier in the Gospel. The linkages between v. 5 and other parts of the Gospel are even more intricate, however. The verb to wipe appears elsewhere in John only in reference to the anointing of Jesus (11:2; 12:3). The common pattern of anointing/washing and wiping of feet leads the reader to view the footwashing in the light of the preceding anointing of Jesus' feet. Jesus, who has been anointed for his burial (12:7), now interprets the meaning of his death by washing the disciples' feet and prepares them to follow his example by laying down their lives for others.[8] If these implications were obvious, however, there would be no need for the dialogues that follow. The dialogues with Peter, the disciples, the Beloved Disciple, and Judas serve to interpret the meaning of the action, just as the author has previously used dialogues and discourses to unpack the meaning of Jesus' signs.

3. THE FIRST CONVERSATION WITH PETER (VV. 6–11)

In the first three verses the narrator reported what Jesus knew and what the Devil had decided. In vv. 4 and 5 Jesus' action is reported. The first five verses provide a narrative frame which introduces the reader slowly and deliberately to this scene. The use of present tense verbs in vv. 4 and 5 further heightens the reader's sense of the immediacy of the scene. V. 6 finally introduces the first dialogue with a question.

The first conversation with Peter involves three statements by Peter and three responses from Jesus (numbered below). The awkwardness with which this conversation is introduced has led to two textual variants in v. 6 which attempt to provide a smoother transition to Peter's first statement.

Peter (1): "Lord, do you wash my feet?"

Peter's first statement expresses wonder and amazement. Given the assumptions surrounding footwashing in the first century, Peter's statement expresses a response that would be readily appreciated by first-century readers. Peter's first statement, resisting the footwashing, arises from his acceptance of the social norms which reinforce superior and inferior social standings. Jesus, by laying aside his garments and beginning to wash the disciples' feet, has displaced those norms and is responding to a different mandate, a different way of ordering his relationships with other persons.

Jesus (1): "What I am doing you do not know now, but afterward you will understand."

Jesus' response strikingly asserts Peter's ignorance of what Jesus was doing. Since the scene was introduced by the narrator with a report of what Jesus knew, the contrast between Jesus and Peter could not be put any more sharply. The phrase "afterward" functions as a prolepsis, an allusion to events that have not yet been narrated. It opens a gap which the reader may or may not be able to fill at this point in the narrative. The implication is that if Peter knew about Jesus' hour and his return to the Father, he would understand the meaning of the footwashing.

The importance of the footwashing as an aspect of Jesus' completion of the mission for which he had been sent by the Father is implied but not explicitly stated. The promise that although Peter does not understand now he will understand "afterward" echoes other statements that contrast what the disciples knew at the time and what they later understood:

> John 2:22 "When therefore he was raised from the dead, his disciples remembered that he had said this; and they believed the scripture and the word which Jesus had spoken."
>
> John 12:16 "His disciples did not understand this at first; but when Jesus was glorified, then they remembered that this had been written of him and had been done to him."

"Afterward" clearly means "after Jesus has completed his mission and returned to the Father." The act of footwashing, therefore, cannot be understood apart from Jesus' death on the cross.

Various disciples and others around Jesus in the Gospel of John do not understand some aspect of Jesus' role and revelation. Nathanael does not understand where Jesus is from, his origin from the Father. Martha does not understand that in Jesus the hope of life is already fulfilled. Thomas does not understand the resurrection. As we discover later, Peter does not understand the need for Jesus to die (13:36-38; 18:10-11). It is appropriate, therefore, that Peter should be singled out as the one to represent the disciples' lack of understanding. Because Peter does not understand Jesus' imminent death and glorification, he cannot understand the footwashing. Only when he understands that Jesus' death completed his mission to reveal the Father (1:18) and take away "the sin of the world" (1:29) will he understand the meaning of footwashing.

The next two exchanges underscore Peter's lack of understanding and provide further clues to the meaning of Jesus' action. As we, the readers, overhear this exchange we are drawn to accept the knowledge shared by Jesus and the narrator and to distance ourselves from Peter. In truth we may not understand much more than Peter at this point in the narrative, but we are enticed to want to understand the action from the vantage point of what Jesus knows and what the narrator has reported.

Peter (2): "You shall never wash my feet."

As usual, to interpret this statement we must ask what it does. What is its impact or effect on the reader? Peter does not respond by asking what it is that he does not understand. Instead, he adamantly persists in refusing to let Jesus wash his feet. As readers we know, of course, that Peter is stubbornly pursuing a response that grows out of ignorance. Peter's statement therefore serves to underscore that refusing to accept Jesus' love (footwashing/death) is a mistaken response that grows out of ignorance.

Jesus (2): "If I do not wash you, you have no part in me."

Jesus' response further elevates the importance of allowing Jesus to wash the disciples' feet. The footwashing is required if one is to "have a place" with the Lord. This idiom does not occur elsewhere in John, but one does find it in Revelation 20:6, "Blessed and holy is he who shares [i.e., "has a place"] in the first resurrection" (cf. Rev 21:8; 22:19). Again, we must ask what this assertion does in the reading process. The reader cannot literally allow the Lord to wash his or her feet, but the reader can understand and believe that Jesus' death revealed the love of God for his own in the world *eis telos* ("completely," "finally") and that Jesus was the Christ, the Son of God. The footwashing scene, therefore, functions metaphorically and proleptically in relation to Jesus' death.[9] It clarifies in advance the meaning of Jesus' death (so the reader will be better able to understand its significance when it is narrated) and be further disposed to respond with belief. By such a response the reader may "have a part" in Jesus and this story.

Peter (3): "Lord, not my feet only but also my hands and my head!"

Impulsively Peter shifts to the opposite extreme. Having first demanded less than Jesus offered, Peter now requests more than Jesus offered. Again, as with Peter's first statement, the reader may appreciate the piety of Peter's request, but again Jesus' response demonstrates that Peter's request rises from his lack of understanding. Jesus was not perpetuating the practice of ritual washings.

Jesus (3): "He who has bathed does not need to wash, [except for his feet], but he is clean all over; and you are clean, but not all of you."

The difficulties in interpreting this verse have led to the introduction of textual variants which have further compounded the problems facing the interpreter. The basic textual issue concerns the phrase in brackets, "except for his feet," which is omitted by Codex Sinaiticus, the Vulgate, some Old Latin texts, Tertullian, and Origen. Resolution of the textual issue depends heavily on arguments over internal considerations: Is it more likely that the tension with v. 8b led to the addition of the longer reading, or that the tension with the remainder of v. 10a [*alla*, but] led to its omission? And further, does the narrative flow of vv. 6–11 point to the inclusion or the exclusion of the phrase?

The shorter reading probably fits the narrative flow of vv. 6–11 better.[10] It is also as likely that the tension with v. 8b led to the addition of the longer reading as it is that the tension with the remainder of v. 10a led to its exclusion. Without the offending phrase, Jesus' third response affirms that one who has been washed (by Jesus' death, which is interpreted by the footwashing) has no need for any further washings, such as Peter was requesting (his hands and head).

Jesus has washed the feet of the disciples, but they are not all clean. Not all of them will respond to Jesus' salvific death in faith. V. 10b refers to Judas, as the narrator explains in v. 11, but perhaps also to those who would deny the salvific significance of Jesus' death and go out into the world (1 John 2:19; 4:1).

The conclusion of this conversation between Jesus and Peter returns again to the theme of knowledge. Jesus knew of his coming death and return to the Father; Peter could not understand the meaning of the footwashing because he did not share in this knowledge. Similarly, Jesus knew that Judas would betray him. Presumably, the disciples did not understand the meaning of what Jesus had just said because they did not share in this knowledge either. By reporting this "inside information" to the reader in v. 11 the narrator moves the reader from the vantage point of the disciples' ignorance to the informed vantage point of Jesus and the narrator. The reader is thereby drawn into the circle of those who share in Jesus' revelation. As the reader moves on through the text, he or she watches from this informed vantage point while the disciples grope for understanding. Again, the narrative's handling of information complements and supports its development of the theme of knowledge (revelation and belief) vs. ignorance (rejection and unbelief).

4. Jesus' Exhortation to the Disciples (vv. 12–17)

Verse 12 marks the end of the footwashing and a transition from Jesus' conversation with Peter to his instruction for the disciples. Again the introductory, transitional question concerns their knowledge or understanding: "Do you know what I have done to you?" The question introduces a subtle tension. In v. 7 Jesus promised that Peter would understand the meaning of what he had done "afterward." Did this phrase refer simply to the footwashing? Will they now be able to understand? On the other hand, if the phrase refers to Jesus' death and resurrection, what is the point of asking the disciples if they understand? Jesus is actually asking not only if the disciples understand the footwashing but whether they understand what is about to happen. Do they understand the meaning of his coming hour, his glorification?

If the tension between the question in v. 12 and the earlier statement in v. 7 represents a breakdown in the narrative logic at this point, one might conclude that it is due to the juxtaposition of material from different sources (e.g., Hultgren:540), or the work of the evangelist adding material that was not in his sources. On the other hand, the narrative logic may break down because the real audience for this instruction is not the disciples but the readers of the narrative, who already know of Jesus' death and resurrection, though it has not yet been reported in the narrative.

Jesus now clarifies the implications of his rejection of the prevailing norms of social standing. First, the footwashing does not mean that Jesus is not to be honored as teacher and Lord (v. 13). Second, because the disciples acknowledge his authority as their teacher, they are to follow his teaching and example and do for each other as he did for them (v. 14). On a metaphorical level this mandate would mean simply to be willing to set aside regard for one's own position in order to serve others. If taken literally, it could mean that the followers of Jesus are to continue the practice of washing one another's feet. The Johannine community may have actually continued this practice,[11] but those who take Jesus' metaphorical statements literally in John are usually those who misunderstand. The connection between the footwashing and Jesus' death raises the alternative possibility that Jesus was exhorting his disciples to be ready to die for one another. This interpretation receives further support from statements later in the Gospel:

> Greater love has no man than this, that a man lay down his life for his friends (15:13).
>
> Indeed, the hour is coming when whoever kills you will think he is offering service to God (16:2).
>
> This he said to show by what death he [Peter] was to glorify God (21:19).

Peter cannot understand the significance of Jesus' death because he is still tied to the world's norms regarding honor and shame. He is not ready to follow Jesus, as the second conversation between Jesus and Peter will confirm (vv. 36–38). Therefore, he cannot understand the footwashing. Neither Peter nor the rest of the disciples understand that Jesus' death should mean for them a complete rejection of the world's norms and the conferring of a new set of values under which they will serve one another even to the point of laying down their lives, as Jesus did.

The unusual term *hypodeigma* ("example") occurs in the Septuagint in well-known passages that exhort the faithful to mark an exemplary death. This is not the only context in which this term appears in ancient texts, but it is common enough in the Septuagint to merit our attention:

> Eleazar: "Therefore, by manfully giving up my life now, I will show myself worthy of my old age and leave to the young a noble example [*hypodeigma*] of how to die a good death willingly and nobly for the revered and holy laws." (2 Macc 6:28)
>
> "So in this way he died, leaving in his death an example [*hypodeigma*] of nobility and a memorial of courage, not only to the young but to the great body of his nation." (2 Macc 6:31)
>
> A mother and her seven sons: "And through the blood of those devout ones and their death as an expiation, divine Providence preserved Israel that previously had been afflicted. For the tyrant Antiochus, when he saw the courage of their virtue and their endurance under the tortures, proclaimed them to his soldiers as an example [*hypodeigma*] for their own endurance." (4 Macc 17:22–23)

Enoch: "Enoch pleased the Lord, and was taken up; he was an example [*hypodeigma*] of repentance to all generations." (Sir 44:16)

The occurrence of the term in these significant passages shows that one of the established contexts in which it was used was in accounts of exemplary deaths which served as models for others to follow.[12] This connotation of the term *hypodeigma* further links the footwashing with Jesus' death, but more significantly the term appears in vv. 12–17, which have customarily been read as a second interpretation of the footwashing which treats it not as an interpretation of Jesus' death but as an example of humble service for others to follow. If vv. 12–17 continue to treat the footwashing as a symbolic action pointing to the meaning of Jesus' impending death, then much of the perceived disjunction between vv. 12–17 and vv. 6–11 evaporates.[13] A similar linkage of Jesus' serving and giving his life is found in Mark 10:45, "For the Son of man also came not to be served but to serve, and to give his life as a ransom for many."

Vv. 14–15 contain the formulas that form the basis of the Johannine ethical imperatives (Schnackenburg:24):[14]

"If I then . . . you also ought to . . ." (v. 14).

"For I have . . . that you also should . . ." (*hina kathōs*, v. 15).

The love command employs the formula found in v. 15: "*that* you love one another, *even as* I have loved you" (13:34). Not only do these formulas recur in the Johannine epistles ("ought": 1 John 2:6; 4:11; 3 John 8; "just as" with an ethical exhortation: 1 John 2:6, 27; 3:3, 7, 12, 23; 4:17), they are explicitly related to the command that members of the community should be willing to die for one another: "By this we know love: that he laid down his life for us; and we ought to lay down our lives for the brethren" (1 John 3:16).

Similarly, the synoptic-like double *amēn* saying which follows (v. 16; cf. Matt 10:24; Luke 6:40) does not function just as an exhortation to humility but as a reminder that because Jesus laid down his life for the disciples they should be prepared to die also. The following passages show how appropriate such an understanding of the comparative axiom in John 13:16 is.

"If the world hates you, know that it has hated me before it hated you" (15:18).

"Remember the word that I said to you, 'A servant is not greater than his master.' If they persecuted me, they will persecute you" (15:20).

"Indeed, the hour is coming when whoever kills you will think he is offering service to God" (16:2).

Jesus' death, therefore, as it is here interpreted through the footwashing, is the norm of life and conduct for the believing community. This is a radical ethic, but one that accords well with the widely accepted view that the Johannine community experienced persecution and conflict with the synagogue.

This section closes by returning again to the issue of the disciples' knowledge of what Jesus was doing.[15] As the preceding material has shown, they did not, indeed they could not, understand what Jesus had done. Only after his death would they understand. Then they would see the need to accept Jesus' death as revelatory and salvific and to revolutionize their understanding of status, honor and shame, and their calling as apostles. Blessing comes to those who live out an ethic based on the *hypodeigma* of Jesus' death.

5. THE FORECAST OF BETRAYAL (VV. 18–20)

Again, the dialogue calls attention to what Jesus knew and, by implication, the consequences of the disciples' ignorance. Jesus knew that not all of the disciples would be able to accept the ethic based on his radical love and expressed in the footwashing and in his death. He knew those whom he had called out. He knew that Judas would betray him, but ironically the betrayal would lead to the completing of Jesus' mission at his death. V. 19 again links what Jesus says at this point in the narrative with his coming death. At that time the disciples will be able to understand what he is saying in this scene. Then they will be able to believe that *egō eimi* ("I am"). This revelatory formula has by now become a cipher for the identity of Jesus as it is interpreted by the entire Gospel.

V. 20, another synoptic-like double *amēn* saying, seems unrelated to its context. This saying, however, authorizes the work of the disciples. Those who receive them receive Jesus and the Father who sent him. The disciples are sent to do as Jesus did (cf. 13:14–15). The sacrifice required by this radical Johannine ethic is warranted, therefore, by the promise that those who receive the disciples (who carry on Jesus' revelatory and sacrificial mission) also receive Jesus.

6. JESUS AND JUDAS (VV. 21–30)

The narrative has prepared for Jesus' confrontation with Judas first by reporting that the Devil had decided that Judas should betray Jesus (v. 2), then by an allusion to Judas in v. 10 which is interpreted by the narrator in

v. 11, and again by the proleptic interpretation of the betrayal by means of Jesus' quotation of Psalm 41:10 in v. 18. Now Jesus says plainly that one of the disciples will betray him (v. 21). His statement is met with lack of comprehension by the disciples. The narrator establishes their lack of understanding by reporting that they were looking at one another, being "uncertain" about whom he meant.

At this point the Beloved Disciple is introduced. Peter, who obviously does not understand what Jesus has said, signals for the Beloved Disciple to ask Jesus who he was talking about. In response to the question, Jesus takes bread, dips it, and gives it to Judas, fulfilling Psalm 41:10, quoted in v. 18. Now the narrator reports that Satan entered into Judas. Still, it is not Satan that prompts Judas to leave and carry out his betrayal. Jesus' initiative in laying down his life is maintained by his words, "What you are going to do, do quickly" (v. 27). The repetition of the verb *to do* resonates with its earlier occurrences in this scene:

"What I am *doing* you do not know now" (13:7); "Do you know what I have *done* to you?" (13:12);

"For I have given you an example, that you also should do *as I have done* to you" (13:15);

"If you know these things, blessed are you *if you do them*" (13:17).

The whole of John 13 turns on the relationship between knowing and doing.[16] Because Jesus knows that his hour has come, he interprets his death by washing the disciples' feet and instructs them to accept his death on their behalf and be ready to die for one another. Judas, like Peter, acts out his lack of understanding. He responds to the spirit (Satan) that dwells within him, in contrast to the disciples who will respond to the abiding presence of the Holy Spirit. Refusing to accept Jesus' redemptive death as the basis for an ethic of love leads Judas (another exemplary or representative figure) to act out betrayal that is based on rejection of Jesus' revelation (knowledge) as it is revealed in the footwashing and in his death.

Immediately, the story returns to the theme of knowledge: "Now no one at the table knew why he had said this to him" (v. 28). This report explains why neither the Beloved Disciple, nor Peter, nor any of the others acted to stop Judas. It also reinforces the disciples' lack of understanding. Ironically, Judas was able to betray Jesus because the others did not understand. Their erroneous assumptions are reported in v. 29, driving home the narrator's report that they did not understand. Not all interpreters have been convinced by the narrator, however, and some have demanded that at least the Beloved Disciple must have understood; but that is an effort to change the story and retell it in a different way, not an effort to interpret the story as told by the narrator. V. 30 closes this part of the scene by referring to the morsel (cf. vv. 18, 26–27), by reporting Judas' obedience (going out quickly), and by interpreting the event symbolically ("it was night"). The implication is clear: Acting out of ignorance or refusal to accept Jesus' revelatory act places one in the realm of darkness (cf. 3:19–21).

7. THE NEW COMMAND AND THE SECOND CONVERSATION WITH PETER (VV. 31–38)

This section is composed of further instruction, including the new commandment, and the second conversation with Peter. Both have significant but overlooked connections with the footwashing.

Jesus' death is characterized as his "glorification." As in the footwashing, however, the glory of his death will be veiled by the cross. His death is also his departure to the Father. Jesus repeats the *mashal*, or riddle, that he had used on two previous occasions (7:33–36; 8:21–22). This time Jesus does not say that they will not be able to find him (cf. 7:34) or that they will die in their sin (8:21). Neither of these consequences will apply to the disciples; they will not be able to come where he is going.

Jesus leaves the disciples a new commandment, however, one that has taken on new significance following the footwashing. Through the footwashing and his coming death, Jesus would love his own "to the end" (13:1). After the footwashing, which foreshadowed his death, Jesus instructed the disciples to wash one another's feet. Now he commands them to love one another as he has loved them. The close association of love with the footwashing and Jesus' death conveys the implication that Jesus was charging his disciples to love one another even if such love requires that they lay down their lives for the community. This inference will later be reinforced by the association of keeping the new commandment (15:12, 17) with laying down one's life for his friends (15:13) and bearing fruit (15:16). For a grain of wheat to bear fruit it must fall into the ground and die (12:24).

Jesus' death is the model for community. The footwashing and the new commandment are related as two facets of the same instruction for the community: Do (footwashing/love/die) for one another as I am doing for you. By such imitation of the pattern of Jesus' life and death all will know that they are his disciples (13:35). This commissioning is a prolepsis expressing divine intent—that all may know. The Gospel promises that although the disciples did not understand, by their obedience to Jesus' example (*hypodeigma*) and the love command their knowledge of God would be displayed before the world. The Gospel narrative is therefore an extension of Jesus' revelatory function.

Throughout this chapter and again in John 18:10–11 Peter is characterized as one who does not understand Jesus' death. He therefore does not understand where Jesus was going (i.e., his return to the Father) nor why he cannot follow him. Because he did not understand that Jesus was going to his death, he could not understand the footwashing (13:6–11). Now he cannot understand Jesus' departure. The irony of Peter's pledge of loyalty is pointed. He cannot follow—that is, he cannot discharge his duty as a disciple—because he does not understand the meaning of Jesus' death. Peter's pledge that he would lay down his life is ironic because Peter does not understand either that Jesus was laying down his life for the disciples, or that "where Jesus was going" was to the Father by means of his death and departure from this world, or that eventually he would indeed lay down his life (cf. 21:19). Jesus confronts Peter with reality: that very night he would deny Jesus three times. The contrast between knowledge and ignorance of the revelation conveyed by Jesus' death is complete.

8. REFLECTIONS

Our reading of this chapter, though it has dealt with only certain aspects of the text, has shown that the chapter presents a coherent development of the contrast between Jesus' knowledge and the disciples' lack of understanding. This contrast is fundamental to the plot of the entire Gospel. Jesus has come as Word incarnate to reveal the Father (1:18). His revelation is light in darkness, but his own do not receive him. Even the disciples do not understand until after his death. Because Jesus knows the Father he is able to face his own death. Jesus' knowledge is closely related to his love for his own, the footwashing, and his death. The contraries are also true. Those who do not receive Jesus' revelation cannot live out the ethic of his example. Because Peter does not understand that the hour of Jesus' death has come, he cannot understand the footwashing, and he is not ready to lay down his life.

Jesus' death, his instruction that the disciples wash one another's feet, the love command, the betrayal by Judas, and Peter's denials cannot be understood in isolation from one another. The footwashing is a proleptic and metaphorical interpretation of Jesus' death. Moreover, because the term *hypodeigma* ("example") elevates a virtuous and noteworthy death, the interpretation in vv. 12–17 is closely related to vv. 6–11 and points to Jesus' death as a model for the Johannine community as it faced persecution and the threat of death. Only when one sees how John 13 relates these distinct elements thematically can one begin to understand the narrative strategy of this chapter, and perhaps by understanding be ready to live out the revelation that is conveyed by the footwashing.

NOTES

[1] The significance of the theme of knowledge in John 13 is recognized by F. J. Moloney, who expresses his indebtedness to Y. Simoens. My own analysis of this chapter may confirm aspects of their work, but I wrote the first draft of this paper without consulting their work. In particular, my analysis of the units within this chapter, the issue of whether it contains a chiastic structure, and the significance of the placement of the *amēn, amēn* sayings differ from theirs.

[2] The unity of John 13:1-38 is defended by F. Manns on formal (chiasm and inclusio) rather than narratological grounds.

[3] M. Sabbe has argued that John 13 makes use of material drawn from Mark 14, Luke 22, and Luke 7; and K. T. Kleinknecht independently concluded that the structure of John 13 depends on the synoptics.

[4] R. Bultmann (465) comments: "*Eidōs* will be used again three times [13:1b, which Bultmann takes to be the introduction to the farewell prayer; 18:4; and 19:28] . . . The purpose of this repetition is to characterize everything that happens here as revelation-event: Jesus acts as the one who 'knows,' as the perfected 'Gnostic' . . . ."

[5] R. M. Ball argues that *eis telos egapēsen autous* means that Jesus instituted the eucharist, but such an explicit eucharistic interpretation is at best secondary to the connection between this phrase and Jesus' death.

[6] This scheme, in a slightly different form, was suggested to me by J. A. du Rand.

[7] Cf. Culpepper (24), where the various readings are presented and discussed. The external evidence (p66, Sinaiticus, and B) favors Barrett's solution. The internal evidence is more difficult in that it confronts the interpreter with a difficult choice: did a scribe encounter an idiom he did not understand and smooth out the text so that it read like v. 27, thereby introducing the difficulty; or did the scribe recognize the tension in the text and seek to relieve it by introducing the Semitic idiom? On balance the former, supported by the mss. listed above, is more likely.

[8] A. J. Hultgren (541-42) has collected the relevant passages that document the practice of footwashing as a gesture of hospitality: Gen 18:4; 19:2; 24:32; 43:24; Judg 19:21; 1 Sam 25:41; Luke 7:44; Test Abr 7:44; Joseph and Asenath 7:1; 13:12; 20:1-5; 1 Tim 5:10. Weiss (302-305) shows particularly from passages in Philo (*Quaes Gen* IV.5; IV.60; *Quaes Ex* I.2; *De Vita Mosis* II.138; *De Spec Leg* I.206-207) and P Oxy 840 that "in the Hellenistic synagogue the washing of the feet was a preparation for meeting God."

[9] J. D. G. Dunn (247-52) adopts this line of interpretation: "John intends us to see in this narrative a figure of the cross," and cites E. Hoskyns, W. F. Howard, C. H. Dodd, C. K. Barrett, J. H. Lightfoot, R. V. G. Tasker, G. Delling, G. Richter, W. K. Grossouw, and J. Marsh (248, n. 7).

[10] F. F. Segovia (44, n. 33) cites the following arguments in favor of the longer reading: "a. the external attestation is much superior; b. the reading can be satisfactorily explained in the context of the Gospel narrative; c. the shorter reading can be readily explained as an attempt to smooth out what could be construed as an irreconcilable clash with the following *alla* [but]." J. C. Thomas and J. A. T. Robinson (147) also favor the longer reading. On the other hand, the longer reading creates a tension with the remainder of v. 10a, "but he is all clean," and requires that the cleansing (*leloumenos*) refer to some action other than the washing (*nipsasthai*).

Thomas (51, n. 25) declares, "It is now obvious that, despite John's fondness for double entendre and for synonyms, *louō* and *niptō* are distinct in meaning. They appear together in a variety of contexts, but never as synonyms." Relying on J. Owanga-Welo (15-16), he cites T Levi 9:11; Tobit 7:9b; and Plutarch *Moralia* 958B.

Drawing a distinction between the meanings of these two verbs has led to the suggestion that Jesus' response validates a rather developed sacramentalism; i.e., that one who has been baptized (*leloumenos*) needs only to have his or her feet washed (*nipsasthai*). The logic of the internal evidence for the longer reading, therefore, is that the footwashing was distinguished from the cleansing of the disciples, whether by the death of Jesus or by baptism. It was a subsequent washing practiced by the Johannine community. The tension with the following phrase, "but he is clean all over," led to the omission of the phrase, "except for his feet."

The argument for the shorter reading is based on the following considerations: (1) the remainder of v. 10a, "but is clean all over," does not follow easily from the longer reading, "except for his feet"; (2) normally the shorter reading is preferred; (3) the longer reading contradicts the logic of vv. 6-11, which links the footwashing with the death of Jesus; and (4) Jesus' insistence on washing Peter's feet (v. 8b), when misunderstood because the relationship between the footwashing and the death of Jesus was not recognized, led to the addition of the longer reading. Jesus' second response to Peter (v. 8b), however, confirms that the footwashing, related as it is proleptically and metaphorically to Jesus' death, is not a secondary cleansing. It is essential and indispensable (see Barrett:441-42).

G. Richter (320) claims that the longer reading cannot come from the Evangelist or either of the first two redactions that he finds in the composition history of the Gospel.

[11] Thomas (52), who favors the longer reading of 13:10, points out that "Such a reading opens up the possibility that not only did the Johannine community believe that Jesus washed the feet of the disciples, but that they too are to wash one another's feet." H. Weiss (298) reaches a similar conclusion: "There can be no doubt, however, that the Johannine community must have performed this ceremony with some regularity and with a definite purpose in mind," but he does not take a position on the exception clause in v. 10. As Thomas observes, however, his thesis that the Johannine community practiced footwashing as preparation for martyrdom would be strengthened by accepting the longer reading.

[12] I have not found this usage of the term *hypodeigma* discussed in the literature on the footwashing, nor in the article on *hypodeigma* by H. Schlier. Failure to grasp its significance led even Robinson (145) to write: "Indeed, one suspects that the sacramental reference would not have been found necessary were it not that the purely exemplary explanation offered in v. 15 ('I have given you an example [*hypodeigma*], that you also should do as I have done') seems such a weak point after the momentous introduction to the story in vv. 1-3."

[13] Dunn (249) argues for the unity of vv. 12-17 with the preceding verses without noting the significance of the term *hypodeigma* for this issue: "In short, Boismard, and Richter are mistaken in thinking that the soteriological-Christological significance of the first part cannot be harmonized with the moral-ethical interpretation of the second part. On the contrary, the union of the two interpretations in the complete presentation is neither artificial nor unexpected...."

[14] G. F. Snyder (6) overstates the case when he claims, "there is no place in the Gospel of John for an ethical admonition which uses Jesus as the paradigm." He dismisses the relevance of parallels from the epistles. The Gospel and the epistles are not in tension at this point, however. The epistles simply state explicitly the ethical foundation that is at work in this section of the Gospel.

[15] Moloney (4) comments: "The 'knowing' and 'doing' of Jesus opens the section, while a consequent blessing of the 'knowing' and 'doing' of the disciple closes it."

[16] See Moloney (8): "His [Jesus'] knowledge has led him into action: the washing of the feet and the gift of the morsel. The non-knowledge of the disciples will likewise lead them into action: the betrayal of Judas and the denials of Peter."

WORKS CONSULTED

Ball, R. M.
    1985   "S. John and the Institution of the Eucharist." *Journal for the Study of the New Testament* 23:59–68.

Barrett, C. K.
    1978   *The Gospel according to St. John.* 2nd ed. Philadelphia: Westminster.

Boismard, M. E.
    1964   "Le lavement des pieds." *Revue biblique* 71:5–24.

Brown, Raymond E.
    1970   *The Gospel according to John, XIII–XXI.* Anchor Bible 29A. Garden City, N.Y.: Doubleday.

Bultmann, Rudolf.
    1971   *The Gospel of John: A Commentary.* Trans. G. R. Beasley-Murray, et al. Philadelphia: Westminster.

Culpepper, R. Alan.
    1983   *Anatomy of the Fourth Gospel.* Philadelphia: Fortress.

du Rand, Jan A.
    1989   "Narratological Perspectives on John 13:1–38." A paper presented at the Johannine Seminar of the Society for New Testament Studies, Dublin, Ireland.

Dunn, James D. G.
    1970   "The Washing of the Disciples' Feet in John 13 1–20." *Zeitschrift für die Neutestamentliche Wissenschaft* 61:247–52.

Hultgren, Arland J.
    1982   "The Johannine Footwashing (13.1–11) as Symbol of Eschatological Hospitality." *New Testament Studies* 28:539–46.

Kleinknecht, Karl Theodor.
    1985   "Johannes 13, die Synoptiker und die 'Methode' der johanneischen Evangelienüberlieferung." *Zeitschrift für Theologie und Kirche* 82:361–88.

Lindars, Barnabas.
    1972   *The Gospel of John.* New Century Bible. London: Oliphants.

Manns, Frédéric.
1981   "Le lavement des pieds. Essai sur la structure et la signification de Jean 13." *Revue des sciences religieuses* 55:149–69.

Moloney, F. J.
1986   "The Structure and Message of John 13:1–38." *Australian Biblical Review* 34:1–16.

Owanga-Welo, Jean.
1980   "The Function and Meaning of the Footwashing in the Johannine Passion Narrative: A Structural Approach." Ph.D. Dissertation, Emory University, Atlanta, GA.

Richter, Georg.
1967   *Die Fusswaschung im Johannesevangelium: Geschichte Ihrer Deutung.* Biblische Untersuchungen 1. Regensburg: Verlag Friedrich Pustet.

Sabbe, M.
1982   "The Footwashing in John 13 and Its Relation to the Synoptic Gospels." *Ephemerides Theologicae Lovaniensis* 58:279–308.

Schlier, Heinrich.
1964   "hypodeigma." *Theological Dictionary of the New Testament*, 2:32–33. Edited by Gerhard Kittel. Trans. Geoffrey W. Bromiley. Grand Rapids: Wm. B. Eerdmans.

Schnackenburg, Rudolf.
1982   *The Gospel according to St. John*, vol. 3. Trans. David Smith and G. A. Kon. Herder's Theological Commentary on the New Testament. New York: Crossroad.

Segovia, Fernando F.
1982   "John 13:1–20, The Footwashing in the Johannine Tradition." *Zeitschrift für die neutestamentlishe Wissenschaft* 73:31–51.

Simoens, Yves.
1981   *La gloire d'aimer: Structures stylistiques et interprétatives dans le Discours de la Cène (Jn 13–17).* Analecta Biblica 90. Rome: Biblical Institute Press.

Snyder, Graydon F.
1971   "John 13:16 and the Anti-Petrinism of the Johannine Tradition." *Biblical Research* 16:5–15.

Thomas, John Christopher.
1987   "A Note on the Text of John 13:10." *Novum Testamentum* 29:46–52.

Thyen, Hartwig.
1971   "Johannes 13 und die 'kirchliche Redaktion' des vierten Evangeliums." Pp. 343–56 in *Tradition und Glaube: Das frühe Christentum in seiner Umwelt, Festgabe für K. G. Kuhn.* Ed. G. Jeremias, H.-W. Kuhn, and H. Stegemann. Göttingen: Vandenhoeck & Ruprecht.

Weiss, Herold.
1979   "Foot Washing in the Johannine Community." *Novum Testamentum* 21:298–325.

Wojciechowski, Michal.
1988   "La source de Jean 13.1–20." *New Testament Studies* 34:135–41.

"I HAVE OVERCOME THE WORLD" (JOHN 16:33): NARRATIVE TIME IN JOHN 13–17

Gail R. O'Day
Candler School of Theology

ABSTRACT

Recent literary critical studies of John have identified and analyzed the temporal figures used in the Fourth Gospel narrative. The fluidity with which the fourth evangelist uses time in chapters 13–17 suggests the need to move beyond taxonomic study of temporal order to a study of the literary and theological functions of time in the farewell discourse. Through its use of narrative time, the farewell discourse demonstrates what is the overriding theological reality for the community of believers: God and Jesus are not limited by conventional constructions of past, present, and future.

The farewell discourse (John 13–17) is a rich text to investigate from the perspective of narrative time. Throughout the discourse, the temporal focus seems to shift constantly. At times Jesus speaks as if the crucifixion/resurrection/ascension were a past event (e.g., 16:33; 17:11), at times he speaks as if his departure from the world is imminent (e.g., 13:33; 14:3), and at still other times he speaks as if he were in the process of departing at that very moment (e.g., 13:31; 16:15, 28; 17:13).[1] The narrative function of time and temporal sequence thus is a pivotal concern for the farewell discourse.

1. NARRATIVE TIME AND THE FOURTH GOSPEL

Alan Culpepper has interspersed comments about the farewell discourse in his general survey of narrative time in the Fourth Gospel (51–75: Chap.3, "Narrative Time"). Culpepper draws on the critical categories developed by Gérard Genette in his seminal study of Proust's *A la recherche du temps perdu*.[2] Culpepper, following Genette, investigates order (i.e., temporal sequence), frequency, and duration as the constitutive elements of narrative time. While frequency and duration have their own interpretive potential,[3] order seems the most promising category through which to study the temporal idiosyncrasy of the farewell discourse.

Genette (35) proposes that

> To study the temporal order of a narrative is to compare the order in which events or temporal sections are arranged in the narrative discourse with the order of succession these same events or temporal segments have in the story. . . .

To that end, Genette identifies two broad modes of temporal ordering in narrative: "retrospection" or "temporal analepsis," in which the narrated sequence of events moves backward in time from the temporal locus of the main narrative line; and "anticipation" or "temporal prolepsis," in which the narrated sequence of events jumps forward (40). An analepsis may refer back to events within the construct of the narrative (internal analepsis) or to events that occurred prior to the starting point of the narrative (external analepsis) (49). Similarly, a prolepsis may anticipate events that will occur within the narrative proper (internal prolepsis) or events whose consummation lies outside the conclusion of the narrative discourse (68). Genette's categories provide a way to analyze methodically the temporal movement and sequences within a given narrative.

What do these theoretical categories look like in an actual narrative? Genette draws on Proust to provide concrete examples of these temporal figures. For our purposes, however, the examples Culpepper adduces when he applies Genette's categories to the Fourth Gospel are more immediately relevant. Culpepper's application of Genette's categories of temporal order to the Fourth Gospel provides some clues to how the story of Jesus is ordered to create the narrative discourse of the Fourth Gospel. The following chart highlights examples of each of Genette's temporal figures identified by Culpepper in the Fourth Gospel (Culpepper:56–67):

Analepsis	Prolepsis
Internal: They came to John and said to him, "Rabbi, *the one who was with you across the Jordan, to whom you testified,* here he is baptizing and all are going to him." (3:26)	... just as the Father knows me and I know the Father. And *I lay down my life for the sheep.* (10:15)
External: Isaiah said this because he saw his glory and spoke about him. (12:41)	*They will put you out of the synagogues.* Indeed *an hour is coming when those who kill you will think that by doing so they are offering worship to God.* (16:2)

John 3:26 is an internal analepsis because it refers back to something that has already occurred within the narrative itself (cf. 1:19–34). John 12:41 is an external analepsis because the testimony of Isaiah occurred prior to the story of Jesus. John 10:15 is an internal prolepsis because the events that it anticipates will be narrated in the gospel Passion narrative. John 16:2 is an external prolepsis because it anticipates an event that will occur after the close of the narrative.

Culpepper further refines Genette's categories of "internal" and "external" to reflect more accurately the temporal field of the Fourth Gospel. Culpepper therefore also speaks of "historical" and "pre-historical" analepses and "historical" and "eschatological" prolepses. "Historical" analepses "recall moments in the history of Israel." "Pre-historical" analepses refer to events "in the relationship between Father and Son in the indefinable past of the incarnate *logos*" (Culpepper:57). "Historical" prolepses refer to "events which will occur among the disciples and later believers," and "eschatological" prolepses refer "to 'the last day,' the end of time" (Culpepper:64). The following chart illustrates these temporal figures:

Analepsis	*Prolepsis*
Historical: If you believed Moses, you would believe me, *for he wrote about me.* (5:46)	But *when you grow old, you will stretch out your hands, and someone else will fasten a belt around you and take you where you do not want to go.* (21:18)
Pre-historical: ... for I *have come down from heaven,* not to do my own will, but *the will of him who sent me.* (6:36)	*Eschatological*: ... for the hour is coming when all who are in their graves will hear his voice and will come out ... (5:28–29)

As Culpepper's analysis of time in the Fourth Gospel proceeds, however, it becomes clear that the Fourth Gospel resists precise categorization by even these refined forms, and Culpepper must also identify "mixed forms." For example, he identifies mixed prolepses as "progressive," that is, "the conditions for their fulfillment are established by the end of the narrative, but their fruition lies beyond it." John 14:19 is a mixed prolepsis according to Culpepper, "In a little while the world will no longer see me, but you will see me; because I live, you also will live" (63). The line between narrative future and the future beyond the narrative is not as clear-cut in the Fourth Gospel as Genette's categories would suggest. Most suggestive for the present study, the heaviest concentration of temporal figures that stretch the basic categories, particularly figures of anticipation, are lodged in the farewell discourse (Culpepper:63).

2. Narrative Time and the Farewell Discourse

Culpepper's use of Genette's categories provides a helpful tool in surfacing the function of temporal figures in the farewell discourse. The temporal ambiguity of the farewell discourse does not rest exclusively in the apparently shifting locus from which Jesus speaks of his departure from the world.[4] The examples Culpepper cites suggest that complex temporal relationships are an essential characteristic of the narrative fabric of the farewell discourse. Yet the concentration of mixed and complex temporal figures, particularly proleptic figures, suggests that the identification and classification of those figures only begin to probe the question of time in the farewell discourse. The fluidity with which the fourth evangelist uses time in chaps. 13–17 suggests the need to move beyond taxonomic study of temporal order to a study of the literary and theological functions of time in the farewell discourse.

In a very real sense, the whole farewell discourse is out of place in the progression of narrative time in the Fourth Gospel (an "anachrony," to use Genette's term; Genette:35–36). It is not simply that certain parts of the farewell discourse disturb the temporal sequence of the narrative, but rather the discourse itself disturbs the sequence of the gospel narrative. Chaps. 13–17 do not merely contain prolepses; they are themselves proleptic in the larger Johannine narrative. These chapters bring the future and the present together in one narrative moment in ways that challenge conventional notions of time. In chaps. 13–17 the future is thus an essential element in the narrative construction of the present.

The farewell discourse provides many markers that point to its proleptic function. The most explicit markers announce the anticipatory purpose of the discourse in the words of Jesus:

13:19   I tell you this now, before it occurs, so that when it does occur, you may believe that I am.

14:29   And now I have told you this before it occurs, so that when it does occur, you may believe.

15:11   I have said these things to you so that my joy be in you, and that your joy may be complete.

16:1,4 I have said these things to you to keep you from stumbling (v.1) . . . But I have said these things to you so that when their hour comes you may remember that I told you about them (v.4).

16:33   I have said this to you, so that in me you may have peace.

Closely related to these verses are:

14:2–3 In my Father's house there are many dwelling places. If it were not so, would I have told you that I go to prepare a place for you? And if I go and prepare a place for

> you, I will come again and take you to myself, so that where I am, there you may be.

14:25–26 I have said these things to you while I am with you. But the Advocate, the Holy Spirit, whom the Father will send in my name, will teach you everything and remind you of all that I said to you.

Jesus declares that through his words he is bringing the future into the present, so that when the future arrives, the disciples will recognize it and embrace what it offers.

The farewell discourse therefore explicitly acknowledges that it is a narrative out of place, a narrative discourse that is paradoxically, if we may borrow freely from Proust and Genette, a remembrance of things hoped for. It is the thesis of this study that this intrinsic temporal paradox is best understood when we recognize that the voice of Jesus conveyed by the farewell discourse is not the voice of the pre-crucifixion/ pre-resurrection Jesus. Rather, as the verses cited above suggest, the voice of Jesus speaks from a post-resurrection vantage point.[5] That is, the voice that we hear throughout the farewell discourse is the voice of the risen Jesus. As we shall see as this study progresses, it is this post-resurrection perspective that makes the farewell discourse a narrative out of time.

Meir Sternberg has suggested that in all narrative representation, "the future has already been determined—by nature or by poetic license—and only its mode of disclosure remains to be fixed upon" (Sternberg:265). In the farewell discourse, the fourth evangelist has chosen to disclose the future by putting it in the present tense. He has brought the future into the present of the narrative through the "temporal omnipresence" of the voice of Jesus in the farewell discourse.[6] The fourth evangelist thereby anticipates the future of the gospel narrative—and the readers' future—on the basis of Jesus' authority, not the narrator's own.[7] The events of the future may lie outside the end of the Fourth Gospel narrative, but the literary construction of the farewell discourse assures the reader that any future is nonetheless fully envisioned by the narrative. We will examine how the farewell discourse creates this new temporal world, as well as the larger literary and theological functions of this melding of narrative present and future. We will begin with the temporal event that determines the perspective of the farewell discourse: the arrival of the "hour."

3. THE "HOUR" AS TEMPORAL CATEGORY

The immediate narrative context for the farewell discourse (the footwashing, John 13:1–30) announces a decisive shift in the temporal perspective of the gospel: "Now before the feast of Passover, when Jesus knew that *his hour had come* to depart out of this world to the Father, having loved his own who were in the world, he loved them *to the end*" (13:1). Both the arrival of the "hour" and the use of "to the end" indicate temporal completeness.

From the opening miracle of Jesus' ministry, the transformation of water into wine at Cana (2:1-11), the fourth evangelist has interspersed into the narrative account allusions to Jesus' impending hour (2:4). The reader is led to anticipate the arrival of the hour. At 7:30 and 8:20 the failure of the Jewish leadership is explained by the comment, "because his hour had not yet come," thus establishing an explicit link between the events of the Passion and Jesus' hour. The public ministry comes to a conclusion in chap. 12 with a reference to the hour: "Now my soul is troubled. And what should I say—'Father, save me from this hour'? No, it is for this reason that I have come to this hour" (12:27). As noted, the foot-washing scene and Passion sequence that begin in chap. 13 open with Jesus' recognition that the hour has come.

The evangelist thus makes explicit use of time as a metaphor for the approach of Jesus' crucifixion/resurrection. The metaphor of the "hour" is tensive, not static. It communicates the urgency of time in the Fourth Gospel and the movement of time toward a critical moment. The metaphor contains within itself the seeds of narrative suspense and anticipation.[8] "The hour" directs the reader forward from the events of chaps. 1–12 to another place in time. This metaphor provides the fourth evangelist with the means of representing in narrative form the dramatic overlay of story time (the events of the Passion) with narrative time (the progress of the "hour").

This dramatic overlay of the metaphor of "the hour" with the events of the Passion reaches its narrative climax in the farewell discourse proper. Jesus begins the discourse with the words, "Now the son of man has been glorified, and God has been glorified in him" (13:31). The concluding section of the discourse, Jesus' prayer, identifies the "now" of 13:31 with the arrival of the hour: "Father, the hour has come; glorify your son that the son may glorify you" (17:1). Taken together, 13:31 and 17:1 establish the framework in which all temporal references in the farewell discourse are to be read. This frame explicitly locates all of chaps. 13–17 within the consummation of the "hour." The "hour" of glorification is *now*, played out in the words of the farewell discourse. All notions of present and future in the discourse are recast against the arrival of the hour. All adverbs of time, particularly adverbs of temporal immediacy (*nun, arti, euthus*; e.g., 13:31-33; 16:22, 31-32; 17:5,13) reinforce the arrival of the hour.

Once we enter the farewell discourse, then, all preparatory time has passed and the "hour" of reckoning has arrived. Time is no longer relative; it is refracted through the decisive moment of the hour. In many ways, chaps. 13–17 can be understood as the fourth evangelist's attempt to freeze the time of the hour in order to explain what the hour will mean before the events of the hour play themselves out in full. Once the events of the hour are put in motion, there will be no time for explanation.

The arrival of the hour indicates a radical new temporal orientation. The gap between the present moment and the impending future has been closed by the "now" of 13:31. The variety of verb tenses used by Jesus to refer to his relationship to the world and his departure from the world, as well as the use of temporal adverbs of immediacy and urgency can be understood as semantic markers to indicate that the arrival of the hour is the governing narrative reality of the discourse. It is also the governing theological reality. Time—the immediacy of the hour, the decisiveness and urgency of the present moment—is the central theological category of the farewell discourse, and the use of temporal figures is its most self-conscious literary device. What we see in the form and substance of the farewell discourse, then, is a perfect melding of narrative form and theological claim.[9] The use of temporal language and figures creates the arrival of the hour for the reader of the gospel. The arrival of the hour then determines how we read the narrative present and how we envision the move from narrative present to narrative future.

4. Present and Future in the Farewell Discourse

The arrival of the hour thus signals a new relationship between narrative present and future. Even though the actual events of the hour, that is, the events of crucifixion/resurrection/ascension, will not be narrated until after chap. 17, the temporal perspective of the farewell discourse presupposes that the glorification of God and Jesus effected by those events is already a reality (13:31). In the farewell discourse, therefore, Jesus speaks not only of the arrival of the hour, but also speaks with certainty about the shape of life in and beyond the hour. He does not speak tentatively about the future, nor offer hypothetical projections, but speaks as one for whom the future is as real as the present moment.

The vision of the future articulated by Jesus in chaps. 13–17 encompasses what almost appear to be two futures: an immediate future and the future beyond that future. Jesus' words about the immediate future include his departure from the world and the events most readily associated with the hour. These events are still future in terms of story order, but Jesus addresses the disciples as if that future is part of their immediate experience. For example, in 16:28 Jesus speaks of his own future as if it were present: "I came from the Father and have come into the world; again I am leaving the world and going to the Father." John 16:16–22a and 16:32 demonstrate the transformation of the immediate future into the present moment most vividly. In 16:17–18 the disciples are confused by Jesus' talk of the future, "What does he mean by this 'a little while'? We do not know what he is talking about." Jesus knows their questions (v.19), yet his answer (vv.20–22) collapses their categories of present and future: "Very truly, I tell you, you will weep and mourn, but the world will rejoice; *you will have pain*, but your pain will turn into joy . . . So *you have pain now* . . . ." The disciples' future (their pain) is read into their present.

In 16:32, what is still future in terms of the narration of events in the gospel is the present reality of the discourse: "The hour is coming, *indeed it has come*, when you will be scattered, each one to his home, and you will leave me alone." Once again, the governing reality is the arrival of the hour, which shifts the balance between the present moment and future actualization. Jesus' prediction of Peter's denial falls into the same category. The source of Peter's bravado lies in his misperception of the changes that have been wrought in the present through the arrival of the hour. Peter's insistence that he can follow Jesus *"now"* (13:37; cf. the "now" and "afterward" of 13:36) evokes Jesus' prediction of the denial. Peter's mistake is that he thinks he understands the present moment, but he does not. Only Jesus understands the present because of the link forged with the future by the arrival of the hour.

When Jesus speaks of the future beyond the immediate future, of the future that follows the immediate events of the hour, his words encompass his return (14:3), the transformation of the disciples' sorrow to joy (16:22), the new relationship the disciples will have with God (14:14; 16:23–24), but also the disciples' experience of the world's hatred and persecution (15:18–20; 16:2–3). The events of this future have a partial fulfillment within the narrative proper (e.g., 20:19–20), but also have a life beyond the gospel narrative. Culpepper notes that these words of Jesus ". . . have the effect of collapsing or compressing narrative time. That which was expected in the future of the story may have already occurred in the reader's past"(68). Jesus speaks about one event of the future, however, that breaks down this seeming distinction between an immediate and a second future, or between a future contained within the narrative and a future that moves beyond the narrative. The relationship between present and future, or future and future, is most multi-layered when Jesus speaks of the Paraclete. Jesus' words about the gift of the Paraclete are consistently in the future tense (14:15, 26; 15:26; 16:13), yet the presence of the Paraclete is also narrated in the present tense (e.g., 14:17). That the

Paraclete is part of the present reality of the gospel narrative is confirmed by the narrative itself. For example, one of the promised functions of the Paraclete is "to bring to your remembrance all that I have said to you" (14:26). In 2:22 and 12:16 we find references to the post-resurrection "remembering" of the disciples, clear evidence of the presence of the Paraclete.

Yet the Paraclete also belongs to the future that moves beyond what is narrated in the gospel, to the future both of hatred and persecution, and of new life with God. Careful delineation of temporal boundaries breaks down at Jesus' words about the Paraclete. Jesus speaks in an unchanging future tense about the Paraclete, even when the narrative simultaneously attests to the Paraclete's present reality, in order to assure the reader of the unfailing availability of the Comforter/Counselor. No present moment can consume the Paraclete. On the contrary, each present moment is reopened to the future through the presence of the Paraclete. That the Paraclete crosses temporal boundaries within the narrative structure of the farewell discourse provides literary confirmation of a theological reality. The Paraclete is not time-bound, but belongs to all times and places.

Jesus' words about the future in chaps. 13–17 involve himself and his own future as fully as they involve the disciples' future. Jesus' promise in 14:18, "I will not leave you orphaned," is shown to be reliable by the comprehensiveness of his vision of the future. The lives of Jesus and his disciples will be intertwined in the future just as they have been in the present (cf. 15:1–10). Jesus' promises about the future are also shown to be reliable in another way. The gospel narrative itself (20:19–23) shows that Jesus' words about his return (16:16), the gift of peace (14:27), the transformation of sorrow into joy (16:22), even the gift of the Spirit (16:7) are trustworthy. When the gospel narrative shows that Jesus can be trusted about the future, a continuum is established between the future that the gospel narrative can verify and the future that only the reader's experience can verify.

The link between these two futures is an essential literary and theological component of the farewell discourse. The narrative present of the farewell discourse is opened up to include the future, a future that is decisively shaped by the arrival of the hour. The present moment is redefined by the arrival of the hour, as are all the futures envisioned by the farewell discourse. The narrative future and the future that lives beyond the narrative are both determined by the hour and are shaped by Jesus' promises. The farewell discourse shows that there is nothing capricious about the future because it is already known in the present words of Jesus. Jesus' words guarantee his abiding presence that knows no temporal restrictions. The future is thus grounded in and governed by the authority of Jesus, to which the reader is given unlimited access through the farewell discourse.

5. THE VOICE OF THE RISEN JESUS IN THE FAREWELL DISCOURSE

The next step in understanding narrative time in the farewell discourse is to ask how the narrative discourse establishes the authority of Jesus over the future. Our previous discussion indicated one way: Jesus' authority is established because what he says about the future is shown to be reliable. The warrants for Jesus' authority in the farewell discourse are more far-reaching than that, however. The most telling way in which the fourth evangelist establishes Jesus' authority is to allow him to speak with an unassailable voice. That voice, as suggested earlier, is the voice of the risen Jesus.

John 16:33 is the clearest example of the voice of the risen Jesus in the farewell discourse:

> I have said this to you, so that in me you may have peace. In the world you face persecution. But take courage; *I have conquered the world*.

Only the voice of the risen Jesus can speak of the victory over the world in the past tense because in terms of story time it is only after the events of crucifixion/resurrection/ascension that the victory is accomplished. It is only the Jesus who has made it through to the end of the story who can speak with certainty about the outcome. The fourth evangelist has not constructed his narrative according to the logic of story time, however. Before the story arrives at its conclusion, Jesus already speaks with confidence of its outcome.

We could read 16:33 as a simple prolepsis, a temporal figure that jumps ahead of the time sequence of the main narrative line, but such classification seems inadequate. John 16:33 is more than (or other than) proleptic because it does not anticipate or look ahead to the moment of Jesus' victory. Instead, it announces that *this* is the moment of victory. It does not bring the narrative present into the future, but brings the future into the narrative present. This is different from speaking of the overlap between the future envisioned by Jesus and the present experience of Johannine community (Culpepper:37). A temporal link is established between the narrative and the reader's experience, but it is established by changing the shape of the narrative present, not simply by using the future tense to point to the reader's present.

John 16:33 is the most telling temporal statement in the farewell discourse and the most revealing of the way the farewell discourse holds together narrative form and theological content. The fourth evangelist uses *temporal figures* to evoke *theological reality*. John 16:33 gives narrative embodiment to the realized eschatology that is so characteristic of the Fourth Gospel. It shows how God's new age has entered the present. Jesus' announcement, "I have conquered the world," asserts that the "future" victory is in fact the present reality. Jesus' victory over the world is not to be deferred to a then and there, but is always available in the here and now. This victory colors the whole discourse.[10] The reason that Jesus can speak with such confidence to the disciples about their future is that it is the risen Jesus who speaks, the Jesus who has already conquered the world. John 16:33 makes categories of prolepsis, anticipation, and retrospection essentially non-functional because it establishes its own temporal order. The temporal figures of the farewell discourse convey its central theological conviction: the future is assured because the victory has already been won.

Chap. 17 is a thoroughgoing example of the way in which the new temporal reality announced by the discourse governs the shape of the narrative. The prayer of chap. 17 is both theologically and narratively dependent on the assertion of 16:33. It evokes both the moment of glorification (17:1–5,11) and the aftermath of the glorification, the unity of all believers (17:20–23). All the different threads of the future: the disciples' joy (17:13), the disciples' persecution (17:14–16), and the new life with God (24–26) are brought together in Jesus' prayer at the moment of his glorification. This prayer is the place in the farewell discourse where form coheres with content most intensely. The voice of the risen Jesus (17:12) draws together past, present, and future in one narrative moment. The story of Jesus, the story of his immediate disciples, and the story of disciples still to be are united in this prayer. Jesus places all time into God's care.

The audience of the prayer also contributes to the disclosure of the temporal perspective of the farewell discourse. From 13:31 to 16:30, the disciples have been Jesus' full conversation partners, the recipients of his words, his interlocutors at crucial points. After Jesus' statements of 16:33, however, the disciples disappear from the purview of the narrative. John 17:1 tells the reader explicitly that Jesus no longer addresses the disciples because "he looked up to heaven." Jesus' immediate listeners are reduced to one: God.

Why does Jesus' orientation change at this moment? Why do the disciples, characters in the story, drop out at this point? The discourse concludes with these words spoken by Jesus solely to God in order to reinforce that the future known and assured by Jesus is neither exclusively linked nor limited to those characters present in the narrative setting. The present moment of chap. 17 is the decisive access point to the future for any potential subjects of Jesus' prayer, not just for those disciples who are on the scene. The future of the believing community is not dependent upon the community's temporal location, on whether or not they "heard" Jesus. Rather, it is dependent on the relationship between God and Jesus that is at the heart of this prayer and that transcends and transforms time.

6. THE VOICE OF THE RISEN JESUS AS GUARANTOR OF THE PRESENT

The farewell discourse thus demonstrates through its narrative form what is the overriding theological reality for the community of believers: God and Jesus are not limited by temporal categories. The presence and interaction of God and Jesus are not restricted by conventional notions of past, present, and future, nor is the community's access to that presence bound by time. The farewell discourse glides between present and future in order to show that a new age has begun. The Paraclete, promised by the voice of the risen Jesus, is the guarantor of this new temporal reality.

If the promises of the farewell discourse are the promises of the risen Jesus, grounded in his victory over the world (16:33), sustained by the gift of the Spirit (e.g., 14:26; 16:12–15), why does the fourth evangelist place them where he does in the gospel narrative? Why does the voice of the risen Jesus speak out of time and place? By placing the promises and words of assurance before the Passion narrative, not after, the fourth evangelist emphasizes that these words are part of present reality for the disciples rather than part of some distant future. The risen Jesus speaks to the disciples *before* they suffer—suffer his death, suffer persecution. The words of promise and assurance are available in advance of the moment of crisis. In this way, not only is the disciples' present changed, but their future is also transformed. The voice of the risen Jesus offers them new categories with which to meet their future, categories that promise that the victory over the world is already available, at any given moment.

What is true for the disciples as characters in the story is also true for any and all subsequent readers of the gospel narrative. Before the readers meet their suffering—be that persecution, martyrdom,[11] or whatever struggles the life of faith holds—they, too, have the advance assurance and guaranteed presence of the risen Jesus. They, too, can be confident that the victory over the world has already been won.

The same comfort and hope that is extended to the disciples within the narrative world is thus extended to the readers of the gospel narrative: the disciples hear the voice of the risen Jesus, the readers hear the voice of the risen Jesus. One of the central purposes of the Fourth Gospel is to assure its readers in all future generations that they can have the same experience of Jesus as the characters in the narrative, that their experience of Jesus is not diminished because they are not first generation believers (20:29). The fluidity of movement between present and future in the farewell discourse and the presence of the strong voice of the risen Jesus combine to give the reader of chaps. 13–17 in any generation full access to the presence of Jesus.

NOTES

[1] Culpepper (63) speaks of the "ambiguity of the point which Jesus `goes to the Father.'"

[2] Marcel Proust's novel is available in English under the title *Remembrance of Things Past* (New York: Random House, 1934, 1970).

[3] Culpepper applies all three categories to the Fourth Gospel in his study.

[4] For a discussion of the descent-ascent pattern in the Fourth Gospel, see Nicholson. Nicholson's primary concern is with understanding the death of Jesus through the descent-ascent schema, not with the mixed temporal location from which Jesus speaks of his ascent.

[5] Culpepper (37) identifies the "retrospective statements" of John 17 (vv. 4, 5, 11) as Jesus speaking from "the position of the risen and exalted Lord." Such statements "characterize the significance of Jesus' life." I want to suggest that the voice of the risen Jesus is not restricted to such retrospective statements in the farewell discourse, but is decisive for the entire discourse.

[6] "Temporal omnipresence" is Genette's characterization of Proustian narrative (Genette:41). It also aptly describes the temporal position of Jesus in the farewell discourse.

[7] Sternberg (268) discusses the authority to which a narrator appeals for the outcome of the narrative.

[8] For a discussion of the creation of suspense in biblical narrative, see Sternberg (264-83).

[9] For a discussion of the interrelationship of narrative mode and theological claim in the Fourth Gospel, see O'Day.

[10] Cf. 14:30 and its statements about the power of "the ruler of this world."

[11] Culpepper (68) points in this direction, but concentrates on individual references to persecution (e.g.16:3) rather than the function of the larger discourse. Paul Minear suggests that the Gospel of John is intended as a conversation between the evangelist and a community facing martyrdom.

WORKS CONSULTED

Culpepper, R. Alan
    1983   *Anatomy of the Fourth Gospel*. Philadelphia: Fortress.

Genette, Gérard
    1980   *Narrative Discourse: An Essay in Method*. Trans. Jane E. Lewin. Ithaca: Cornell University Press.

Minear, Paul
    1984   *John: The Martyr's Gospel*. New York: Pilgrim.

Nicholson, Godfrey C.
    1983   *Death as Departure: The Johannine Descent-Ascent Schema*. Chico, Ca: Scholars.

O'Day, Gail R.
    1986   *Revelation in the Fourth Gospel*. Philadelphia: Fortress.

Sternberg, Meir
    1985   *The Poetics of Biblical Narrative: Ideological Literature and the Drama of Reading*. Bloomington: Indiana University Press.

THE FINAL FAREWELL OF JESUS: A READING OF JOHN 20:30—21:25

Fernando F. Segovia
The Divinity School, Vanderbilt University

ABSTRACT

This study advances a literary-rhetorical reading of John 20:30–21:25, the final narrative scene of the Gospel, based on the following methodological criteria: the Gospel as an example of ancient biographical literature; the Gospel's use of the common literary technique of patterns of repetition and recurrence in ancient narrative; and the Gospel's use of a common type-scene, the farewell scene, in ancient narrative. Following generic conventions, the study argues for John 20:30–21:25 as the final scene both within the Gospel's narrative of death and lasting significance (18:1–21:25) and its concluding narrative section, namely, the aftermath of death in the form of resurrection appearances (20:1–21:25); as such, this scene, the fourth and final resurrection appearance of Jesus, is said to be particularly concerned with the lasting significance of the figure of Jesus as the Word of God. Following narrative conventions, the study also argues for John 20:30–21:25 as both a coherent and meaningful narrative scene and an example of a farewell type-scene after death; as such, the scene is said to focus on the lasting significance of Jesus by way of the disciples' own praxis in the world after Jesus' departure to the Father and, in so doing, to reveal a variety of highly interrelated and interdependent strategic functions. The study further provides a brief response of the author as a socially conditioned reader to this final farewell of Jesus in the Gospel.

1. INTRODUCTION

In the scholarly literature on John 21, a twofold focus of attention can be readily discerned: a wide consensus regarding its provenance as a late addition to an already fairly complete and extensive Gospel narrative as well as a further search for its constitutive literary strata in the form of sources and redactions.[1] The present reading of John 20:30–21:25, my own proposed delimitation of this narrative scene, is not at all interested in diachronic concerns, whether with regard to the specific location and role of this scene in a proposed compositional history of the Gospel or with regard to its proposed character as a literary composite. It is not that I rule out in principle the validity or usefulness of such excavative concerns, but rather that I believe the present narrative scene to be quite meaningful and coherent in the Gospel narrative as it presently stands. This reading is interested, therefore, in concerns of a synchronic order: in the narrative scene as it presently stands in the Gospel as well as in its specific location and role within the present Gospel narrative as a whole.

This reading of John 20:30–21:25 is by no means presented as the sole, definitive, and objective reading of this narrative scene but as only one possible reading of it. It is a reading that is variously informed by reader response criticism, liberation theology, and a literary-rhetorical methodology. I shall provide a brief explanation of all three theoretical orientations in the present section and shall then pursue the third, the literary-rhetorical analysis, at greater length in the second section.

a. As argued in the essay on plot, I believe, with pragmatic or reader response criticism (Abrams:3–29; Freund:1–20), the reader to be a very important pole of the reading task, with all readings as perspectival, as a negotiation between text and reader in the construction of meaning. In such a negotiation, once again, the reader becomes as important as the text: while various features of the text (e.g., plot, characters, point of view, narrator, implied audience, literary conventions, sociocultural conventions, rhetorical functions) serve to guide the reader in the process of reading, the very identification, emphasis, and interpretation—both semantic and affective—of the features in question by the reader are influenced by a number of highly complex and interrelated factors (e.g., gender, race or ethnic origins, sociocultural conventions, class, education, religious affiliation and theological position, ideological stance). Consequently, no reading is seen as objective and scientific, and hermeneutical questions become as important as questions of methodology. The present reading is offered, therefore, as but one reading, comprehensive and coherent, of this narrative scene.

b. From such a theoretical perspective, the social location of the reader emerges as not only of enormous interest but also crucial importance. In the present study I shall confine myself almost entirely to a literary-rhetorical reading of the text as such; at the same time, however, I should also like to devote some attention, though limited, to certain aspects of my own social location as reader in the reading of this text, especially from the point of view of my affective response to such a reading.[2] As such, a brief reading of my own social location as reader is in order at this point; I shall focus particularly on ethnic origins and theological stance.

On the one hand, I would describe my social location, from the point of view of ethnic origins, as one of an engaged outsider, as one of the perennially colonized: born and reared in the Third World, in one of the last colonies of a moribund Spanish empire, which then became subject to the political and economic control of two other empires of the Northern hemisphere: first, a rising American empire with a global manifest destiny, and, subsequently, an expansionist Soviet empire with a similarly global socialist destiny; forced to emigrate by political reasons to the most affluent nation of the First World; and now a member of what I refer to as the Fourth World—the children of the colonized Third World who, for one reason or another, have had no choice but to reside in the lands of the colonizing First or Second World. As such, I form part of a group—the Hispanic Americans—whose very origins, language, and culture are considered by the dominant culture as inferior by nature; it is from within such a locus that I read, interpret, and theologize—as if not "of this world" (John 15:19). On the other hand, I would further describe my social location, from the point of view of theological position, as one of liberation: the sustained and explicit uncovering of dehumanizing and oppressive structures; the critical empowerment of my people; and the radical affirmation of all peoples, all languages, all cultures as belonging to and in the Reign of God. From such a stance, I would argue, the Scriptures must be subjected to a critical analysis that I would call intercultural criticism, analyzed as it were in the light of praxis, to sift out what can still be liberating from what can serve to enslave—"a truth that liberates" (John 8:32).

c. From such a theoretical perspective, furthermore, the features of the text that guide the reader in the process of reading must also be directly addressed and analyzed. In fact, the present study will be primarily concerned with what I regard as a beginning stage in intercultural criticism, namely, a literary-rhetorical analysis of John 20:30–21:25. This analysis will deal specifically with the following three methodological criteria: (1) the Fourth Gospel as an example of ancient biography; (2) its use of the common technique of patterns of repetition in ancient narrative; and (3) its further adoption of a common type-scene, the farewell scene, in ancient narrative. At the end, I shall return briefly to what I see as the final stage in such criticism, the critical search for liberation.

2. LITERARY-RHETORICAL METHODOLOGY: FUNDAMENTAL CRITERIA

a. *The Fourth Gospel as Ancient Biographical Narrative.* The first methodological criterion has to do with matters of genre and generic conventions regarding the Fourth Gospel as a whole. As argued in the previous study on plot, I believe that the Fourth Gospel represents an example of ancient biography and, as such, follows the basic conventions of ancient biographical writing (Scholes and Kellogg:210–218; Fairweather:266–75; Cox:45–65; Aune:46–63). In the light of these conventions, the portrayal of

Jesus in the Fourth Gospel may be summarized as follows: (1) all three divisions of the standard structural framework are present, though their precise demarcation is very much open to discussion and interpretation—the Fourth Gospel does have a beginning narrative of origins (1:1–18), a central narrative of the public life or career (1:19–17:26), and a concluding narrative of death and lasting significance (18:1–21:25); (2) a chronological type of development is followed throughout; (3) and the type of the holy man is used and, more specifically, the subtype of the son of god—Jesus as the preexistent Word of God in the world. From such a perspective, therefore, John 20:30–21:25 forms part of the Gospel's narrative of death and lasting significance: the scene portrays the final appearance of Jesus as the risen Word of God. In the next section of this study, I shall pursue in much greater detail the precise location and role of this scene within the concluding narrative of the Gospel.

b. *The Fourth Gospel and Patterns of Recurrence.* The second methodological criterion has to do with matters of literary style and technique. Once again, as argued in the essay on plot, the Fourth Gospel has recourse to a very common literary technique of ancient narrative, namely, the use of patterns of repetition or recurrence at both the macrostructural and microstructural level (Kawin:34–59; Miller:1–21; Alter:88–113), with such patterns ranging from the very small to the very large and encompassing a wide variety of different features; such patterns of recurrence also involve a very important element of variation as well, whereby a significant measure of richness and diversity is introduced in the very midst of recurrence and repetition. In the Fourth Gospel such repetitive patterns are quite prominent and encompass the full range of the spectrum (Mlakuzhyil:87–135). A proper attention to and analysis of such patterns can be of immediate advantage in coming to terms with the literary structure and development of any one narrative division or subdivision. To be sure, John 20:30–21:25 is no exception in this regard: several such patterns can be readily discerned.

c. *The Fourth Gospel and the Farewell Type-Scene.* The third methodological criterion has to do with matters of literary form. One can readily observe in the Fourth Gospel a common convention of ancient narrative: the use of what R. Alter has recently called, with regard to biblical narrative and borrowing traditional terminology from Homeric studies, the "type-scene" (Alter:47–62). One finds in ancient narrative the frequent repetition of more or less the same story with different characters or with the same characters but in different sets of circumstances; a wide number of such recurrent episodes or narrative scenes in the lives of the heroes can be readily identified. Each type-scene follows its own conventions, that is to say, its own fixed number of constitutive and predetermined motifs. However, not all of these motifs need be present in every example of the type-scene, in the same order, to the same extent, or with the same force; in fact, it is the manipulation of these motifs within the different examples of the same type-scene that ultimately accounts for the artistic individuality and uniqueness of each example, for richness and diversity in the very midst of repetition and recurrence.

A common example of a type-scene is that of the testament or farewell of the dying hero, quite prominent in both the Jewish literary tradition, biblical as well as pseudepigraphical, and the wider Greco-Roman literary tradition. Three subtypes may be distinguished within this tradition of the hero's "last words": (1) a final cry or brief saying on the part of the dying hero containing a final summation of his life (Schmidt); (2) a longer farewell before death (Stauffer:29; Munck:156; Kurz:262–63); and (3) a longer farewell after death, that is to say, in the form of an appearance of the hero after death and prior to a final ascent or apotheosis (Stauffer:30; Munck:165; Michel:120). Two observations are in order with respect to the recurrent motifs involved. First of all, there is no significant difference between the motifs of the farewell before death and the farewell after death: the former are simply transferred and applied to the new situation. Secondly, the difference in motifs between the final brief sayings and the longer farewell scenes is simply one of number: while the former contain one or two such motifs, the latter display a multiplicity of these motifs.

Within the longer farewells, both before death and after death, I would also add a formal distinction between the farewell context and the farewell speech or conversation (Segovia). Such a distinction is very useful for purposes of analysis and interpretation; in effect, the context sets the stage for the speech or conversation, the central component of the farewell. As such, I find a further distinction between the recurrent motifs of the farewell context and the recurrent motifs of the farewell speech or conversation proper to be quite useful as well.

The identification of these motifs has ranged from a minimalist perspective (Munck; Cortès), with a very limited number of such motifs by means of deliberately wide categories, to a maximalist perspective (Stauffer; Michel; Kurz), with the selection of a much larger number of recurrent motifs. Such an identification has also been based on either the Jewish literary tradition alone (Munck; Cortès; Michel) or both the Jewish and the Greco-Roman tradition (Stauffer; Kurz). I would argue for a maximalist approach, for as comprehensive a listing as possible, and for a proper grounding of such a listing in both literary traditions, though the two traditions are indeed quite close to one another. At the same time, I would also argue, again from the point of view of analysis and interpretation, that such a comprehensive approach should exhibit a very definite sense of order and avoid too extensive or disjointed a listing (Stauffer; Kurz).

In this regard I find the proposed identification of the farewell motifs by H.-J. Michel to be the most satisfactory. Though quite comprehensive in scope, Michel avoids too disjointed or extensive a listing by bringing together similar farewell motifs under the same category; as a result, a very orderly and controlled classification and arrangement of the motifs is provided. However, given his sole reliance upon the Jewish tradition of the farewell, the proposal must be properly complemented by a corresponding integration of the Greco-Roman tradition, readily provided by the work of E. Stauffer (Kurz). With such an integration, the basic categories outlined remain the same, but the number of motifs encompassed within some of these categories is correspondingly widened. In all, Michel's proposal outlines a series of thirteen categories, of which four have to do with the farewell context and the other nine concern the farewell speech.

1. Of the four categories that have to do with context, only one (c) represents a grouping of similar motifs: (a) the presence of a circle of confidants; (b) a blessing upon those gathered together as a gesture of farewell; (c) other farewell gestures (e.g., a kiss, an embrace, weeping and laments, a meal, a common posture, dialogue); (d) the arrival of death (or final ascent), which need not be portrayed immediately after the speech itself or before the assembled gathering.

2. Of the nine that concern the speech proper, four (b, c, d, g) represent groupings of similar motifs: (a) the announcement of approaching death (or final ascent); (b) parenetical sayings or exhortations (theological overviews of history; the use of figures from the past as models for imitation or examples to be avoided; moral exhortations; words of encouragement and consolation; promises and woes); (c) prophecies or predictions; (d) retrospective accounts of the individual's life and didactic speech; (e) determination of a successor; (f) a prayer; (g) final instructions; (h) instructions concerning burial; (i) promises and vows demanded of the gathering whereby the observance of the preceding exhortations and commands are secured and guaranteed.

In the Fourth Gospel one finds all three subtypes of the "last words": brief final sayings before death, a longer farewell before death, and a longer farewell after death. While the farewell before death consists of one single and quite extensive narrative scene (13:1–17:26; cf. 13:30), the farewell after death involves a lengthy narrative section (20:1–21:25), encompassing a number of different narrative scenes and containing four resurrection appearances in all. From this perspective, therefore, John

20:30–21:25 forms part of Jesus' farewell after death and represents the fourth and final resurrection appearance of Jesus.

3. LITERARY-RHETORICAL ANALYSIS OF JOHN 20:30–21:25

A. The Narrative Context of John 20:30–21:25

In keeping with the threefold structural pattern of the Fourth Gospel as an example of ancient biography, I see John 18:1–21:25 as the Gospel's narrative of death and lasting significance. Within this concluding narrative I would identify five self-contained narrative sections, with all but the first involving several narrative scenes. These five sections follow a linear and progressive development. The first three sections depict the preparatory events for Jesus' death: while the first section portrays Jesus' arrest at the hands of the ruling authorities of Jerusalem (18:1–12), the other two describe his appearance before the ruling authorities in Jerusalem: first, before the Jewish authorities (18:13–27) and, then, before the Roman authorities (18:28–19:16). The last two sections focus on the death itself (19:17–42) and its immediate aftermath, resurrection and resurrection appearances (20:1–21:25).

This last narrative section reveals in a very direct and concrete way the lasting significance of Jesus as the Word of God: in rising from the dead, his mission of revealing the Father is fully and triumphantly accomplished; his status and role vis-à-vis the world and its rulers are vindicated; and a successor is granted to the disciples so that they can proceed to undertake their own assigned role in and to the world. This section also makes for a very unusual narrative of death and lasting significance: though an apotheosis of the hero and appearances after death are by no means unknown in the literature (Fairweather:274–75), resurrection appearances certainly are. This section contains four such appearances in all and through them the fundamental assurance of victory and vindication introduced from the very beginning of the Gospel (1:5) comes true: Jesus has survived death at the hands of his enemies and can now return to the world of God, the world from which he came.

John 20:30–21:25 forms part, therefore, of this final narrative section of John 20:1–21:25 and thus further reveals the lasting significance of the figure of Jesus. I believe that this narrative section consists of three self-contained narrative scenes, each with a number of narrative units: (1) The Empty Tomb and the Appearance of Jesus to Mary Magdalen (20:1–18); (2) The Appearances of Jesus to his Disciples in Jerusalem (20:19–29); and (3) The Appearance of Jesus to his Disciples in Galilee (20:30–21:25). This final narrative section also reveals a linear and progressive development:

the first scene establishes and proclaims the resurrection itself; the second scene begins to bring about the promised change of perception and understanding among the disciples, provides the occasion for the bestowal of Jesus' promised successor, and proceeds to outline the proper and correct role of the disciples in the world; the third scene provides a further development of the proper and correct role of the disciples in the world by focusing on the need for mission and on their relationship with regard to one another, especially those under their guidance or authority.

B. Literary Structure and Development of John 20:31–21:25

I have referred throughout to John 20:31–21:25 as the concluding narrative scene of John 20:1–21:25, the final section of the narrative of death and lasting significance. I would argue for such a proposed delineation of this scene on the following grounds. First of all, I see the preceding narrative scene of John 20:19–29 as a self-contained and coherent literary unit, governed by an overall pattern of inclusion: while the outer components describe two different resurrection appearances of Jesus to a group of disciples, one without and one with Thomas present (20:19–23; 20:26–29), the central component focuses on the figure of Thomas (20:24–25). Secondly, with 20:30–31 one finds a direct address by the narrator to the narratees, the only such address in the Gospel (cf. 19:35), followed by a change in characters as well as a change in time and place.[3] With respect to the characters involved, one now finds, instead of the unidentified group of disciples present in 20:19–25, seven disciples specifically mentioned, though only five are ultimately identified (21:2): Simon Peter; Thomas, "the one called 'the twin'"; Nathanael, "the one from Galilee"; the sons of Zebedee; and two of his disciples. Of these seven only two play a distinctive role in the scene: Simon Peter and the beloved disciple ("the disciple whom Jesus loved"), only introduced as such later on (21:7). On the other hand, with respect to time and place, the scene is now located by the Sea of Tiberias in Galilee (21:1), away from the unidentified room—presumably in Jerusalem—of the preceding scene, and explicitly identified not only as a further appearance of Jesus and thus following upon the earlier appearances but also as the third such appearance to his disciples (21:1, 14). Finally, the scene comes to a close as it began, that is to say, with another comment by the narrator, who now proceeds to embrace and include the narratees themselves within this concluding affirmation of the Gospel (21:24–25).

As such, I consider 20:30–21:25 to be a self-contained and coherent narrative scene of the Gospel. With regard to literary structure and development, I see this scene as consisting of three self-contained units governed by an overall pattern of inclusion: while the outer units contain explicit comments by the narrator (20:30-31; 21:24-25), the central unit portrays the fourth and final resurrection appearance of Jesus (21:1-23). I also see the outer units as arranged in chiastic fashion, in the form of an A B B A pattern: the outer components (20:30; 21:25) contain very similar comments regarding the specific character of Jesus' biography as but a very brief account of the whole of his mission and ministry; the inner components (20:31; 21:26) not only proceed to outline the fundamental purpose (20:31) and origins of such a biographical account (21:24), but also deal directly with the narratees. The proposed structure may be readily outlined as follows: (1) The Character and Purpose of Jesus' Biography (20:30-31); (2) The Final Farewell of Jesus (21:1-23); (3) The Origins and Character of Jesus' Biography (21:24-25).

1. The Character and Purpose of Jesus' Biography (20:30-31)

The first narrative unit is quite brief and consists of a direct address by the narrator to the narratees; again, the unit begins with a description of the very character of the biographical account itself (20:30) and then proceeds to a formulation of its fundamental purpose (20:31).

First of all, following immediately upon the blessing pronounced by Jesus on all those who do not see and yet believe in him (20:29), the narrator specifies that Jesus performed many other "signs" in the presence of his disciples which are not included in "this book," in this biographical account of Jesus' life (20:30). In so doing, the narrator not only establishes the fact that "the book" itself represents but a minor part of Jesus' mission and ministry as a whole, but also affirms the greatness of that mission and ministry and hence of Jesus himself—in other words, much more could be included and narrated, given all that he did. Secondly, the narrator proceeds to give the fundamental purpose for what has been selected and provided in the Gospel (20:31). This purpose is presented as twofold: belief in Jesus as the Christ and Son of God; "life" in his name as believers in Jesus, as disciples of Jesus. Only in Jesus, therefore, is there "life" (14:6, 19)—and this Jesus is far greater than depicted in the preceding narrative.

With 20:30-31, therefore, the narrator reinforces the blessing of 20:29 by exhorting and enticing the narratees to believe in Jesus, without seeing and on the basis of the biographical account itself, by claiming that only in Jesus can they ultimately find "life" in this world and indeed a "life" that surpasses anything described in these pages. With 20:30-31, furthermore, the narrator proceeds to introduce one more "sign," the final sign, of Jesus in the presence of his disciples.

2. The Final Farewell of Jesus (21:1-23)

The central narrative unit is quite extensive and describes the last "sign," the final resurrection appearance, of Jesus; two major sections can be readily distinguished in terms of the characters involved: the first section, somewhat longer than the second, deals with the group of disciples as a whole, though both Simon Peter and the beloved disciple play a distinctive role in it (21:1-14); the second section focuses specifically on these two disciples, Simon Peter and the beloved disciple (21:15-23). While no change in location is registered between the two sections (cf. 21:20), a change in time is briefly noted: "after they had eaten" (21:15).

a. Jesus and the Disciples (21:1-14)

The first major section is demarcated by an inclusion specifying the timing of the appearance: an introductory statement (21:1) describes the timing in rather general terms, along with the location of the appearance and an introduction to the appearance itself—"After these things Jesus showed himself again to the disciples by the Sea of Tiberias, and he showed himself in this way"; a concluding statement (21:14) provides a more specific timing in terms of the number of appearances to the disciples, bypassing therefore the initial one to Mary Magdalen—"This was the third time that Jesus showed himself to the disciples after his resurrection from the dead."

The section follows an overall pattern of inclusion: while its outer components (21:1-3; 21:6d-14) deal with the fishing of the disciples and its aftermath, the central component contains Jesus' specific instructions concerning such fishing (21:4-6c). The section also consists of two literary forms, a miracle story and a meal story, with the latter functioning as a direct expansion of the former. Though both Simon Peter and the beloved disciple play a distinctive role in this first section, that of Peter is much more prominent and active than that of the beloved disciple.

1. The first subsection is quite brief (21:1-3). After the introductory statement of 21:1, the subsection further identifies the characters involved (21:2)—the seven disciples of Jesus—and describes the setting for the miracle story that follows in a series of short, undeveloped statements (21:3). The narrator swiftly records an exchange between Simon Peter and the other disciples, initiated by Peter, in which a decision to go fishing is made (21:3a-d); describes their boarding of a boat for this purpose (21:3e); and establishes their failure to catch any fish that night (21:3f). The setting is thus quite terse and to the point.

2. The second subsection is also quite brief (21:4-6). The subsection contains the miracle proper: after introducing the figure of Jesus (21:4), a twofold interchange between Jesus and the disciples in the boat, initiated

by Jesus, is recorded (21:5–6). The narrator suddenly introduces the figure of Jesus, specifically noting the timing of the appearance ("at daybreak"), its location ("on the shore"), and the frame of mind of the disciples on the boat ("no recognition of Jesus"). Then, the twofold interchange is described: the first exchange (21:5), consisting of a brief question and a brief response, establishes once again the failure of the disciples to catch any fish, setting the stage thereby for the second exchange; the second exchange (21:6), consisting of a command by Jesus and a notice of its fulfillment by the disciples, records the miracle proper (21:6): upon casting the net on the right side of the boat, as instructed, the disciples now catch so many fish that they are unable to haul in the net. As with the setting, the miracle proper is also quite terse and to the point.

3. The third subsection is much more extensive (21:7–14). The subsection not only provides the reaction of the disciples to the miraculous catch of fish (21:7–8) but also extends the miracle story by means of a meal story (21:9–13), in itself bearing a certain miraculous dimension as well, with a concluding statement to the section as a whole (21:14).

The narrator begins by describing the different reactions of the various disciples in question (21:7–8): (a) first of all, the "disciple whom Jesus loved" is introduced as one of the seven disciples on the boat: on the basis of the miraculous catch, he is the first to identify the figure on the shore as Jesus ("It is the Lord!"; cf. 20:9), which knowledge he readily shares with Peter (21:7a–b); (b) as a result, Peter is described as immediately abandoning the boat and the others and plunging into the water, clearly in order to meet Jesus on the shore (21:7c–e); (c) finally, the others—including the beloved disciple himself—are portrayed as remaining in the boat, heading for shore with the net full of fish (21:8). With mention of "the land" in 21:8, along with the distance between the boat and shore, the miracle story comes to an end: not only is there a return to "the shore" of 21:4, but also the very possibility of the intervening dialogue is ultimately explained—the boat was not far from the shore.

The narrator then continues by presenting the expected and climactic meeting on the shore quite unexpectedly in terms of a meal (21:9–13), without any reference to Peter and without any greeting whatsoever (cf. 20:19, 26); this meal provides an expansion of the beginning miracle story which extends right into the next major section as well.

First of all, Jesus is described, through the eyes of the disciples who now arrive at the shore, as having already prepared some food, some fish and bread, for the disciples (21:9).[4] Secondly, a twofold interchange between Jesus and the disciples is recounted (21:10–12). The first exchange, consisting of a request by Jesus and a notice of its fulfillment by the disciples, reintroduces the figure of Peter (21:10–11): when the disciples are asked by Jesus to bring some of their own fish for the meal, Peter is portrayed as going aboard the boat and hauling the net ashore by himself, the very same net that the group had been unable to haul into the boat after the catch. In fact, both the miraculous nature of the catch and the weight of the net are further emphasized by explicit reference to the kind of fish caught ("large fish"), their exact number ("one hundred and fifty-three"), and the condition of the net ("not torn"). The second exchange, consisting of a further request by Jesus with no response, sets the stage for the meal by way of an invitation on the part of Jesus (21:12). The narrator, returning to the previous observation of 21:4b, proceeds to describe the disciples' frame of mind at this point: there was no need for the disciples to ask concerning the identity of Jesus, since, in keeping with the previous identification of the beloved disciple, they now knew that it was indeed the Lord. With the miraculous catch and the meal, therefore, there is a progression from a failure to identify Jesus to a full recognition of him. Finally, the meal itself is briefly described (21:13): Jesus is portrayed as taking first the bread and then the fish and giving it to the disciples (cf. 6:11).

This first major section may be read from a variety of different though interrelated perspectives:

1. The section provides yet a further appearance of Jesus leading to a further recognition of Jesus by the disciples as the risen Lord. As in the first appearance (cf. 20:19–20), recognition is not immediate, despite the previous appearances of Jesus and the present address of "little children" (21:5; cf. 13:33); such failure to recognize Jesus at this point is apparently due to the distance of the boat from the shore. Recognition now takes place on the basis of a miraculous deed (cf. 2:1–11), and such recognition is formulated specifically in terms of the first part of Thomas' confession in 20:26–29: It is the Lord!

2. The section also places such an appearance within the framework of a common metaphorical contrast of the Gospel, light and darkness, thereby returning at the very end of the Gospel to its very beginnings, to the narrative of origins itself (1:1–18; cf. 1:4–5, 6–9): the night of fishing is immediately followed by an encounter with Jesus at the break of light (cf. 20:1). As such, the episode immediately takes on a highly symbolic dimension: with the break of light and the appearance of Jesus, the failure of the night before is radically reversed—from no fish at all to an enormous catch. In other words, the section pointedly teaches that it is only with Jesus that the disciples can prosper and succeed (cf. 15:4–5).

3. The section further pursues the proper and correct role of the disciples in the world, especially with regard to their assigned mission in and to the world—formally disclosed, inaugurated, and empowered in

the first appearance (20:21–23) and then further addressed by means of the Thomas episode and the second resurrection appearance (20:29). This role is addressed in two ways. First of all, if the "fishing" is taken as literal, then the section ironically portrays the disciples as being in the safety of Galilee and as going fishing on their own, ignoring thereby Jesus' command of mission in and to the world. Secondly, if the "fishing" is taken as metaphorical, with reference to the mission itself, then the section also shows that the disciples can have no success whatever aside from Jesus. As such, the section makes it very clear that the disciples must carry out their assigned role in and to the world and that they must do so under the guidance and direction of Jesus himself.

4. The section introduces as well a meal between Jesus and his disciples, not unlike that of 6:1–15, in which the disciples themselves played a prominent role (6:4–10, 12–13). Thus, for example, this meal also takes place in Galilee (6:1); involves bread and fish (6:11); reveals a very definite miraculous dimension—preceded as it is by the miraculous catch of fish and involving a seemingly miraculous preparation on the part of Jesus (6:11–13); entails a confession of Jesus—a full recognition of Jesus as Lord (cf. 6:14–15); and reveals a certain missionary dimension as well—in and through the "fishing" of the disciples (6:2–5). With this meal, therefore, the recognition of Jesus as Lord, again following the previous confession of Thomas, is repeated and confirmed.

5. Finally, the section sets the stage for the second section that follows in a number of rather concrete ways: (a) a certain contrast between the beloved disciple and Peter is introduced; (b) Peter's actions—his plunging into the water and his dragging of the net ashore—reveal a certain disregard for the other disciples in the course of his own devotion to and following of Jesus; (c) the meal itself provides a literal example of a "feeding/tending" of the "sheep/lambs" on the part of Jesus.

b. *Jesus and the Two Disciples: Peter and the Beloved Disciple (21:15–23)*

The second major section provides a further expansion of the meal story introduced in 21:9–14. The section focuses specifically on the two disciples that play a distinctive role in the first section: Simon Peter and the beloved disciple. As in the first section, the role of the beloved disciple is less prominent and even less active than that of Peter, insofar as he is mentioned only by way of Peter. The section again follows an overall pattern of inclusion: while the outer components deal with the envisioned "following" of each disciple in question (21:15–19; 21:22–23), the central component brings the two disciples together by means of their present "following" of Jesus (21:20–21).

1. The first subsection is the most extensive (21:15–19). The meal, now concluded, is expanded by means of an extended dialogue between Jesus and Simon Peter; the dialogue itself has two parts: an initial questioning of Peter (21:15–17) followed by a concluding declaration on the part of Jesus (21:18–19). The interchange is initiated and led throughout by Jesus.

The initial questioning (21:15–17) consists of a threefold repetition of three components: the same question by Jesus, the same response by Peter, and the same instruction by Jesus; to be sure, such repetition also contains considerable stylistic and strategic variations as well. The first component addresses the question of love on the part of Peter for Jesus. One strategic variation should be noted: the comparative of the first question—"do you love me 'more than these'?"—is dropped from the other two questions. The middle component repeats the affirmative response of Peter, phrased throughout in terms of Jesus' own knowledge of Peter's love for him. Again, one strategic variation should be noted, at the end rather than at the beginning. This variation is introduced by a comment from the narrator explaining Peter's frame of mind at this point: sorrow at such a repeated questioning by Jesus. Then, the variation takes place: the affirmative response is preceded and strengthened by a declaration regarding the very nature and scope of Jesus' knowledge—"Lord, you know all things." The final component provides a definition of the first component, of the meaning and consequences of love for Jesus—"feed/tend my sheep/lambs."[5]

The concluding declaration (21:18–19) is twofold, consisting of a prediction regarding Peter's fate as a disciple of Jesus (21:18) and an exhortation "to follow" him regardless of the consequences involved, as foreseen in the prediction (21:19b). A comment by the narrator (21:19a) interrupts the declaration in order to provide a proper and correct interpretation of its first part: the given contrast between "young"/"old," "girding oneself—walking where one wills"/"stretching one's hands—being girded—being taken where one wills not" refers not only to Peter's death but also to his mode of death, given the specific introduction of the one element without parallel, "the stretching of the hands," which I take to serve as a metaphorical description of such a death.

This first subsection, therefore, defines love for Jesus in terms of praxis by way of a metaphor: there is no love for Jesus apart from the "feeding/tending" of the "sheep/lambs," thereby indirectly conferring upon Peter the role of "shepherd." Moreover, such a role, such love for Jesus, is further described as ultimately entailing for Peter death itself (10:11–17)—this is, in fact, the nature of his "greater" love. The subsection ends with an exhortation to Peter "to follow" Jesus, to love Jesus and to serve as "shepherd," despite the inevitable consequences involved.

Though specifically addressed to Peter and serving as a direct counterpart to his earlier threefold denial of Jesus (13:36–38; 19:25–27), I see the dialogue as encompassing all other disciples as well, above all those exercising a certain amount of responsibility within the community itself: to love Jesus means to function as a "shepherd"; to function as a "shepherd" means to care for "the sheep/lambs"; to care for the "sheep/lambs" may lead to death itself.

2. The second subsection is quite brief (21:20). The subsection seemingly opens with a change of place, a movement away from the meal, thus providing a physical or literal enactment of the exhortation "to follow" Jesus. This change of place sets the stage for the reintroduction of the beloved disciple: as Peter "follows" Jesus, he turns and sees the beloved disciple—explicitly identified in terms of his role at the earlier farewell meal (13:21–30)—"following" as well (cf. 1:35–42). Such a "following" sets the stage in turn for the final subsection concerning the fate of the beloved disciple.

3. The third subsection is also quite brief, consisting of an exchange between Jesus and Peter, now initiated by Peter himself (21:21–23). With the observed "following" of the beloved disciple, Peter raises the question of the fate of this disciple, of such a "following" of Jesus on his part (21:21). Jesus' response (21:22), formulated in terms of a question, not only bypasses the question altogether but also provides a critique of it. In effect, Peter is told that the fate of the beloved disciple, the nature of his "following," is of no concern to him; his only concern should be that of his own "following" of Jesus regardless of the consequences involved. That Peter's question has to do with the ultimate consequences of such "following"—the death of the disciple—is clear from the very formulation of Jesus' response: it is of no concern whatsoever to Peter if the beloved disciple should "abide" until his return—a reference to a final coming of Jesus—that is to say, if the beloved disciple does not lose his life in his own role as "shepherd."

As in the previous declaration concerning the fate of Peter, the narrator once more intervenes in order to provide a proper and correct interpretation of this further declaration of Jesus concerning the fate of the beloved disciple, though now by way of a direct response to a very different and widespread interpretation of this saying: whereas "the brethren" took the saying to mean that the beloved disciple would not encounter death, the narrator corrects such an interpretation by emphasizing the exact wording of the saying and its conditional formulation—Jesus did not say, "he will not die," but rather, "if I wish that he abide until I return." Such a comment seems to point—though this is not altogether clear—to an unexpected and perhaps recent death of the beloved disciple himself.[6]

This second major section provides a further development of a number of issues raised in the first major section:

1. First of all, the section continues with the contrast between Peter and the beloved disciple. This contrast is now pursued in terms of their respective "following" of Jesus and the ultimate consequences of such "following": while that of Peter entails death, that of the beloved disciple seems to imply an abiding until the return of Jesus, and the difference is said to be of no concern to Peter whatsoever. Quite ironically, to be sure, this contrast is only apparent in nature: in the end such a presumed difference is characterized as incorrect and attributed to a widespread misunderstanding on the part of the disciples—the "following" of the beloved disciple ultimately entails death as well. As such, the apparent contrast is used to specify that the "following" of Jesus may demand death of some but not of others and that such a difference in "following" is of no concern to the disciples.

2. The section also addresses the previous disregard of Peter for the other disciples in the course of his own devotion to Jesus. In fact, the section now specifies that a confession in Jesus as Lord entails a love for Jesus which involves acting as a "shepherd" with regard to the other members of the community, caring for them—and especially for those under their authority—to the point of death if necessary. In so doing, such teaching repeats and reinforces the farewell instruction of Jesus before death, the one preeminent and distinguishing command of Jesus: to love one another as he had loved them (cf. 13:34–35; 15:9–17).

3. Finally, the section returns to the meal of the first section as an example or pattern for such "shepherding" and love on the part of the disciples: through this final meal on the shore, Jesus in effect proceeds to "feed/tend" his own "sheep/lambs," his own "little children." As a result, the disciples are once again asked to do unto others what Jesus himself has done unto them, including death for one another if need be.

Concluding Comments. With 21:1–23, therefore, the narrator proceeds to describe a final "sign" of Jesus in the presence of his disciples. This sign specifies in a very concrete and direct way that belief in Jesus as the Christ and Son of God (20:30–31), as the risen Lord (20:28), entails a love for Jesus on the part of those who believe in him which demands a very specific role in the world—a role involving an active mission to the world and a "shepherding" of the disciples of Jesus to the point of death if necessary; without such love for Jesus, the sign further specifies, there can be no "life" in his name. With 21:1–23, furthermore, the narrator sets the stage for a final comment regarding all such "signs" of Jesus narrated in the Gospel.

3. The Origins and Character of Jesus' Biography (21:24–25)

The third narrative unit, like the first, is quite brief and consists of another direct comment by the narrator. Again, the same two components of the first unit may be discerned, though now in inverse order and no longer in the form of direct address to the narratees. The unit begins, therefore, with a description of the origins of the biographical account (21:24) and then proceeds to a further description of its very character as a biographical account (21:25).

First of all, following immediately upon the final "sign" of Jesus of 21:1–23 and the appearance of the beloved disciple in the course of this sign, the narrator begins by identifying this disciple as the one who not only has given "witness" concerning "these things"—all of the narrated "signs" of Jesus—but has consigned them to writing, that is to say, as the source for and author of the biographical account itself (21:24a). The narrator, now speaking corporately in the first person plural (cf. 1:14, 16), proceeds to emphasize the character of this "witness" given by the beloved disciple as "true" (21:24b); in so doing, I would argue, the narrator deliberately draws into the circle of believers for a final and joint affirmation the very narratees who were addressed directly in the first major section—"'we' know that his witness is true."

Secondly, the narrator concludes by specifying, once again, that what is written in this biographical account represents but a minor part of all that Jesus did during his entire mission and ministry (21:25). In fact, this relationship of the written account to the actual life of Jesus is now further intensified by means of hyperbole: Jesus did so "many other things" in the course of his mission and ministry that, if consigned to writing, the world itself could not contain "the books" that would be written. In so doing, moreover, the narrator again affirms the greatness of that mission and ministry and hence the greatness of Jesus himself—given all that he did, much more could be included and narrated.

With 21:24–25, therefore, the narrator highlights the figure of the beloved disciple from the central unit: not only is he the source and author of the biographical account itself, but his "witness" concerning Jesus is "true," as all believers, now including the narratees themselves, readily acknowledge. With 21:24–25, furthermore, the narrator returns to the first unit of 20:30–31, further exhorting and enticing the narratees by claiming that all that is written in "this book"—all of Jesus' "signs"—is "true," thereby leading to "life" all those who believe in Jesus and love Jesus, all those who accept its "witness."

4. Strategic Concerns and Aims of John 20:30–21:25

The preceding literary-rhetorical analysis of John 20:30–21:25 shows that this final narrative scene can indeed be seen as a self-contained artistic whole, highly unified and carefully developed from beginning to end. I believe that this narrative scene can also be seen as a unified strategic whole, with very clear concerns and aims at work through the very use and deployment of such a literary structure and development. First of all, such concerns have to do with the final event of Jesus' mission and ministry and involve a specific focus on the proper and correct role of the disciples in the world after his return to the Father. Secondly, such concerns are guided and informed by a number of interrelated and interdependent aims, yielding a variety of strategic functions for the section as a whole: didactic and exhortative as primary; admonitory, consolatory, and polemical as secondary or subordinate.

The didactic and exhortative functions readily emerge as primary. On the one hand, the disciples receive further teaching, directly and indirectly: the need for mission in and to the world; the message that without Jesus nothing is possible; love for Jesus or "following" Jesus as entailing a "shepherding" of Jesus' disciples, with loss of life as a possibility; a correction of a widespread belief concerning the ultimate fate of the beloved disciple. On the other hand, the disciples are also urged to follow Jesus regardless of consequences and without concern for the following of others. Such functions may also be observed at work with regard to the narratees: on the one hand, there is teaching concerning the purpose, origins, and nature of the biographical account itself; on the other hand, there is a clear call to believe in Jesus. The admonitory, consolatory, and polemical functions clearly emerge as secondary: first of all, the disciples are warned that without Jesus they can do nothing; secondly, they are reassured that with Jesus all is possible; thirdly, the fishing of the disciples in the safety of Galilee and the very possibility of death in the "following" of Jesus indicate a sharp differentiation from the world at large involving opposition and conflict.

The specific character of this unit as a strategic whole points to a twofold rhetorical situation or view of the implied readers (and narratees) by the implied author (and narrator). On the one hand, the disciples are viewed in a very positive light: their status as disciples of Jesus—as the "little children" who fully recognize Jesus as the risen Lord—is acknowledged and reaffirmed; their status in the world is also set off against an unbelieving and hostile world. On the other hand, the disciples are also viewed as under duress and in need of further teaching and exhortation regarding their proper and correct role vis-à-vis the world and vis-à-vis one another as disciples of Jesus: to proceed with their appointed mission to the world; to care for the other disciples, particularly those under their guidance and authority, as "shepherds." Such a rhetorical situation points to a community which, while basically firm and united, is seen as grappling with the fundamental consequences of belief in Jesus and love for Jesus, with the way of discipleship in the world, in the light of highly unfavorable circumstances. The message from the implied author, therefore, is primarily one of teaching and exhortation: believe in the Lord, carry forth his mission, and care for his disciples regardless of consequences.

C. John 20:30–21:25 as the Final Farewell of Jesus

To begin with, the direct comments by the narrator that form the framing units for this narrative section (20:30-31; 21:24-25) do not form part of the farewell type-scene as such. Such comments, having to do with the biographical account as a whole and addressing the narratees as such, are meant to signal the conclusion to the entire Gospel narrative. In so doing, however, these comments do place special emphasis on the enclosed resurrection appearance of Jesus (21:1-23) as his final farewell to the disciples prior to his final ascent to the Father and his full glorification or apotheosis with the Father (17:1-5)—after a long farewell before death, farewell words at the scene of death, and three resurrection appearances in the farewell after death. Within this final farewell appearance, I see the first major section as providing the farewell context (21:1-14) and the second major section as containing the farewell conversation (21:15-23).

1. John 21:1-14 as Farewell Context

Of the four recurrent motifs proper to the farewell context, only two are present in this appearance: (a) the presence of a circle of confidants—in effect, a rather small circle of seven disciples; and (b) common farewell gestures—as in the case of the farewell before death, one finds not only the context of a meal but also the use of dialogue between the hero and the assembled confidants.

One also finds, however, a rather unique feature for a farewell context: the inclusion of a miracle story involving a miraculous catch of fish. This miracle story fulfills several aims: it serves to identify the figure on the shore as that of Jesus, their risen Lord; it sets the stage for their final farewell conversation; and it introduces a number of other farewell motifs as well, to be more fully developed in the farewell conversation: (a) the question of succession—the figures of Peter and the beloved disciple and their different reactions to the appearance of Jesus; (b) didactic speech: the need for mission to the world; the centrality of Jesus—whereas aside from

Jesus they can do nothing, with Jesus all is possible; and the life of the hero as an example—Jesus' own "feeding/tending" of the disciples.

2. John 21:15–23 as Farewell Conversation

Of the nine recurrent motifs proper to the farewell speech or conversation, five are present here: (a) parenetical sayings or exhortations; (b) prophecies or predictions; (c) teaching; (d) question of succession; (e) final instructions.

First of all, one finds a moral exhortation: a call to Peter—and through Peter to all the other disciples as well (21:20)—to follow Jesus, regardless of consequences. Secondly, one also finds a prediction with regard to Peter, not only concerning his death but also the very manner of his death ("the stretching out of the hands"). Thirdly, one also finds didactic speech: (a) a definition of love for Jesus in terms of "feeding/tending" the "sheep/lambs," thereby bringing to the fore a motif already introduced within the context itself—the disciples are to do unto others as Jesus has done unto them; (b) a proper interpretation of two sayings of Jesus, one with reference to Peter and one with reference to the beloved disciple. Fourthly, the question of succession, already introduced within the context itself, is now brought to the fore as well: the "following" of both disciples ultimately entails death. Finally, a parting instruction is included: the disciples are to "feed/tend" the "sheep/lambs."

This final appearance of Jesus contains, therefore, a solid nucleus of farewell motifs, both with regard to context and conversation. The most important of these, as their threefold repetition itself indicates, are those of teaching and final instruction: the definition of love for Jesus or "following" Jesus in terms of "shepherding" the disciples of Jesus, to the point of death if need be. In fact, the issue of succession is ultimately not as important as that of "following"—the disciple must be ready "to follow" Jesus in whatever path is required, regardless of the consequences involved and without concern for the "following" of others.

The major thrust and role of this final farewell appearance is quite clear. This final farewell proceeds to specify much more concretely the proper and correct role of the disciples in the world: a fulfillment of the command to go into the world and a "following" of Jesus which is patterned after and grounded in Jesus' own role with regard to them—a "feeding/tending" of the "sheep/lambs" of Jesus that demands total service, even death itself. As such, this last narrative scene brings the entire narrative of death and lasting significance as well as the biographical account of Jesus as a whole to a close by showing in a very concrete way that the lasting significance of Jesus' mission, ministry, and death lies in the very praxis of the community itself, in their own mission to the world and relationship to one another, in their own love for one another as Jesus himself had loved them.

4. CONCLUSION: A BEGINNING EXERCISE IN INTERCULTURAL CRITICISM

As mentioned in the introductory section, I will limit my remarks concerning the complex relationship between interpretation and social location to my own affective response as reader of this text to the text as an artistic and strategic whole, that is to say, to my own critical appropriation of this text as an engaged outsider in the search for liberation. In so doing, I will limit my remarks as well to the primary didactic and exhortative functions of the text by way of the praxis enjoined upon the disciples as disciples of Jesus, namely their missionary task and relationship to one another whereby the lasting significance of Jesus as the Word of God continues to be present in and conveyed to the world. In fact, I will limit my remarks to the very prominent metaphor of "shepherding" used with regard to such praxis in the course of the threefold instruction of Jesus to "feed/tend the sheep/lambs."

On the one hand, the use of this metaphor does encompass, as the subsequent instruction of 21:18–19 makes very clear (cf. 10:11–17), the very possibility of death in the exercise of such "feeding or tending": if need be, the disciple must give up his or her life for others, especially those under his or her guidance and authority, in the following of Jesus. On the other hand, the use of this metaphor also introduces in and of itself a very definite measure of élitism and subservience in community relations: the shepherd leads, tends, and feeds; the sheep follow and obey.

From the point of view of both a Third and Fourth World Christian, I would argue that the latter dimension of this metaphor—its inherent element of élitism and subservience—has in fact dominated the relationship between the First and the Third and Fourth Worlds, between the colonizing and missionary church and the colonized or mission church: "truth" as carried out to the confines of the earth by the North Atlantic civilizations so that the poor "savages," "primitives," and "immigrants" might be "enlightened" and "saved"—by force if necessary, for their own good. I would further argue that the former dimension of the metaphor—the service unto death—has applied for the most part to the "sheep/lambs" rather than the "shepherds," as the widespread silence and cooperation of the churches in the face of the enslavement of millions of the black peoples of Africa, the decimation of millions of the indigenous peoples of the Americas, and the long period of colonial exploitation and suppression readily testify. This situation, furthermore, still continues, both in the Third World and in the Fourth World, with continued silence and cooperation in the face of an "enslavement," a "decimation," an "exploitation," and a "suppression" now carried out for the most part at the cultural, political, and economic level rather than at a physical level as such.

I see this metaphor of shepherding as highly dangerous, therefore, given its reception and application in history, and perhaps best put aside: for many it has not been and is not a source of freedom and liberation, but of enslavement and oppression, paternalism and condescension. Yet, there is a dimension to it that cannot be surrendered but must be translated into or conveyed by means of a more adequate metaphor: Christian discipleship—the "following" of Jesus—as implying and entailing total service unto others to the point of death, especially on the part of those who hold positions of authority. That I do find most liberating, indeed at the very heart of John 20:30–21:25 and of the Fourth Gospel as a whole.

NOTES

[1] For a general overview of recent contributions to these two foci, see Neirynck.

[2] All I wish to do at this point is to broach the question regarding the very complex relationship between interpretation and social location. Again, as I point out in the essay on plot, this is a project which I intend to pursue in a much more systematic and comprehensive fashion in the future.

[3] I am using the term "narratees" here to mean the audience of the narrator as inscribed in the text, which in this case is not represented as a character (Prince:56; Baldick:145). As such, it is to be distinguished from the "implied reader," the audience of the implied author, which is inferable from the entire text. In the case of 19:35, one finds a much more indirect reference to the narratees: the narrator provides an insight into the mind of the one male disciple at the scene of the crucifixion, the disciple whom Jesus loved (19:25-27), disclosing thereby the very purpose behind the witness of this disciple to the events at the crucifixion, namely, "that you may believe." To be sure, this is is the same purpose identified by the narrator for the biographical narrative as a whole in 20:30-31 as well as the same disciple later identified by the narrator as the source for and author of the biographical narrative itself in 21:24-25.

[4] The character of this meal is ambiguous. It is not clear whether its preparation—the securing of the bread and the fish by the risen Jesus—should be seen as a miraculous deed in and of itself. I favor such a reading: the meal itself is not only introduced by a miracle story but also has a miraculous grounding or dimension to it.

[5] The variation here is strictly stylistic or terminological in character: two different terms are used for both the object of the shepherding ("sheep" and "lambs") and the activity of the shepherd ("feed" and "tend"); moreover, these terms are intermixed throughout.

[6] If such a death is indeed presupposed and in view, its cause—whether as a result of natural causes or of the Christian mission—is simply beyond resolution. In any case, the main point is that the specific "following" required of any one disciple should be of no interest or concern to the others.

WORKS CONSULTED

Abrams, M. H.
    1953   *The Mirror and the Lamp: Romantic Theory and the Critical Tradition*. London-Oxford-New York: Oxford University Press.

Alter, Robert.
    1981   *The Art of Biblical Narrative*. New York: Basic Books.

Aune, David E.
    1987   *The New Testament in Its Literary Environment*. Library of Early Christianity. Philadelphia: Westminster.

Baldick, Chris.
    1990   *The Concise Oxford Dictionary of Literary Terms*. Oxford and New York: Oxford University Press.

Cortès, Enric.
    1976   *Los discursos de adiós de Gn 49 a Jn 13–17. Pistas para la historia de un género literario en la antigua literatura judía*. Colectánea San Paciano 23. Barcelona: Herder.

Cox, Patricia
    1983   *Biography in Late Antiquity: A Quest for the Holy Man*. Berkeley-Los Angeles-London: University of California Press.

Fairweather, J.
    1974   "Fiction in the Biographies of Ancient Writers." *Ancient Society* 5:231–275.

Freund, Elizabeth.
    1987   *The Return of the Reader: Reader-Response Criticism*. New Accents. London and New York: Methuen.

Kawin, B. F.
    1972   *Telling It Again and Again: Repetition in Film and Literature*. Ithaca, N.Y.: Cornell University Press.

Kurz, William J.
    1985   "Luke 22:14–38 and Greco-Roman and Biblical Farewell Addresses." *JBL* 104:251–68.

Michel, H.-J.
    1973   *Die Abschiedsrede des Paulus an die Kirche, Apg. 20,17–38. Motivgeschichte und theologische Bedeutung*. Studien zum Alten und Neuen Testament 35. Munich: Kösel-Verlag.

Miller, J. Hillis.
    1982   *Fiction and Repetition: Seven English Novels.* Cambridge: Cambridge University Press.

Mlakuzhyil, G.
    1987   *The Christocentric Literary Structure of the Fourth Gospel.* Analecta Biblica 117. Rome: Pontifical Biblical Institute.

Munck, Johannes.
    1950   "Discours d'adieu dans le Nouveau Testament et dans la littérature biblique." Pp. 155–70 in *Aux sources de la tradition chrétienne: Mélanges offerts à M. Maurice Goguel.* Bibliothèque théologique. Neuchâtel and Paris: Delachaux & Niestlé.

Neirynck, Frans.
    1990   "John 21." *New Testament Studies* 36:321–36.

Prince, Gerald.
    1987   *A Dictionary of Narratology.* Lincoln and London: University of Nebraska Press.

Schmidt, W.
    1914   *De ultimis morientium verbis.* Marburg: Chr. Schaaf.

Scholes, Robert and Robert Kellogg.
    1966   *The Nature of Narrative.* London-Oxford-New York: Oxford University Press.

Segovia, F. F.
    (1991)   *The Farewell of the Word: A Johannine Call to Abide.* Minneapolis: Fortress Press (forthcoming).

Stauffer, E.
    1950   "Abschiedsreden." *RAC* 1:29–35.

RESPONSE FROM A EUROPEAN PERSPECTIVE

Johannes Beutler
Philosophisch-Theologische Hochschule
Sankt Georgen

It is a privilege for me to respond to the papers submitted to *Semeia* 53. International scholarship in Johannine studies can profit considerably by the eight contributions collected in this remarkable volume. It is the genuine expression of a new branch of international criticism of the New Testament, which originated predominantly in the United States of America. So I see my own contribution as a token of dialogue across the Atlantic, based on personal acquaintance with more than one of its distinguished contributors. I should like to structure my response in three sections: (1) Method and Hermeneutics; (2) History; (3) Theology.

1. METHOD AND HERMENEUTICS

1.1 *Method*

1.1.1 The Synchronic Approach

There is no doubt that the shift from diachronic to synchronic methods of interpretation has contributed considerably to our insight into New Testament texts. It is the last consequence of a development which started with redaction and composition criticism in the mid-fifties and which led progressively to an analysis of New Testament texts in their own right. A decisive step was the discovery that even texts which have been incorporated into a new document become fully part of their new context. So the intentions of the author cannot be identified only by way of a substraction of his or her "additions" to the traditions received or the recognizable "alterations" of a *Vorlage*, but by the complete work as it stands today. It has become and is now his/her text, literary work, and can be studied as such.

There is, however, a crucial point in the attempt to describe a New Testament text in merely synchronic terms. Insofar as the contributions of this volume confess themselves committed to a "rhetorical approach" to the Gospels (see below, 1.1.3), they also have recourse to the use of some form of form criticism. Texts are ascribed to the "genre" of "ancient biography," to "metaphors," to the "farewell" speech, to the "*hypodeigma*," and by this procedure the purely synchronic approach seems to have been replaced by a method of study which includes elements of comparative research. Literary genres of classical antiquity (or Semitic poetics) are introduced in order to favor the comprehension of texts or parts of texts. The reader may ask him/herself to what extent it is possible to renounce source and tradition criticism while including form criticism in the interpretation of Gospel texts. Can the two elements be separated? Is the "divine man" and his biography a purely formal element, or does it include material elements which are realized outside and inside the Gospels? This problem of the methodological place of form criticism concerns not only New American criticism but also contemporary approaches on the European continent (cf. Berger:1977, 128–36; 1980).

1.1.2 Reader Response

What is called reader response in New American criticism can be compared with the quest for the "pragmatics" of a text in the continental European schools. If we take one of the more recent manuals of New Testament methodology from the German-speaking area, W. Egger's *Methodenlehre zum Neuen Testament* (1987), the student is asked to distinguish three main steps of synchronic exegesis: syntactical analysis, semantics, and pragmatics. The latter would mean the quest for the intention of the (implied or real) author of the text, the "message" for the (implied or real) "narratee." There are different schools of European scholarship which have specialized in this field, some of them being directly or indirectly influenced by the communication theory of J. Habermas. As one example of this method of research, we may point to H. Frankemölle's *Biblische Handlungsanweisungen. Beispiele pragmatischer Exegese* (1983).

Whenever the "semantics" and the "pragmatics" of a given text are considered as successive steps in its interpretation one can get the impression that the meaning of this text can be determined independently from the question of its purpose for the reader. In fact the succession of "semantics" and "pragmatics" in central European research seems to originate in the combination of two different approaches: French semantics or semiotics and German pragmatics. The seam of both schools can still be noticed in Egger's book on methodology: while his observations on the "meaning" of the signs used in a text are mainly based on French structuralism, his remarks on pragmatics are more strongly influenced by German scholarship.

As far as the contributions to the present volume are concerned, there is a consistent emphasis on reader response comparable with European research regarding the pragmatics of a text. One difference seems to be that in the present volume more than one author emphasizes the fact that the relationship of the reader towards his or her text is constitutive for the establishment not only of the purpose but also the meaning of the text. This means that the reader is constitutive not only for the pragmatics, but also for the semantics of the text. This aspect has been underlined by both F. F. Segovia (Introduction) and R. Kysar. The latter underlines the fact that of course the reader alone does not suffice for creating the meaning of the text but only contributes to it. The importance of the given text for the creation of meaning remains indispensable.

It is true that authors like H. Frankemölle see the importance of the reader for the construction of the meaning of a text. However, insofar as they distinguish between the "semantics" and the "pragmatics" of a given unit as successive steps in its interpretation, this reminder of the connection between the meaning and the purpose of a text seems to be appropriate. For authors on either side of the Atlantic, the step from the implied or real author of New Testament times to the actual reader of our days remains of course the decisive and at the same time the most difficult one (see below 1.2).

1.1.3 The Rhetorical Approach

Most of the collected papers in the present volume confess themselves indebted to the rhetorical approach to the text. This can mean two different things: the quest for the role of the reader in the establishment of the meaning and purpose of the text or the quest for the rules of classical rhetorics as relevant for the understanding of our text.

As far as the latter are concerned, I see some limits in the applicability of these rules to a text like the Fourth Gospel. In the strict sense, the laws of rhetorics in antiquity were developed for the writing of speeches. They help to organize a speech in as successful a way as possible (cf. Quintilian, *Inst. Or.* X 3–5). Now a gospel text is not necessarily to be understood as a speech in this strict sense. It is a narrative, which may contain speeches, in our case particularly discourses or sermons of Jesus. So the laws of classical rhetorics can be applied to our gospel as a whole only with some caution, and the same holds true for parts of the Fourth Gospel which combine narrative with speech.

The same reserve has to be observed whenever the laws of poetics are invoked for the establishment of the meaning and purpose of a gospel text (see Staley). So the reference to ancient biography seems to be of primary importance for the establishment of the meaning of the Fourth Gospel. The laws of rhetoric can be applied in the strict sense only to the discourses of our gospel, unless it could be proved that the gospel as a whole is a speech.

1.2 Hermeneutics

1.2.1 Original Meaning and Setting of the Text

As has been pointed out by F. F. Segovia (Introduction), little attention has been paid in the present volume to the original setting of our Gospel texts, to the social conditions of the author and the readers. Questions regarding the *Sitz im Leben* of the author or of the community form part of traditional "form criticism." It has been replaced in the present volume by considerations of style and structure as elements of new literary criticism. The "reader" remains a rather abstract figure, as has been pointed out by F. F. Segovia (loc. cit.). There is a different school of contemporary New Testament research which is more interested in the social conditions of the authors and the original readers of the New Testament writings. It seems rather to walk side by side with the new literary criticism (see Elliott).

Of course, the quest for the concrete social conditions out of which our New Testament texts originated and for which they were written may remain a purely historical one. As such, it would be part of the historical critical method, which tries to establish "how it really happened" ("wie es wirklich gewesen ist"). But it may be also part of a hermeneutic approach which tries to uncover the social conditions of the original text and its readers as a paradigm for an understanding of the text. On the one hand, the limits of our text would appear more clearly, for instance, the "sectarian" ring of the Fourth Gospel. On the other hand, its effort to give answers to open questions of the milieu would become more obvious. They may range from questions concerning living in a world of religious syncretism to concrete questions regarding the role of women in society, of church leaders, or of the needy.

1.2.2 History of Interpretation

Between the text and its original readers and ourselves there is the long history of successive interpretations of our text. For a long time the denomination of the Christian interpreter played a decisive role in his or her work of explaining the text. A Lutheran would stand in the Lutheran tradition and be influenced by it in his or her work of interpreting the text. The same would hold true for the adherents of other churches and denominations. Since the origin of modern biblical research from the time of the Enlightenment, scientific schools played an increasing role in the hermeneutics of a given author. Such schools would sometimes go beyond the boundaries of certain denominations, as in the case of the "Tübingen school" of the early 19th century. It is to the credit of twentieth-century hermeneutics to have made such influences more conscious. Hans-Georg Gadamer, perhaps the most influential representative of the Heidegger school of our days, has taught us to integrate the *Wirkungs-*

geschichte (history of impact) of a given text into the task of its interpretation for today (Gadamer:270, 312). The influence of this approach can be noticed in the well-known commentary series, "Evangelisch-Katholischer Kommentar zum Neuen Testament," now reaching completion.[1] Of course, most contributors to this volume limit themselves to examples of previous interpretations, but at least the task to be fulfilled has been noticed. I think that a complete survey of the history of interpretation can be given only on the basis of interdisciplinary research done by exegetes as well as church historians, philosophers, and sociologists, who supply the exegete with the knowledge of the changing philosophical background and social setting of the various phases of the "history of the text."

1.2.3 Reading the Text Today

While all of the contributors to the present volume make clear their position with regard to method of interpretation, only a few of them reflect about themselves as the subjects of interpretation. It is interesting to notice that the two authors who do so most clearly have a Third World or colonial background: F. F. Segovia (Cuba) and W. Wuellner (South Africa). J. L. Staley may be added, with his emphasis on the context of persecution for the understanding of the Fourth Gospel.

Hermeneutics has played a key role in biblical interpretation in the second half of this century. The debate began with Bultmann's "existential interpretation," as expressed for example in his fundamental article, "Neues Testament und Mythologie" (1941), and centered on the individual as subject in the interpretation of texts. How to break up the "hermeneutical circle" between text and reader, or better, how to get into it: that was the question. Eventually the debate turned more and more into a discussion on philosophical and theological anthropology. One branch of existential theology (represented also by Karl Rahner) turned into the political theology of the late sixties. The main representative of this school was J. B. Metz (Münster), who had some influence on Latin American liberation theology. The quest for the human existence of the individual trying to "understand" was now replaced by the quest for society as conditioning texts and readers. In exegesis only marginal groups adopted this approach for the interpretation of biblical texts. The main shift, particularly in the North Atlantic area, was from hermeneutics to method. Only under the influence of feminism and Third World theologies has a new quest for hermeneutics come to the fore once again.

Indeed, such a change of "paradigm" seems unavoidable for me. I write these lines one year after the day when six of my fellow Jesuits, all members of the University of Central America, were shot dead in San Salvador, together with two women in their employ. I got the news of their violent death twenty-four hours later, during a period of guest lectures in West Africa. It has become increasingly clear to me since that day that my own work as a theologian and an exegete has to be rethought. Where are our own coresponsibilities for violence in the Third World, be it Africa, Asia, or Latin America? Could it be true that my—our—own interest in formal questions in the interpretation of texts is made possible by the fact that I belong to the "wealthy," to those who do not have to fear hunger, persecution, and death? If I compare the subjects treated at the annual meetings of the Studiorum Novi Testamenti Societas (S.N.T.S.), which I regularly attend, with those raised in Third World theological publications, the difference is obvious. In fact, the meetings of the S.N.T.S. reflect faithfully the dichotomy in current theological research: a theology of the rich, mainly centered around historical or literary questions and represented by the great international societies; and a theology of the poor and the powerless, gathering in the comparatively humble meetings of the Ecumenical Association of Third World Theologians (EATWOT)—and all this in spite of remarkable efforts on the part of the staff of the S.N.T.S. to overcome this gap.

I do not have a solution to this problem. I can only take up W. Wuellner's invitation to reflect critically on our own "critical approach" to the gospels and F. F. Segovia's appeal to integrate our own social position into our investigation of the relationship of the reader to the gospel texts. I do in fact think that an increasing readiness to face persecution as a consequence of Christian confession in a non-Christian environment may be one of the teachings of the Fourth Gospel for the readers of our days (see Staley).

2. HISTORY

2.1 *The Gospel as Witness*

The rhetorical approach of the present volume considers the Fourth Gospel as a literary document. Its orientation is at the same time artistic/ aesthetic and pragmatic: how does the organization of the material serve the purpose of the (implied or real) author in influencing the (implied or real) reader? This way of asking abstracts from the historical reality of the persons mentioned in the text and of the facts and speeches reported.

This perspective is in contrast with the intention of the author expressed in the Fourth Gospel itself. At the end of the gospel text, a group of disciples declares solemnly: "This is the disciple who is bearing witness to these things and who has written these things; and we know that his testimony is true" (21:24). It is not quite clear whether this statement refers only to the words of Jesus about the Beloved Disciple, to the whole of chapter 21, or to the entire Fourth Gospel, as traditionally understood. In any case, it expresses the conviction that the text of the Fourth Gospel has to be considered as a witness—a witness to facts and not just to convictions (Segovia, "Farewell," B.3; Beutler:1972; Painter).

The consequence of this observation is that a purely literary or aesthetic approach to the Fourth Gospel does not do it full justice according to its own standards. Any "rhetorical approach" reveals itself as one method of Johannine research, but never *the* approach for now and for the future. I see this thinking behind many of the contributions to the present volume, particularly in F. F. Segovia's stress on the gospel as an example of ancient biography.

2.2 The Gospels as History

Also from a scientific point of view, the study of the New Testament texts as documents of history cannot be abandoned. No doubt there is a crisis in the so-called historical critical method of biblical research. It would be incorrect to use the biblical texts only as sources of information about the history of Israel, of Jesus, or of the early church. This was the mistake of part of biblical research in the nineteenth and early twentieth century. It can be seen very clearly in Synoptic Gospels research where the main interest of many scholars, particularly in Germany, seems to have been the reconstruction of the original message and self-understanding of Jesus and his "very deeds." In contemporary criticism I see a sound reaction against this historicizing perspective of gospel research.

On the other hand it would be wrong to deny any historical value to our New Testament documents. European and international scholarship has profited greatly from the historical work of exegetes and church historians on the early Christian documents. Reconstructing the history of the early Christian communities has helped us to see the conditions and limits under which our New Testament texts originated. Even reader response criticism could hardly dispense from this work. It has enabled us to recognize the New Testament documents as witnesses of a process of interpretation of the Jesus kerygma which can serve as an example for similar developments in our days. It has warned us about delivering ourselves to any kind of fundamentalism which takes historical texts as supra-historical authorities which cannot be questioned—a particular danger in our generation and not only in Islamic countries. So it appears indispensable.[2]

2.3   The Role of Time

There is an interesting focus on time in G. R. O'Day's article, "I Have Overcome the World" (John 16:33). It is qualified as "narrative time" in the farewell discourses of Jesus. This shows already that the main emphasis is on the text as text. How do "internal" and "external" time relate, or—in order to dialogue with R. A. Culpepper—what is the relationship between prehistory, history, and eschatology in our text? We notice with O'Day a problem of shift from the literary to the historical level, but also from the historical to the metahistorical.

The focus of O'Day's contribution remains on the literary level. She shows convincingly the central role of the "hour" of Jesus in the Fourth Gospel. It is not only the fulfillment of his own career but also of history. So it includes and concludes the life and destiny not only of Jesus but of the disciples as well. The "Paraclete" will keep the "hour" present after the departure of Jesus for the coming generations.

This coherent perspective has been made possible by the abandonment of diachronic methods of interpretation inside and outside the farewell discourses. Authors who accept layers of composition in the farewell discourses would see a development in the "hour" announced by Jesus—from "his" hour to the hour of the disciples, an hour of death and childbirth (John 16:2, 4, 21, 32). Both "hours" are related not only to a text world, but also to the world of antiquity, to the history of the Roman Empire in the first century and the time to follow.

3.   THEOLOGY

All of the contributions in this volume consider "the Fourth Gospel from a literary perspective." This raises the question how a literary and a theological perspective could be related. I think that all of the authors agree that there is no alternative between the two ways of studying our text. They are complementary to each other; theological work supposes literary analysis. But literary research will also lead to theological insight. Let me show some theological perspectives arising from the reading of the literary approaches of the present volume.

3.1   Anthropology and Ecclesiology

Reader response criticism is centered on an author who wants to communicate a message to a reader. So the role of the (implied or real) reader becomes central in the contemporary approach to the gospels. He or she appears as a rather abstract being. What is decisive is the response of faith to the message of faith communicated by the author. The reader belongs to the "text world," and his or her roots in concrete history are either neglected or treated only secondarily. What comes out in reader response criticism are the categories of theological anthropology as contained in our text. The readers are led from "darkness" to "light," from (apparent) "knowledge" to "faith," from pride to serving. This perspective could lead to the shortcoming that the ecclesiological aspect of the gospel text is being neglected. The Shepherd Discourse of John 10 can be read as an example of metaphorical speech, moving readers towards a decision of faith in Jesus the Good Shepherd. But it can also be read as a text speaking to the leaders of the People of God and drawing the outlines of a new community based on mutual service unto death according to the example of Jesus (Beutler:1991). It finds its continuation in John 13–17 and in the dialogue between Jesus and Peter in John 21.

If we return from here to reader response criticism, we may ask: who is the reader? Is it the individual reading his or her book, or is it rather the community reading it together or hearing it in liturgy? The answer to this question, which may be affirmative for both alternatives, is of importance also for churches striving for liberation in many parts of the world today.

3.2 Christology

Theological work on the Gospel of John in the past was strongly centered around questions of christology. Scholars mainly interested in systematic theology would ask for the particular Johannine type of christology as compared with the Jesus of the Synoptic Gospels or of Paul. Those coming from comparative studies of religion would relate Johannine christology to myths of the Redeemed Redeemer, the Apocalyptic Son of Man, or the Divine Agent. More recent literary criticism in Germany and other countries has distinguished between different successive christologies in the Fourth Gospel: from a Jewish-Christian messianic model towards a "high christology," based on the incarnation of the Divine Word, which was corrected still inside the Johannine school by an antidocetic tendency, visible in texts ascribed to the "ecclesiastical" or "Johannine redactor" of the Gospel and to the Johannine Letters (Richter; Haenchen; Becker). It is fully understandable that such an approach would lead to increasing criticism in international scholarship. In fact, the history of Johannine christology remains highly speculative even after decades of competent research.

A first answer of reader response criticism to this problem seems to have been a shift of interest from christology to a theology of discipleship. This is in line with the emphasis of new criticism on the reader. I think that the work dedicated to the role of the disciple or the faithful in the Synoptics and in the Fourth Gospel until now (last but not least in the

United States of America) has been very rewarding. Two fine examples in our volume are the paper on John 9 by J. L. Staley and the interpretation of John 11 by W. Wuellner. They strengthen our conviction that the Fourth Gospel was written not to communicate knowledge about Christ but to lead to faith in him.

There arises, however, a perspective on Christ in the different papers which allows for a description of his career and his message. It is particularly F. F. Segovia who in his three contributions has tried to see Christ in the perspective of ancient biography. According to the rules of this literature, the life of Christ seems to have been described in three phases: origin and youth; public life and activity (in the center); death and abiding importance. The discussion may go on about all three of these phases. I wonder whether the prologue of the Fourth Gospel can simply replace a report about childbirth and youth of the hero Jesus (as compared for instance with the report given in the gospel of Luke in Luke 1–2 or the one about the youth of Moses in Acts 7:20–23: "he was born . . . brought up . . . instructed"). On the other hand, the death and abiding significance of Christ seem to characterize not only the third and last phase of his career, but also the central one, if not all the three of them. One should think in this regard of the "lamb of God" of John 1:29, 36 and the first mention of death and resurrection of Jesus in John 2:19–22. G. R. O'Day has correctly underlined the dominating role of the "hour" of Jesus in the Fourth Gospel, focusing all time in one decisive moment, which sums up the past and anticipates the future.

3.3 Theology *(in the strict sense)*

There is a final point in reader response criticism as applied to the Fourth Gospel which makes me think. The new form of criticism is mainly interested in the relation between author and reader and in the reaction of the reader intended by the author. If this approach is misunderstood, one might question whether the main purpose of the Fourth Gospel is a human activity—the response of the reader. This activity could be understood as opposed to the activity of God as center of the Fourth Gospel (as of any other book of the Bible). God's love for the world (John 3:16) or Jesus' love for his own (John 13:1) have been considered by many to be the focus of the Gospel of John. If the main emphasis of the Gospel of John becomes the response of the reader, it must remain clear that this response is a response of faith equal to the acceptance of God's love and saving word. Theologically speaking, even the response of faith is not a human achievement but God's gift: "No one can come to me unless the Father who sent me draws him" (John 6:44).

NOTES

1 Zürich: Benziger; Neukirchen: Neukirchener Verlag.
2 For the abiding role of historical critical exegesis, cf. Merk; Müller.

WORKS CONSULTED

Becker, Jürgen.
1979–81   *Das Evangelium des Johannes.* 2 vols. Ökumenischer Taschenbuchkommentar zum Neuen Testament 4. Gütersloher Taschenbuchkommentar Siebenstern 505–506. Gütersloh: Mohn; Würzburg: Echter.

Berger, Klaus.
1977   *Exegese des Neuen Testaments.* Uni-Taschenbücher 568. Heidelberg: Quelle & Meyer.
1980   *Formgeschichte des Neuen Testaments.* Heidelberg: Quelle & Meyer.

Beutler, Johannes.
1972   *Martyria. Traditionsgeschichtliche Untersuchungen zum Zeugnisthema bei Johannes.* Frankfurter theologische Studien 10. Frankfurt am Main: Knecht.
1991   "Der alttestamentlich-jüdische Hintergrund der Hirtenrede in Johannes 10." Pp. 18–32 in *The Shepherd Discourse of John 10 in Its Context.* Ed. J. Beutler and R. T. Fortna. Society for New Testament Studies Monograph Series 67. Cambridge: Cambridge University Press.

Egger, Wilhelm.
1987   *Methodenlehre zum Neuen Testament.* Freiburg-Basel-Vienna: Herder.

Elliott, John H., ed.
1986   *Social-Scientific Criticism of the New Testament and Its Social World. Semeia* 35. Atlanta: Scholars.

Frankemölle, Hubert.
1983   *Biblische Handlungsanweisungen. Beispiele pragmatischer Exegese.* Mainz: Grünewald.

Gadamer, Hans-Georg.
1990   *Hermeneutik I. Wahrheit und Methode. Grundzüge einer philosophischen Hermeneutik.* Tübingen: Mohr.

Haenchen, Ernst.
1980   *Das Johannesevangelium. Ein Kommentar.* Ed. U. Busse. Tübingen: Mohr.

Merk, Otto.
1980   "Bibelwissenschaft II. Neues Testament." *Theologische Realenzyklopädie* 6, 375–409. Berlin-New York: de Gruyter.

Müller, Karkheinz.
1984   "Exegese/Bibelwissenschaft II." Pp. 332–53 in *Neues Handbuch Theologischer Grundbegriffe.* Ed. Peter Eicher. München: Kösel.

Painter, John.
1990   *John: Witness and Theologian.* Mitcham: Beacon Hill.

Richter, Georg.
1977   *Studien zum Johannesevangelium.* Biblische Untersuchungen 13. Ed. J. Hainz. Regensburg: Pustet.

A Response from a Literary Perspective

Mary Ann Tolbert
The Divinity School, Vanderbilt University

1. Introduction

Literary studies of biblical texts, employing contemporary theories and techniques developed by other disciplines in the humanities like English literature, comparative literature, and linguistics, are relative newcomers to the world of biblical criticism. Although a "Bible as Literature" movement gained some popularity earlier in this century, especially in departments of English in the United States, it was conceived primarily as an appreciative approach to biblical stories from the King James Version and to their influence on the development of English literature since the seventeenth century. The critical use of literary theory to analyze biblical texts dates only from the mid to late 1960s and is still concentrated in North American biblical circles. However, as the essays in this volume witness, the exegetical benefits of such approaches are numerous, making it very likely that literary studies will continue to be important components of biblical research for many years to come.

Since biblical literary criticism bases both its theories and its practices on material outside the realm of biblical studies proper, it is probably occasionally helpful to compare literary work on the Bible with current literary research from other disciplines in order to orient biblical literary criticism within the larger world of literary studies. As a response to this volume on "The Fourth Gospel from a Literary Perspective," I would like to compare and contrast these essays with what I perceive to be some of the dominant perspectives now present in European and North American literary criticism generally. To make this task manageable in a brief space (a full book has recently appeared attempting such a project, see Moore), I will limit my focus to two overlapping issues: 1. text and meaning, and 2. theoretical coalitions and ideological analysis. Further, I want to locate contemporary literary criticism of the New Testament, as represented by these essays, within the recent history of American literary criticism, both biblical and non-biblical.

2. TEXT AND MEANING

Early literary studies of the New Testament (e.g., Wilder; Via, 1967) were heavily indebted to New Criticism, a school of literary criticism that dominated the American scene from the 1930s to the early 1960s. New Criticism was founded upon the premise that each text is an autonomous literary object, which must be investigated on its own terms independent of author, audience, or social and cultural heritage. Following the tenets of New Criticism, New Testament literary criticism began mainly as formalist analyses of the literary dynamics of biblical texts. New Criticism itself had developed in part as a reaction to tendencies in nineteenth and early twentieth century criticism to value a literary text primarily as an expression of its author's biography or its audience's appreciation or its culture's spirit. Since similar tendencies were present in traditional forms of biblical criticism (e.g., form criticism's use of gospel material as a means for reaching the *Sitz im Leben Jesu*), New Criticism's emphasis on interpreting the text *as text* provided an important corrective for biblical criticism as well. Indeed, as long as many biblical critics continue to view the New Testament as a repository for undistorted chunks of early church history or the life of the historical Jesus, the strictures and arguments of the New Critics will continue to be needed in biblical scholarship.

New Criticism's theoretical dominance was broken in the early 1960s by the publication of Northrop Frye's *Anatomy of Criticism*, in which Frye successfully argued that any individual literary work was at the very least connected to the entire literary universe (for how else could literary allusions be explained), if not to the real world of its production. With the stranglehold of New Criticism loosened, new literary theories abounded in the 1970s; perspectives as diverse as Marxism, psychoanalysis, myth criticism, Jungianism, and structuralism formulated major theoretical options for the analysis of texts, and each gained adherents, including some within the guild of biblical scholarship (see, e.g., Patte; Tolbert; Via, 1977). Many of these positions retained New Criticism's focus on the text itself but substituted depth psychology, economics, or linguistics for the solely aesthetic realm in which New Criticism had anchored all literary works.

However, by the end of the 1970s a new critical orientation was growing in influence: reader-response or audience-oriented criticism. While the text was still important, reader-response critics pointed out that no text is read, understood, or interpreted without a reader. Texts do not mean anything alone; they only "mean" when they are read by a reader. Meaning, then, comes from the interaction of text and reader. Reader-response or audience-oriented criticism actually encompasses a range of fairly different views on the relative power of the text or the reader *vis-à-*

vis each other. This range permits reader-response criticism both to maintain many of the formalist features of New Criticism for those who view the text as the more powerful and stable pole in the interaction and also to develop the insights of psychology, sociology, and ideology as they affect readers of texts by those who see the reader as the more dominant one.

All of the essays in this volume owe their theoretical allegiance to reader-response criticism in one way or another. Although Wuellner refers to his analysis as a rhetorical one, his argument that meaning arises in the reader clearly locates his method within the range of audience-oriented criticism. Moreover, all of these articles exhibit strong formalist tendencies as well, linking them both with the first stages of the literary study of the New Testament (and with New Criticism) and also with the more text-dominant positions in the reader-response spectrum. Only Wuellner, at the end of his contribution, and Segovia, at the end of his second article, raise questions about concrete readers in interaction with the text and the different meanings that might arise from such real readers.

Focusing on the necessary interaction of texts and readers allows audience-oriented criticism to explain the existence and indeed the inevitability of multiple interpretations of any one text. Different readers read differently. Analyzing those differences and adjudicating the resulting interpretations is a major concern of contemporary literary criticism (see, e.g., Culler; Flynn and Schweickart). By joining the more formalist, text-centered end of reader-response theory, the authors in this volume, and perhaps many current New Testament literary critics along with them, generally avoid the debate over the differences among readers and the legitimacy of multiple readings. An "ideal" reader, either inscribed in the text or implied by it, is the analytical construct used in most of these essays. While such a construct has exegetical advantages, it also tends to mask important components of the interpretative process. For example, in Jeffrey Staley's "Stumbling in the Dark, Reaching for the Light: Reading Character in John 5 and 9," he investigates how a reader would perceive the development of characters in a linear reading of the miracles in John 5 and 9. His insight into the importance of the belated reference to the Sabbath for altering the reader's understanding of each story is an excellent exegetical point. However, many of the other points he makes depend upon a *very* careful, indeed almost minute, examination of narration and speech throughout the two chapters. What kind of reading is presupposed in this process of teasing out all the tiny details of contrast, pondering the various alternatives of interpretation, and referring back and forth between stories? Most of the Gospel of John's ancient audience probably did not *read* the text at all but *heard* it read to them, and their understanding could hardly be that developed by Staley's linear reader. Even most modern day readers of the Gospel probably do not spend the concentrated time on each phrase, each verse that Staley's reader does. What Staley's generalized reader masks is, of course, the critic himself: Staley's reader reads the way Staley does. His analysis, while enlightening and helpful, is not the reading experience of any reader, but the analysis of the trained modern biblical critic. Let me hasten to say that there is absolutely nothing wrong with such a critical reading; the problem arises only in the fiction of a generalized reader who actually functions as a blind for the author. In the wider world of literary criticism today, critics and readers are being forced out from behind their masks and asked to own their views as their own and not as everyone's or anyone's; such a process for biblical critics might prove very salutary in the increasingly diverse world of New Testament interpretation.

Given the formalist alignment of these essays, another aspect of their common approach stands out in contrast to most textual studies in other disciplines. For the formalist critic, the text to be studied is the final form of the text as it presently exists. While biblical literary critics have regularly appealed to this dictum as a way of eschewing the endless, and often fruitless, arguments over sources, written or oral, for biblical books, their observance of the rule has been less than rigorous. By studying the final form of the text, most literary critics mean the whole text without sections omitted as interpolations or additions. Although all of these essays look at the final form of John as it presently exists without recourse to elaborate schemes for rearranging the material or analyzing various editions, only one of them looks at the *whole* text (Segovia's "The Journey(s) of the Word of God: A Reading of the Plot of the Fourth Gospel"). Especially for reader-response critics, who must acknowledge that a reader's understanding of any section of a text is built upon what the reader has learned up to that point, studying only isolated sections of longer stories is extremely problematic. Actually, the books in the New Testament and even in the Hebrew Bible are hardly longer than brief to moderate short stories. Yet, what literary critic would characteristically write essays on only one or two pages of a short story, much less one or two paragraphs? Indeed, in the world of English literature, one essay might well analyze the plots of several novels, covering considerably more material than is found in the entire Bible.

The essays in this volume are not alone in focusing on fragments of texts, for biblical literary criticism from its beginnings has tended to follow such a practice. Very few articles have attempted literary analyses of whole texts. Why biblical literary criticism displays such a remarkable contrast to other forms of literary criticism is an interesting question. Part of the reason certainly lies in the educational heritage of most current biblical literary critics. Trained as historical critics, form critics, or redaction critics, biblical literary critics may not see any problem with analyzing only one or two chapters of a text, looking at only one motif, or studying only one character, even though such practices conflict with many of the tenets of formalist literary analysis. For biblical scholars form criticism, especially, legitimated such fragmentary research. In addition to education, both practical and economic reasons probably play a role in this practice, as any good Marxist would surely note. Unlike English literary critics who have thousands of books and centuries of literary tradition to roam through, biblical literary critics and particularly New Testament literary critics have a comparatively *tiny* corpus of material to work with. Practically, studying small fragments of texts expands the possible options for scholarly research and thus the possibilities of scholarly publication, a career "must" in the current academic market. Moreover, the dominant use of biblical material in the church conforms to such fragmentary analyses; whether in sermons or in lectionary readings, only short sections of biblical texts tend to be used in church activities. Therefore, ministers are generally searching for fuller studies of these brief units, and their search fuels publications. While the episodic character of ancient writing certainly encourages the examination of textual fragments, the very real, though usually unacknowledged, economic motives behind such practices cannot be dismissed.

The biblical literary critic faces a dilemma: to deal only with whole texts restricts scholarly options and goes against the predominant tradition of biblical criticism in this century; however, to examine fragments of whole texts from a literary perspective runs the risk of undercutting some of the most important rules and exegetical gains provided by that perspective in the first place. At the very least, biblical literary critics should locate their studies of brief units within the context of the overall development of the story, a procedure many of them, including some in this volume, do not always follow.

3. THEORETICAL COALITIONS AND IDEOLOGICAL ANALYSIS

In the early 1980s Jonathan Culler described the beginning coalescence of a variety of perspectives into a body of "theory" that was shared by a growing number of fields of study as traditionally diverse as literary criticism, philosophy, psychology, feminist studies, racial and ethnic studies, and linguistics. Under the pervasive influence of the French deconstructionists, all of these areas had begun to see themselves as text-dependent;

that is, they understood their subject matter to be "texts," whether literary texts, history as text, society as text, or human life as text. Moreover, these texts were human constructions, embodying and supporting certain viewpoints while erasing or negating others. Jacques Derrida, the primary theorist of deconstruction, mounted what was mainly an attack on Western metaphysics, arguing that human language systems did not function to represent some Reality outside of themselves but were instead completely self-referential. Derrida's work, combined with the analyses of discourses of power provided by Michel Foucault, formed the cornerstone of this new body of "theory" Culler described.

Since "texts" of whatever kind require readers to interpret them, the concerns of reader-response criticism also blended into this "theory" but with special attention devoted to those varieties that understand the reader's role as constitutive of the meaning of the text. Readers make meaning out of texts, and in addition those meanings may, indeed almost always do, differ from each other. Arguments for one "right" meaning of a text must assume some transcendent, transhistorical textual essence that immediately comes under attack from Derrida's metaphysical critique. If no transcendent "right" reading exists or has ever existed, how is one to evaluate the many claims to "right" readings—or the many more denunciations of "wrong" readings—to be found throughout the ages? For Foucault, such claims constitute discourses of power. Those with economic, intellectual, or cultural power set the rules of "right" and "wrong" used to judge all others, and they support those rules by arguing for their metaphysical rather than their human basis. Whose discourse is the most powerful, how it gained that power, how it preserves that power, and to whose good it works—all become critical areas for literary as well as political exploration. While what I have presented here is a *very* brief and simplified version of deconstruction's influence on reader-response criticism, it serves to indicate why this new body of "theory" also soon incorporated a vigorous component of ideological analysis.

Under the increased ideological awareness of literary theory in the mid to late 1980s, such issues as gender, race, and cultural prerogatives were all freed from the sphere of "nature" and placed squarely in the sphere of human construction. Feminist scholars in literary criticism, philosophy, anthropology, and psychology have argued for the social construction of gender (see, e.g., Butler), raising crucial political questions about who benefits and who loses in any particular society's gender game. Both race and ethnicity have been analyzed in much the same fashion. Moreover, the influence of these social constructions on the processes of producing and reading texts (see, e.g., Showalter) underscored the perspectival aspect of all textual interpretation: we necessarily read out of our own historical, cultural, and social location; no one reads from a transcendent, uninvolved space. Recognizing the ideological bias present in all readings of all "texts," literary as well as cultural, unmasks the fiction of objective or universal readings. Textual interpretations that are judged "objective" or "unbiased" by a particular group are simply those that most fully agree with the biases of that group. Thus, not only the texts but the readers of those texts themselves need to be analyzed for their ideological allegiances and social locations, since these factors of necessity influence the meanings they create out of texts and probably the acceptance or rejection those meanings will receive by those of the dominant discourse.

With two significant exceptions, all the essays in this volume singularly lack even a hint of this body of "theory." Although Wilhelm Wuellner in "Putting Life Back into the Lazarus Story and Its Readings: The Narrative Rhetoric of John 11 as the Narration of Faith" spends the most time developing what he designates as the first level of rhetoric, "the author and the produced text," his second and especially his third level of rhetoric acknowledge the position of the scholarly critic in the midst of postmodern theory. How such a postmodern stance concretely affects his reading of the Lazarus story is less clear, but the effort to situate himself within the currents of the last decade of literary "theory" is to be commended. The most direct expression of "theory's" influence occurs in the last essay in the volume, Fernando Segovia's "The Final Farewell of Jesus: A Reading of John 20:30-21:25." Segovia explicitly details his own social location as a reader of the Gospel of John and, moreover, takes time at the end of his contribution to evaluate the text's ideology of discipleship and the church's later appropriation of it for the colonized peoples of the third (and fourth) world. Since no other author attempts anything like Segovia's relatively modest ideological critique, his article almost seems out of place in the volume. However, the cause of that disharmony lies in the failure of all the other essays to reflect upon or even acknowledge major critical developments in European and American literary theory over the past decade.

From its inception in the mid 1960s, biblical literary criticism has tended to follow, reflect upon, and adopt most of the significant evolutions in American literary theory. Consequently, it is odd that such impressive and important developments over the last decade as deconstruction, feminist theory, and various other forms of ideological analysis are so markedly absent from much contemporary biblical literary criticism, including most of the essays in this volume. Especially given the dependence of all of these essays on aspects of reader-response criticism, the many critiques of the "ideal," universal reader ought to be included somewhere in the discussion (Staley does attempt something of this in his "A Postscript"). Both ideological and even, again, economic issues may lie at the heart of this failure. Some, though certainly not all, biblical critics work and write out of systems of religious conviction that still privilege authoritarian and hierarchical structures, the very type of structures most susceptible to deconstruction's ruthless opprobrium. For such scholars, to analyze their own ideological commitments and social locations may be viewed as undermining the authority of their beliefs. Far more biblical scholars are financially dependent upon academic or ecclesial institutions or church-related presses whose vested interests run counter to the implicit cultural critique mounted by contemporary "theory." I am arguing here that the absence from much biblical literary criticism of recent trends in literary theory can be explained, not as a thoughtful intellectual rejection of those trends, but rather as the ideological avoidance of what may be perceived as potential threats to vested interests. If such an argument has merit, it also has problematic implications for the future of literary studies of the Bible. Biblical literary critics cannot afford to cut themselves off from the theoretical foundations of their work or isolate themselves from the crucial debates in current literary theory. While biblical literary critics certainly remain accountable to biblical scholarship generally and perhaps also to their own confessional communities, they bear a responsibility as well to engage in their literary task with integrity, which at the very least means to take seriously the positions and issues generated by contemporary literary theory. Failure to do so in itself proclaims a powerful ideological commitment, whether explicitly confessed or not.

4. Conclusion

The essays in this volume present some excellent exegetical insights into the Gospel of John, most of which I have not mentioned in this response. Any reader of the volume will already have discovered the value of formalist literary analysis for the interpretation of many Johannine passages. What I have attempted to do in this response is locate these essays within the history of biblical literary criticism and also within the recent history of American literary theory, pointing out what they do and do not have in common. My reason for choosing such a perspective arises in part from *my own* particular social location as a first world, middle-class, white, feminist biblical scholar, committed to work of human liberation. I have also been from the beginning of my academic career a biblical literary critic, excited by the possibilities for New Testament interpretation available through the application of literary theory. Indeed, I am especially encouraged by the recent developments in postmodern literary theory and feminist theory for liberation concerns and thus am disappointed by the failure of many biblical literary critics to entertain these perspectives. While the essays in this volume are useful and generally enlightening, there is much more to contemporary literary criticism than is presented, suggested, or even dreamt of in most of these discussions.

WORKS CONSULTED

Butler, Judith
    1990   *Gender Trouble: Feminism and the Subversion of Identity*. New York: Routledge.

Culler, Jonathan
    1982   *On Deconstruction: Theory and Criticism after Structuralism*. Ithaca: Cornell University Press.

Flynn, Elizabeth and P. Schweickart, eds.
    1986   *Gender and Reading: Essays on Readers, Texts, and Contexts*. Baltimore: Johns Hopkins University Press.

Frye, Northrop
    1957   *Anatomy of Criticism: Four Essays*. Princeton: Princeton University Press.

Moore, Stephen
    1989   *Literary Criticism and the Gospels: The Theoretical Challenge*. New Haven: Yale University Press.

Patte, Daniel
    1976   *What Is Structural Exegesis?* Philadelphia: Fortress.

Showalter, Elaine, ed.
    1985   *The New Feminist Criticism: Essays on Women, Literature, and Theory*. New York: Pantheon.

Tolbert, Mary Ann
    1977   "The Prodigal Son: An Essay in Literary Criticism from a Psychoanalytic Perspective." *Semeia* 9:1–20.

Via, Dan O., Jr.
    1967   *The Parables: Their Literary and Existential Dimension*. Philadelphia: Fortress.
    1977   "The Prodigal Son: A Jungian Reading." *Semeia* 9:21–43.

Wilder, Amos
1964 *Early Christian Rhetoric: The Language of the Gospels*. Cambridge: Harvard University Press.

www.ingramcontent.com/pod-product-compliance
Lightning Source LLC
Chambersburg PA
CBHW031312150426
43191CB00005B/199